AMERICAN LITERATURE READINGS IN THE 21ST CENTURY

Series Editor: Linda Wagner-Martin

American Literature Readings in the 21st Century publishes works by contemporary critics that help shape critical opinion regarding literature of the nineteenth and twentieth century in the United States.

Published by Palgrave Macmillan:

Freak Shows in Modern American Imagination: Constructing the Damaged Body from Willa Cather to Truman Capote
By Thomas Fahy

Arab American Literary Fictions, Cultures, and Politics
By Steven Salaita

Women & Race in Contemporary U.S. Writing: From Faulkner to Morrison
By Kelly Lynch Reames

American Political Poetry in the 21st Century
By Michael Dowdy

Science and Technology in the Age of Hawthorne, Melville, Twain, and James: Thinking and Writing Electricity
By Sam Halliday

F. Scott Fitzgerald's Racial Angles and the Business of Literary Greatness
By Michael Nowlin

Sex, Race, and Family in Contemporary American Short Stories
By Melissa Bostrom

Democracy in Contemporary U.S. Women's Poetry
By Nicky Marsh

James Merrill and W.H. Auden: Homosexuality and Poetic Influence
By Piotr K. Gwiazda

Contemporary U.S. Latino/a Literary Criticism
Edited by Lyn Di Iorio Sandín and Richard Perez

The Hero in Contemporary American Fiction: The Works of Saul Bellow and Don DeLillo
By Stephanie S. Halldorson

Race and Identity in Hemingway's Fiction
By Amy L. Strong

Edith Wharton and the Conversations of Literary Modernism
By Jennifer Haytock

New Critical Essays on Kurt Vonnegut

Edited by

David Simmons

First published in 2009 by
PALGRAVE MACMILLAN®
in the United States—a division of St. Martin's Press LLC,
175 Fifth Avenue, New York, NY 10010.

Where this book is distributed in the UK, Europe and the rest of the world,
this is by Palgrave Macmillan, a division of Macmillan Publishers Limited,
registered in England, company number 785998, of Houndmills,
Basingstoke, Hampshire RG21 6XS.

Palgrave Macmillan is the global academic imprint of the above companies
and has companies and representatives throughout the world.

Palgrave® and Macmillan® are registered trademarks in the United States,
the United Kingdom, Europe and other countries.

ISBN: 978–0–230–61627–1

Library of Congress Cataloging-in-Publication Data

New critical essays on Kurt Vonnegut / edited by David Simmons.
    p. cm. — (American literature readings in the 21st century)
    ISBN 978–0–230–61627–1 (alk. paper)
     1. Vonnegut, Kurt—Criticism and interpretation. I. Simmons, David,
1979–

PS3572.O5Z793 2009
813'.54—dc22   2009005353

A catalogue record of the book is available from the British Library.

Design by Newgen Imaging Systems (P) Ltd., Chennai, India.

First edition: October 2009

10 9 8 7 6 5 4 3 2 1

Printed in the United States of America.

Transferred to Digital Printing in 2010

This book is dedicated with love and thanks to
my parents, Marlene Anne and David Robert Simmons

CONTENTS

ACKNOWLEDGMENTS

The first debt of any editor of a collection such as this must be to the contributors, who have provided the effort and enthusiasm that have made the production of this volume a pleasure to partake in. I am especially grateful to Elizabeth Abele, Susan E. Farrell, and Robert Tally for allowing me to shamelessly poach many of the most valuable contributions from some of the academics involved in their recent conferences on Vonnegut and his work. My thanks also go to Brigitte Shull at Palgrave for giving me the opportunity to edit the collection in addition to her continued patience and helpful advice. Professor Philip Tew introduced me to the study of Vonnegut; I am grateful for that, and the vivid example of his passion for research. I thank Taco Meeuwsen for his kind donation of the book's cover image. Finally, I must acknowledge my debt to those that persevered with me throughout the process of bringing this collection to fruition: namely my parents, David Robert Simmons and Marlene Simmons; my friends and colleagues, Wasfi Ibrahim, Claire Allen, and Lorna Jowett; and my loving partner, Nicola Allen.

INTRODUCTION

With the death of Vonnegut in 2007, now seems like an appropriate time to set about reassessing the author's extensive body of work. From *Player Piano* (1951) through seminal 1960s' novels such as *Cat's Cradle* (1963) and *Slaughterhouse-Five* (1969) up to the recent success of *A Man Without A Country* (2005), Vonnegut's writing has remained popular, offering a darkly satirical yet largely optimistic outlook on modern life. Though many fellow writers admired Vonnegut—Gore Vidal famously suggested that "Kurt was never dull"—the academic establishment has tended to retain a degree of skepticism concerning the critical validity of Vonnegut's work. Such neglect may have been the result of the author's own continuing humanism that positioned him at odds with an increasingly postmodernist and post-structuralist critical fraternity throughout the 1970s and much of the 1980s. Nevertheless, the essays contained in this collection seek to examine Vonnegut's writing, textually, thematically, and structurally. In particular, they offer a more comprehensive and expansive reassessment of Vonnegut's body of work than has been previously offered, renegotiating the author's writing in light of a changing academic climate that is now beginning to move away from an entrenched critical hegemony of post-structualist and postmodernist debate.

The essays in this collection represent some of the most exciting, current scholarship on the late Kurt Vonnegut, gathering together writing by established experts in the field, such as Lawrence Broer (*Sanity Plea: Schizophrenia in the Novels of Kurt Vonnegut*. Tuscaloosa: University of Alabama Press, 1989); Todd Davis (*Kurt Vonnegut's Crusade, or How a Postmodern Harlequin Preached a New Kind of Humanism*. New York: State University of New York Press, 2006); and Susan E. Farrell (*A Critical Companion to Kurt Vonnegut*. New York: Facts on File, 2008), alongside chapters by a host of lesser known yet intellectually nascent scholars whose work bodes well for the future of Vonnegut studies.

Todd Davis' "Flabbergasted" begins the collection. This short epistolary introduction forms a fitting dedication to Vonnegut, which successfully articulates the emotions that his legions of fans undoubtedly must have felt as a result of the passing of this seminal author. From this point on, the chapters are organized chronologically, following the order in which the books under discussion were published.

The noted scholar Philip Tew revisits *Mother Night* (1961), in "Kurt Vonnegut's *Mother Night* (1961): Howard W. Campbell, Jr., and the Banalities of Evil," rereading the novel in the light of its similarities to Hannah Arendt's reports on Adolf Eichmann, collected together in *Eichmann in Jerusalem: A Report of the Banality of Evil* (1963). Tew chooses to reject much of the overly hagiographical writing on Vonnegut to date, offering instead a meticulous reevaluation that focuses on the text itself and its refutation of simplistic moral positions.

The next chapter takes a similarly contentious approach to Vonnegut's work. "'*No Damn Cat, and No Damn Cradle*': The Fundamental Flaws in Fundamentalism according to Vonnegut" provides a dynamic rereading of religion in *Cat's Cradle* (1963). Though *Cat's Cradle* is one of Vonnegut's earliest novels, Paul L. Thomas' essay explores the current relevance of the novel's ideas concerning (primarily) religious fundamentalism. Thomas, who is a teacher in the Deep South of America, posits that Vonnegut's concerted attempts to decry simplistic, and potentially harmful, monotheistic notions of good and evil, right and wrong, might be of benefit to a contemporary world in which religious conservatism seems to be on the increase.

Rachel McCoppin's "'God Damn It, You've Got to Be Kind': War and Altruism in the Works of Kurt Vonnegut" discusses some of Vonnegut's most well-known and widely read novels, *Mother Night*; *God Bless You, Mr. Rosewater* (1965); and *Slaughterhouse-Five*. McCoppin presents a reading that cleverly builds upon established knowledge to examine the manner in which Vonnegut utilizes War as a literary device through which to promote his belief in the need for an increasingly humanist ideological reformulation of Western society.

Elizabeth Abele also investigates the same texts in "The Journey Home in Kurt Vonnegut's World War II Novels." Abele's approach, which explores the autobiographical nature of some of Vonnegut's better-known novels, discusses how they can be interpreted as responses to wartime experience in light of wider societal and artistic trends. The focal similarity between these two chapters hopefully demonstrates the ideological depth of Vonnegut's novels, and the multitude of possible readings that they allow for.

Though Vonnegut experienced his greatest period of success during the 1960s, he and his writing have retained popularity (with only occasional drops in commercial success) right up to the present, engaging with a range of aesthetic and social issues pertinent to a late–twentieth-century audience. Kurt Vonnegut's later writing demands to be reconsidered in a less retrospective and more openly contemporaneous and contextual manner. This is especially the case when one considers the bias that has typically been displayed toward his more recognized 1960s' output. In contrast to Vonnegut's 1960s' texts, his later works testify to a phase of American writing that has been seen through a particular literary prism since the mid-1970s. Yet, Vonnegut's staunch humanism and idealism have nevertheless found immense success with an audience eager to read something that is optimistic whilst also retaining a level of political engagement.

Susan E. Farrell's "Art, Domesticity, and Vonnegut's Women" opens the second section of the collection. Farrell's chapter provides a comprehensive reading of Vonnegut's representation of women from his early magazine fiction through to some of his later novels such as *Bluebeard* (1987). Though some critics have suggested that Vonnegut's writing has a marked tendency to overlook or sideline female characters, Farrell creates a convincing counterargument, which examines the synchronicity of aesthetics and feminine domesticity in many of Vonnegut's texts.

Robert Tally's "Apocalypse in the Optative Mood: *Galápagos*, or, Starting Over" examines one of Vonnegut's least written about, later novels, offering a detailed consideration of the text that seeks to align *Galápagos* (1985) with Vonnegut's larger body of work, primarily in its humanist depiction of a postapocalyptic world that leads Tally to term it a "hopeful end-of-the-world romance" (176).

Galápagos is also discussed in Lorna Jowett's "Folding Time: History, Subjectivity, and Intimacy in Vonnegut," which takes a multidisciplinary approach in analyzing Vonnegut's (often contentious) relationship to the science fiction genre. Jowett considers a selection of Vonnegut's more overtly sci-fi novels in the context of larger debates in the field. Jowett convincingly argues that Vonnegut consciously utilized many of the particular stylistic devices of the genre as a necessary means of presenting his ideas on America and its history.

"Resilience, Time, and the Ability of Humor to Salvage Any Situation" by Jessica Lingel explores the short fiction collection *Bagombo Snuff Box* (1999). Analyzing selected stories from the volume, Lingel provides a detailed discussion of this often overlooked text, which realigns the stories contained within with the rest of

Vonnegut's canon of work, particularly in terms of the author's pre-occupation with the processes of writing fiction.

Essential to this collection is an exploration of Vonnegut's work that seeks to open up an entrenched propensity toward Vonnegut's 1960s' writing in favor of a more expansive and considered account of the author's continuing relevance in the latter half of the twentieth century.

To this end, the third, shorter section of the collection is devoted to a study of Vonnegut's intertexts. Though a writer who was never shy in utilizing a wide variety of generic tropes, structures, and iconography, there is still very little analysis regarding Vonnegut's specific relationship with other writers, both in terms of his contemporaries and in terms of those later authors that adopted elements of Vonnegut's writing such as his style, structuring, generic interplay, or humor.

Lawrence Broer's chapter, "Duty Dance with Death: *A Farewell to Arms* and *Slaughterhouse-Five*," explores the multitudinous links between Ernest Hemingway and Vonnegut. More specifically, Broer offers a nuanced analysis of these writers' novels, teasing out the parallels between the two while also noting the significant differences existing in texts that were crucial literary staging posts in the American depiction of War and its effects on the individual.

Moving into the contemporary period, Chris Glover's "Somewhere in There Was Springtime": Kurt Vonnegut, His Apocalypses, and His Post-9/11 Heirs" offers a comprehensive exploration of Vonnegut's significant position within the postapocalyptic genre. Charting the changes in the form that were introduced by Vonnegut, Glover goes on to examine how these, often humanistic characteristics, filtered through to the later writing of a host of Anglo-American authors including Don Delillo, Ian McEwan, and Cormac McCarthy.

Finally in this section, Claire Allen's "Wampeters and Foma? Misreading Religion in *Cat's Cradle* and *The Book of Dave*" contains an extended analysis of Kurt Vonnegut's *Cat's Cradle* and *The Book of Dave* (2006) by the contemporary English satirist Will Self. Continuing Chris Glover's interest in the apocalypse in Vonnegut's work, Allen provides a lively yet considered comparison of the two novels, discussing the similarities in their use of satire as a means to explore a host of phenomenological issues related to subjectivity, religion, and narrative (mis)representation.

It is hoped that this collection will prove to be an interesting and engaging reevaluation of Vonnegut's varied oeuvre, demonstrating not only the author's great intelligence and writing ability but also his passionate humanism and belief in the socially beneficial functions of fiction. Indeed, the quality and diversity of the essays collected in this volume perhaps testify to the author's continued hold on the interest of so many scholars and writers. Their collected work offers a contribution to understanding Vonnegut's importance to the American popular psyche and a timely reminder of his undisputable place in an American literary canon in which literary works stand as significant cultural artifacts.

PART I

Vonnegut's Early Writing (1950–1969)

CHAPTER 1

Flabbergasted

Todd Davis

As I write this, today is Kurt Vonnegut's birthday, the first we'll celebrate without him, or at least without his body, since he quietly passed into whatever comes after this life last April. I'm sure there's a joke in there somewhere, one that Kurt would've enjoyed, but I'm not ready just yet to laugh in his absence.

I never met him in person; yet, since his death, I've missed him like I'd miss a favorite uncle. I imagine there are many folks in the same leaky boat as me, and ever since April we've been bailing tears in hopes of passing through this stretch of rough water. What's the reason for all this mourning among strangers? It's simple, really: Kurt's writing made people feel like they belonged to a family of sorts, very much like the folk societies he studied with Robert Redfield and to which he believed we all needed to belong for good mental health and for a feeling of purpose in life. Kurt's writing and speaking persona—one that I believe was as close to the real thing as possible—was two parts Hoosier hospitality and one part depression-era kindness. Kurt never talked down to his reader and seemed to genuinely believe in the words of his son Mark, which he used as the epigraph for his novel *Bluebeard* (1987): "We are here to help each other get through this thing, whatever it is."

While I was writing *Kurt Vonnegut's Crusade, or How a Postmodern Harlequin Preached a New Kind of Humanism* (2006), I made no attempt to contact him. I heard him speak a couple of times in person—once in a gymnasium at William Rainey Harper College just outside of Chicago in Palatine, Illinois, and once at Butler University in Indianapolis. Both times I was among a throng of thousands of adoring fans and had no fear of having an intimate moment with my

favorite author. I suppose I didn't try to correspond with him during the writing of my book because I was afraid everything I loved
so dearly about his work might be undone by the person behind the
language.

I had read enough Hemingway biographies to know that I could
love a writer's stories without loving the writer himself, and I'd studied enough theory—Wimsatt and Beardsley's intentional fallacy chief
among them—to understand that the writer's life or intent mattered
less in literary study than the work of art itself. Thus, with my sense
of intellectual maturity hanging from my shoulders like a doctoral
hood, I vowed that I would separate the artist from the work itself
and keep my distance from him until some later date.

But Kurt didn't seem to give a damn for that kind of maturity
or intellectual sophistry. In fact, he often confessed to retaining an
idealism and a sense of humor best-suited to high school and college
students. It's why he continually argued for artists to be agents of
change. As he explained in an interview with *Playboy*, "My motives
are political. I agree with Stalin and Hitler and Mussolini that the
writer should serve his society. I differ with dictators as to how writers
should serve. Mainly, I think they should be—and biologically have
to be—agents of change. For the better, we hope."

So I wrote my book without consulting the artist, but only the
artist's books and interviews and films, the scholarly detritus that
tries to explicate the imaginative vision of this man's oeuvre. After I
was done, I sent the book away to the presses, hoping to get my literary "testimony" into the public's hands. When I finally did land a
contract for the book, however, I had this wrenching feeling in my
belly—part anxiety, part wayward-son-desires-a father's-blessing—
that I knew could only be satisfied if the artist himself had a chance
to read the manuscript. I'm no saint. I would have published the book
whether Kurt approved of it or not. I'd worked long enough and hard
enough on the manuscript, and I believed what I wrote was as close
to the truth about his stories and his career as I could come. And
besides, I wanted tenure.

But I did send him the book, and for a few weeks I metaphorically
(and, at times, literally) held my breath, until I received a letter written on stationery from a Saab dealership located in West Barnstable,
Massachusetts, and, as the letterhead proclaimed, managed by a fellow named Kurt Vonnegut. I loved that he still had stationery from
his failed attempt at the car business in the 1950s and loved even
more the kind message and self-portrait he had scribbled to me upon
the yellowed paper. Although he said in the note that all he'd "ever

tried to do was the easy stuff," he'd already done the miraculous: He had made a fellow Hoosier believe that what he was trying to do made a difference, if not for other readers of Vonnegut novels, for the artist himself.

Over the next three years, I would find gifts and postcards from Kurt stuffed into my mailbox—once a leather-bound edition of *Welcome to the Monkey House* (1968) with another self-portrait sketched onto its inside cover and another time a signed artist proof of his pen-and-ink illustration, "Three Kings from Viewpoint of Christchild." Some writers are falsely self-effacing, seeking to be praised for their modesty as well as their work. This wasn't the case for Kurt. He literally was flabbergasted—a term he liked to use quite often—at his own success. He was serious and evenhanded when he evaluated his novels. As he said in *Palm Sunday* (1981), *Slapstick* (1976) deserves a "D," *Breakfast of Champions* (1973) a "C," and books like *God Bless You, Mr. Rosewater* (1965) and *Mother Night* (1961) "A's." So there was no surprise when his gifts would come in simple envelopes, with nothing to protect them from being wrinkled or crushed by the other mail. (I had to rush the artist proof to a frame shop in order to have it dry-mounted, removing the wrinkles as best I could.)

Despite his prophetic pessimism, Kurt remained committed to random acts of human kindness right up to his death. When I invited him to give the commencement address at our college, he declined, saying in a note that "standing before an audience nowadays, I would find myself quite speechless. Life is indeed about to end, in a hundred years or less, so I stand mute. Game over!" Yet in the face of such a dire prognosis, he would call and leave phone messages for students in my Vonnegut seminar, responding to notes or illustrations we would send him from various assignments, or he would write postcards to them, each name inscribed, admonishing them to "keep up" with "acts of kindness" because they "really matter." I still scratch my head at how peculiar this all seems. Going through my undergrad- and grad-school years, I never imagined a writer of the stature of Kurt Vonnegut sending a postcard to me or my class, let alone leaving a message on my professor's voicemail for me and my classmates to listen to.

But this was the beauty of Kurt Vonnegut as an artist and as a human being. He really cared. It was no charade. How human beings acted toward one another and the planet really mattered to him, and, whether the odds looked bad or not, he would not change his behavior and join the crowd, lemminglike, in decadent self-gratification. Kurt was forever explaining that he believed "at least half the people alive, and maybe nine-tenths of them, really do not like this ordeal at all. They pretend to like it some, to smile at strangers, and to get up each morning in order to survive, in order to somehow get through it. But life is, for most people, a very terrible ordeal." Such observations were part of his anthropological training. It's the reason he reports in *Slaughterhouse-Five* that Harrison Starr has chided him for writing an antiwar book, saying that one might as well write an "antigla-cier" book. This is, of course, an argument in pragmatism, in moral effectiveness. Kurt was nobody's fool. He wasn't convinced that writ-ing an antiwar book like *Slaughterhouse-Five* (1969) would actually change the course of the world, but he would not allow himself to alter his behavior and the things he believed to be true and right sim-ply because they were not pragmatic or morally effective.

The kindest thing Kurt ever did for me personally—and as you've read, he did so many kind things for me and my students—was to take my own writing seriously. Here, I don't mean my scholarship, but my modest attempts at writing poems. Kurt always addressed me as "The Poet," something that made me blush. (To be called a poet sounds rather grandiose, an oddity that ought to be earned over a lifetime, a moniker for the dead, perhaps?) Yet, when Kurt would encourage me to show him my poems, it meant the world, it meant not giving up on my writing, because here was a man whose work I admired tell-ing me he admired what I was up to as well. His notes were always brief: "Thanks for the perfect poem about the Patriot Act. I needed one," or "Particularly like 'Some Heaven.' My dad shot rabbits down in Brown County, and I could not enjoy his doing that, although he expected me to," or "Please keep sending me your poems, which have special resonance for me."

After my second book of poems, *Some Heaven*, was published by Michigan State University Press in February 2007, Kurt called me on a Saturday afternoon, late in the month. As usual, his phone call came from out of the blue and caught me off guard. In this particular instance, Kurt told me he had read my book and loved it. He said, "Todd, you should be flabbergasted. You've got beautiful poems cap-tured in a beautiful book." As best I can remember, I stammered and stuttered with his praise and said something about how I needed to get on the road to give readings and try to sell some copies in order to repay Michigan State for the kindness of publishing my work. After my yammering, there was a long pause, and then Kurt told me not to worry so much about it. He said, "You don't have control over the way a book will sell. You've done the good work. You've made poems that leave me flabbergasted. In fact, I'm going to go back through the book this afternoon." And with that, he wished me well and hung up. (In my experience with Kurt on the telephone, he would enter a conversation abruptly and end it just as abruptly.)

The rest of the day I worried that I'd given Kurt the wrong impression. I *was* "flabbergasted" to have my second book of poems in the world. I was "flabbergasted" that Michigan State had designed such a beautiful book and that another favorite writer, Jim Harrison, had offered a cover blurb. But Kurt's words kept echoing. He'd given me advice that sounded like a mixture of Hoosier common sense and Buddhism's refrain to empty oneself of self-concern. I slept fitfully that night and woke early to a raging snowstorm. My family and I were supposed to go to a Penn State women's basketball game, but with the roads so treacherous, we were bound to the house for a lazy day of reading and perhaps some afternoon sledding.

As I lay in bed, the phone rang. My wife, Shelly, who was downstairs on the couch, picked up at the same time as I did, and before I could say hello, the voice on the other end said, "Hi, this is Kurt." Shelly was groggy from dozing on and off with her book and assumed that this was our friend, Kurt Engstrom, who we had hoped to meet at the game, not Kurt Vonnegut. She launched into a discussion of the weather and regrets over missing the afternoon together. Ever the gentleman, Kurt apologized for waking her and explained he was another Kurt, not the one she assumed he was. After she hung up, Kurt said he only wished to let me know that upon a second reading of my book, he was even more impressed and wanted to do something about it. "These are real poems, Todd. Important poems. I'm so pleased for you," he said. Again, I mumbled thanks and then launched into a few sentences about how I hoped he hadn't misunderstood me the day before and how I was very grateful to the press and to him. He cut in before I could finish making a fool of myself and said, "The reason I called this morning is to ask a favor of you. Would you mind sending me two copies of *Some Heaven?* I want to give one to my friend John Updike and another to the poetry editor at *The New Yorker.*" My throat constricted and my heart didn't so much race as swell five times its size. Somehow I managed to say it would be my greatest pleasure to do so, and with that Kurt told me to have a good day playing in the snow with my boys and hung up.

That was the last time I talked to Kurt. The next day I sent him the books with a note, and a few days later I received from him an artist proof of "A Tree Trying to Tell Me Something," the perfect picture for someone like me whose poems so often have an oak or elm or serviceberry residing in them. It was signed to the "Altoona Poet" from KV and was dated March 1, 2007. I don't know if he ever sent my books to John Updike or the poetry editor at *The New Yorker*, because shortly afterward he fell and hit his head, drifting for a time in a coma before slipping off the obligations of this fleshly world.

It would be silly to say that I don't care or don't wonder about the fate of the books I sent to him, about the actions of one of my literary heroes in the final days of his life, but it really is only a curiosity, sort of like writing an antiglacier book when you know it won't stop the glacier. The fact that Kurt Vonnegut—a man whose reputation as a master of American letters was more than secure—would take the time to write a fledgling writer like myself, to send notes and phone messages to college students who were reading and thinking about his books, leaves me dumbfounded, or as Kurt would say, flabbergasted. I only hope that the ways Kurt reached out to the world—I'm sure there are many people with stories about him just like mine—won't be forgotten, that some of us will take his example to heart and live our own lives in a way that would make him smile, that would make him laugh hard enough to trigger the smoker's cough that in the end couldn't silence him.

Works Cited

Arendt, Hannah. *Eichmann in Jerusalem: A Report of the Banality of Evil.* London: Viking, 1963.

Broer, Lawrence. *Sanity Plea: Schizophrenia in the Novels of Kurt Vonnegut.* Tuscaloosa: U of Alabama P, 1989.

Davis, Todd. *Kurt Vonnegut's Crusade, or How a Postmodern Harlequin Preached a New Kind of Humanism.* New York: State U of New York P, 2006.

Farrell, Susan E. *A Critical Companion to Kurt Vonnegut.* New York: Facts on File, 2008.

Self, Will. *The Book of Dave: A Revelation of the Recent Past and the Distant Future.* London: Viking, 2006.

Vonnegut, Kurt. *A Man without a Country.* New York: Seven Stories, 2005.

———. *Bagombo Snuff Box.* New York: Putnam, 1999.

———. *Bluebeard.* New York: Delta, 1987.

———. *Cat's Cradle.* New York: Dell, 1963.

———. *Galápagos.* New York: Dell, 1999.

———. *God Bless You, Mr. Rosewater.* New York: Dell, 1998.

———. *Mother Night.* New York: Dell, 1999.

———. *Palm Sunday: An Autobiographical Collage.* New York: Delacorte, 1981.

———. *Player Piano*. New York: Dell, 1952.

———. *Slaughterhouse-Five or The Children's Crusade, a Duty Dance with Death*. New York: Dell, 1991.

———. *Timequake*. New York: Dell, 1997.

———. Welcome to the Monkey House. New York: Dell, 1988.

CHAPTER 2

Kurt Vonnegut's *Mother Night* (1961): Howard W. Campbell, Jr., and the Banalities of Evil

Philip Tew

The recent, much lamented death of Kurt Vonnegut, an iconic American author celebrated throughout the world, ought to have initiated a broad reconsideration of his life and work. As a small part of that process, this essay deploys various theoretical-conceptual and critical sources to analyze *Mother Night* (1961), published as a paperback original almost forty-eight years ago, which as Jerome Klinkowitz explains in "Vonnegut the Essayist," was part of the author's effort as a jobbing writer "to make money when the family weeklies reduced their story acquisitions" (4). Vonnegut's narrative focuses on a potential war criminal, Howard W. Campbell, Jr., an American. During World War II, Campbell had broadcast for the Nazi regime on German radio to an international audience, offering numerous racist invectives as part of his propaganda. The narrative purports to be the confessions written by him while awaiting trial in Israel, evoking a haunting yet elusive concept of evil that permeates the narrative and one's sense of its protagonist.

Unfortunately, Campbell only catches the attention of some Vonnegut aficionados because of his cameo role in revised abbreviated form in *Slaughterhouse-Five* (1969), a far more ridiculous figure when compared to his origins in *Mother Night*. In the earlier novel, as protagonist, he is awarded a full identity and history. He considers, at least obliquely, the moral complexities of negligent choices and support for a murderous regime. In that first narrative, the structure of Campbell's thought is distinctly circuitous and evasive, combining comic overtones, despite its dark subject matter, with episodic vignettes written in a laconic, often epigrammatic style. He describes himself "as a writer and broadcaster of Nazi propaganda. I was the leading expert on American problems in the Ministry of Popular Entertainment and Propaganda" (18), in which institution he is employed directly by Goebbels. Surely as a reader one is meant to intuit a certain pride as regards his eminence; and thus as a subtext to all that occurs, the war is the major historical coordinate of his life, overshadowing everything else, his subsequent life defined by this dubious role despite his claim to have acted as an agent for the Americans, passing coded messages. This essay reads the novel in terms of its narrative structures and strategies, and its underlying kitsch elements' (implied in Campbell's prewar career in Germany as a playwright responsible for appalling romantic plays) relation with evil. Underpinning its ongoing analysis is an implicit question of whether Vonnegut's book can render a viable ethical view with its oblique and darkly comic ruminations or whether it remains finally unable to confront the overwhelming nature of the Nazi regime.

Tom Marvin in "'Who Am I This Time?' Kurt Vonnegut and the Film *Mother Night*" describes this book as "arguably Vonnegut's most difficult and complex novel" (231). *Mother Night* represents Vonnegut's first mature novel, being stylistically assured, pithy, morally inclined yet ambivalent, and thematically sophisticated despite its apparent simplicity of language. Increasingly, this early novel is beginning to draw renewed critical attention, and it remains an intriguing contribution to Vonnegut's oeuvre, partly because it appears so early in the initial phase of his writing career, a period characterized by obscurity. Nevertheless, in many ways it seems to exhibit certain characteristics—mordant humor, a pithy and conversational style, ever present moral ambiguities, ethically neutral characters, and oodles of pathos—that would later elevate this jobbing writer who was, as Donald E. Morse points out in *The Novels of Kurt Vonnegut: Imagining Being an American* (2003), still at this point, before the later publication and positive cultural reception of *Slaughterhouse-Five* (1969), very largely ignored critically (xv). And yet, as Todd F. Davis indicates in *Kurt Vonnegut's Crusade or, How a Postmodern Harlequin Preached a New Kind of Humanism* (2006), *Mother Night* was certainly commercially successful, even if not taken seriously by critics or academics (2). In retrospect, the novel suggests themes, perspectives, and subject matter that would catapult Vonnegut into a kind of critical adulation that persists for many who lived through his rise and peak of fame, so much so that for Morse, he sustains and synthesizes both cultural and literary significance:

> A preeminent American storyteller with a sharp critical, satiric vision, Vonnegut may be seen—as I have argued—as *the* representative American writer of the latter half of the twentieth century in that the concerns articulated in his writing are the great moral, social, and political issues of his time, such as genocide, racism, the destruction of nature, endangered first amendment rights, the need for human community, and the sacredness of all life. (11)

Vonnegut seems to evoke a certain unquestioning, almost pious praise, which at times risks or occasionally even constitutes hagiography. Todd, for instance, recalls a visit to his town by Vonnegut when the author offered a reading, a performance attended by Todd and his wife. Celebrating this occasion, Todd offers a eulogy of the writer, signifying fortuitousness of being able to attend the performance and describing his sense of the writer's charm and homeliness (2–3). This is a dangerous critical strategy. If one is bedazzled by such declarations of the writer's blend of eminence and his absence of ostentation, as a critic one risks obscuring the dynamics of his novels, particularly this early novel with its dark themes and comic ambiguities, perhaps rather seeing the work appropriated by critics in a default "Vonnegutian" paradigm so as to fit into the Vonnegut myth, something I wish to studiously avoid. In this light, I wish to consider the novel itself together with a range of critical responses outside of the peculiarly self-sustaining constraints of the kind of view that partakes of such grandiloquence on behalf of the book's author, and in so doing, hopefully to return us primarily to the strategies and impact of the text itself.

Mother Night's first edition begins with Vonnegut's "Editor's Note," where he stresses Campbell's life as a writer familiar with Platonic lies, but Vonnegut insists "My duties as an editor are in no sense polemic. They are simply to pass on, in the most satisfactory style, the confession of Campbell" (ix). The details of this prefatory excursion allow Vonnegut to amplify his irony, with the admission of certain apparent changes to the original manuscript, including cutting Campbell's pornographic descriptions (x). What then might be the outcome of Vonnegut's apparent role as mediator, his relation to the war crimes? How might this be positioned or comprehended? Vonnegut's strategy seems to imply through its factual allusions something historically and biographically rooted that cannot be ultimately judged. Certainly, William Veeder in "Technique as Recovery: *Lolita* and *Mother Night*" feels that it emphasizes the moral absolutism of those that would so do, stressing "our common guilt" (99), and in this light, he reads the novel so as to suggest that "Vonnegut insists that Hitler's minions were not unqualifiedly loathsome, even as he displays the murderous instincts of 'good citizens' throughout America" (98). However, he also reads the "Editor's Note" as if Vonnegut simply asserts here a contradictory ambiguity, for according to Veeder's account, although Vonnegut concedes that artistic lies may contain a greater truth, Veeder objects that Vonnegut has thus failed to direct the reader as how to interpret Campbell (104–05) and essentially "leaves us largely in the dark" (106). In fact, Vonnegut's "Editor's Note" in some ways echoes both the "Editor's Note" and "The Custom-House" that preface Nathaniel Hawthorne's *The Scarlet Letter*. Like Hawthorne, Vonnegut distances himself, and complicates for the reader matters of accuracy, of factuality. As if outside the narrative frame, Vonnegut warns his reader:

> In preparing this edition of the confessions of Howard W. Campbell, Jr., I have had to deal with writings concerned with more than mere informing or deceiving, as the case may be. Campbell was a writer as well as a person accused of extremely serious crimes, a one-time playwright of moderate reputation. To say that he was a writer is to say that the demands of art alone were enough to make him lie, and to lie without seeing any harm in it. To say that he was a playwright is to offer an even harsher warning to the reader, for no one is a better liar than a man who has warped lives and passions onto something as grotesquely artificial as a stage. (ix)

I contend that Veeder misreads the tone and purpose of this section. Surely the teasing quality of the note (encountered first in the original publication) is predicated on an implied aesthetic defense of the protagonist because of his creativity, a claim that is palpably undermined throughout the text that follows. This creates a certain tension; Vonnegut's prefatory note also purports to invoke variously an implied factuality, an editorial process, and a certain historical relatedness to the narrative, which of course forms part of the elaborate structural joke. The narrative is, thus, layered, and never simply a context where as Veeder claims, "Campbell tells us that many men are guilty of his crime" (106). Interestingly, this section's final supposed quotation has been derived from an apparently "discarded" (xi) chapter where Campbell dedicates his book to himself, an act of astonishing narcissism on Campbell's past, one of complex irony on

Vonnegut's. Hence, the note allows the narrative to engage a broader ethical position concerning both culpability and suffering, which are interrelated. Vonnegut added an introduction written for the hardback edition published in 1966 that centers on his German family and his own experiences in Dresden. This changing of the framing of the text confirms the moral "We are what we pretend to be, so we must be careful about what we pretend to be" (vii).

Such duplicity brings to mind a real war criminal, Adolf Eichmann, whose capture and abduction by Mossad in 1960 surely influenced Vonnegut, suggesting aspects of his plot. Eichman was facing trial in 1961 in Israel for various crimes including those against humanity, just before Vonnegut's composition of his third novel. Jerome Klinkowitz believes in this provenance, explaining in "*Mother Night, Cat's Cradle*, and the Crimes of Our Times" that "the book was published in 1961, when Eichmann was in the news" (82). More specifically, Vonnegut had a particular model readily available for interpreting the contradictory significance of these events, because they famously attracted the attention of Hannah Arendt, who reported in 1961 on the legal proceedings for *The New Yorker*. Subsequently, she published her slightly longer account with its now celebrated subtitle, *Eichmann in Jerusalem: A Report of the Banality of Evil* (1963).

There remains a displaced and oddly reflexive quality to Campbell's narrative, a macabre version of Vonnegut's own task, and Campbell's activity (if not Vonnegut in his allusion to editorial intervention) echoes in many ways Adolf Eichmann's attempt at writing a memoir that he had begun before his abduction and had continued during his incarceration. This is alluded to by Hannah Arendt in her book. As Marvin says, "The novel constantly reminds readers that Campbell is typing his memoirs in an Israeli prison cell and reflecting on his experiences as he goes along" (233). This process first indicates "an average, 'normal person'...perfectly incapable of telling right from wrong," (23) and second evokes a seemingly normal individual, apparently without guilt or even hatred of Jews (22). Again, this reflects the observations of Arendt, who noted of Eichmann that "his was obviously no case of moral let alone legal insanity" (22) and who much later adds that from his police examinations, one might observe that "the horrible can not only be ludicrous but outright funny" (41) and that from his way of talking conclude that he lacked empathy (44). Both of these latter aspects appear clearly relevant to the characterization of Campbell, as similar incapacities lurk in the interstices of Vonnegut's description of the working of Campbell's memory. The reader reconstructs these failings. Even the novel's comic tone may allude to the realities that Arendt observed in Eichmann. Campbell seems capable of levels of apparent normality, functioning on the fringes of postwar America, odd and reclusive, but not monstrous to outward appearances. As Arendt says of Eichmann who functioned apparently as a normal family man before his abduction, "Everybody could see that this man was not a 'monster.' But it was difficult indeed not to suspect that he was a clown" (49).

Clearly in support of this supposition, there are numerous explicit allusions in *Mother Night* to events that evoke Eichmann's crimes and his time in Israel, including Campbell's meeting with Eichmann in prison, one of his guard's descriptions of fastening a strap around Rudolf Hoess's ankles as part of the execution of the commandant of Auschwitz. However, as I will suggest, there is more to the implicit references to Eichmann than simply a matter of inspiration; rather, a deeper and darker aspect to the overlapping set of implicit comparisons or affinities exists. Campbell's associational method leads him to recall a New Year's party in Warsaw at the start of 1944 where on meeting Hoess, the two discuss a pageant Goebbels wanted Campbell to write honoring German soldiers killed in suppressing the uprising by Jews in the Warsaw ghetto. According to Campbell's account, Goebbels envisaged a macabre annual event drawing on Campbell's kitsch tendencies in his so-called art:

> Letting the ruins of the ghetto stand forever as a setting for it.
> "There would be Jews in the pageant?" I asked him.
> "Certainly—" he said, "thousands of them."
> "May I ask, sir," I said, "after the war where you expect to find any Jews after the war?"
> He saw the humor in this. "A very good question," he said, chuckling. "We'll have to take that up with Hoess," he said. (12)

The implications of this exchange are chilling, the humor morally suspect and mordant. Again the tastelessness is suggestive. As Hermann Broch says in "Evil in the Value-System of Art" (1933), "There is probably no place where the restructuring of value-standards, where the effective reach of evil in the world is so pronounced as in the existence of kitsch, which significantly, is an offspring of the bourgeois age" (7).

A curious yet terrible associational logic underlies the sequence of recollections that come to Campbell during his time in prison, which itself represents a distinct phase of his life and his account, to which he intermittently returns. Vonnegut's book reflects three other major overlapping periods: Campbell's time in prewar Germany when initially encountering Frank Wirtanen, "the blue fairy godmother" (23), the American, Major Frank Wirtanen, who recruits Campbell to spy for his country of origin, partly by appealing to his vanity and performative nature; the years during the war itself, haunted by atrocity and with examples of inhumanity constantly at the fringes of his consciousness; and, the period in the early 1960s in New York when he meets George Kraft/Iona Potapov, a Russian spy who is a "sleeper," reencounters his Resi, only for her to betray him, and a hodgepodge of American fascists. In the prewar period, as Will Kaufman makes clear in *The Comedian as Confidence Man: Studies in Irony Fatigue* (1997), Campbell is "not at all part of the real world" (156). Kaufman suggests that during this time, Campbell is more concerned with his fantasies of romance and the intense love of his young wife, and he reads Campbell's subsequent "performance" as an elaborate comedy, which has a serious element, becoming "an American patriot, a spy who in spite of his patriotism has managed to give aid and comfort top his enemies, and—as even the American intelligence officer admits—a de facto Nazi" (157).

The main narrative follows an added introduction and the preface, and begins with the protagonist's deceptively simple declaration:

> My name is Howard W. Campbell, Jr.
> I am an American by birth, a Nazi by reputation, and a nationless person by inclination.
> The year in which I write this book is 1961. (3)

As Gholson indicates, the addition of Vonnegut's introduction may subtly mediate and ameliorate how one positions Campbell's crimes and transgressions (155), as the addition certainly defines the actuality and relevance of the text. The original text was more equivocal, and its readers "were confronted with the task of deciphering the 'truth' of Vonnegut's position as an editor, and the likelihood that Campbell had existed ever as a 'real' person" (155).

After Campbell declares his presence, Vonnegut has him next describe his surroundings in four short vignettes, each structured around an encounter and exchange with each of his four guards as they change shifts. As Marvin comments, "These stories create multiple perspective on the question of Campbell's guilt or innocence" (234). They describe first Arnold Marx who is disinterested in the war, without any recent history, ignorant of Goebbels, rather pursuing the past in archaeological excavations. The remaining three are variously Andor Gutman, an Estonian survivor of Auschwitz; Arpad Kovacs, a Hungarian Jew who masqueraded as an SS officer; and Bernard Mengel, a Polish Jew who helped with the hanging of Rudolf Hoess. Far from being the straightforward act alluded to by Campbell in his opening, this section, in fact, both reinforces a sense of historical specificity and also, in some sense, indicates the shifting possibilities of historiography. Campbell's single term "nationless" subtly evokes Arendt's book, in which she makes it clear that the declaration of the statelessness of the Jews was one of the central legalistic strategies by which the Nazis engineered their deportation not only from Germany but all across Europe and beyond.

Campbell's vicarious and perhaps apparently subliminal identification undermines him from the start. And importantly, the allusion in this sense subtly reminds the reader that the Holocaust haunts the text. Early on, it is specifically alluded to by Gutman, who admits to Campbell that in Auschwitz he had volunteered for the *Sonderkammando*, the detail who cleared the corpses and were then killed, only to be saved by Himmler's order to close the ovens. He feels it is shameful, while Campbell purports to understand, an early indication of his moral malleability, his absence of ethical engagement. For Marvin,

> His story suggests that it is possible to be a victim and a villain at the same time, and this is how Campbell chooses to portray himself in his confessions....Being a "victim" as well as an "agent" does not excuse either Gutman or Campbell, but it does suggest that conventional notions of guilt and innocence are inadequate to deal with the complexities of human behavior. (234)

There is another example of such inadequacy in the episode concerning Kovacs, who after joining the SS supplies information to the underground and fools his platoon with his invective. Kovacs was recommended by Eichmann for catching and executing fourteen potential soldiers. Ironically so, as Campbell discovers,

> "You met him, did you?" I said.
> "Yes—" said Arpad, "and I'm sorry I didn't know at the time how important he was."
> "Why?" I said.
> "I would have killed him," said Arpad. (9)

In this episode there is a further irony, since the Israeli jailer Arpad also belittles Campbell's broadcasts as weak after reading the transcripts offered to him as evidence of the American's crimes.

Bleak humor offsets Campbell's culpability, allowing him to memorialize at length his function as an insider in the Nazi regime. Only a fraction of a page considers the most horrific of the Nazi crimes. Campbell recalls being captured near Hersfeld and being forced by the Americans to visit the Ordhruf death camp where he "was forced to look at it all—the lime pits, the gallows, the whipping posts—at the gutted and scabby, bug-eyed, spavined dead in heaps" (19) and to watch the camp guards getting hung as he was photographed with his captor Lieutenant Bernard B. O'Hare, "lean as a young wolf, as full of hatred as a rattlesnake" (19). One wonders whether it is just Campbell or additionally Vonnegut who seems determined to avoid any binary sense of evil, where the Germans would be vilified and the victors celebrated. Clearly, to have done so would also have distorted the historical contexts. One wonders whether Vonnegut might have possibly adopted a more balanced sense of culpability. The survivors of the war generally do not seem to thrive. One example is Campbell's captor, O'Hare, who becomes inadequate and disillusioned, still trying to sustain a perverse notion of rational justice. In contrast, Campbell has willfully withdrawn from any idea of causality and consequences, avoiding any moral decision. The contrast is interesting. O'Hare rages and fulminates, verging on incoherence. In contrast, Vonnegut, by giving voice to Campbell, demonstrates how he is capable of using his persuasive intelligence, doing so to avoid the implications of his own actions by the pithy and entertaining nature of his words; yet in the interstices, Vonnegut seeds doubt, indicating through the manner of Campbell's tale, his underlying duplicity. The ruminations of Campbell in his cell reflect on the small but growing evidence of his account, culminating at the end with Wirtanen's account of their relationship.

Campbell, rather than admit the horrors of war, emphasizes the quotidian, the banalities of the Nazi era: ping pong competitions and drinking with his friend, Heinz. The comedy of the narrative is predicated on a series of contradictions, both minor and major, which recur throughout the narrative, as increasingly the core ironies multiply. Much later, for instance, toward the novel's end, in a passage much quoted or alluded to by critics, Vonnegut has Campbell forward certain ideas concerning the totalitarian mind when a G-man, who is arresting the American fascists, asks how Lionel Jones, a racist critical of Catholics and Negroes, can have made common cause with Father Keeley and the so-called Black Fuehrer:

> I have never seen a more sublime demonstration of the totalitarian mind, a mind which might be likened unto a system of gears where

teeth have been filed off at random. Such snaggle-toothed thought machine, driven by a standard or even by a substandard libido, whirls with a jerky, noisy, gaudy pointlessness of a cuckoo clock in Hell....

Jones wasn't completely crazy. The dismaying thing about the classic totalitarian mind is that any given gear, though mutilated, will have at its circumference unbroken sequences of teeth that are immaculately maintained, that are exquisitely machined....

The missing teeth, of course, are simple, obvious truths, truths available and comprehensible even to ten-year-olds, in most cases.

The willful filing off of gear teeth, the willful doing without certain obvious pieces of information— (145)

The section seems central to understanding Campbell himself, so elaborate is the underlying metaphor. Curiously the very lacuna or absence that Campbell identifies about the Nazi mentality seems to characterize him in a subtle fashion. The sublime nature of the lacunary thought process he identifies brings to mind Arendt's description of Eichmann, with his elaborate—and she feels possibly fundamentally truthful (22)—claim he was never anti-Semitic. And surely Campbell's description represents an act of projection on his part, having witnessed the Nazi leaders in Germany at such close quarters and passing convincingly among them. In a curious reading of the novel, Gilbert McInnis, in "Evolutionary Mythology in the Writings of Kurt Vonnegut, Jr.," regards Campbell's comments here as evidence of totalitarianism being part of a "random thought machine" (386) where in our universe, chance rules and serves as "a substitute for God" (386). Perhaps this too glibly tidies up the chaos and the pain. More acutely as regards wartime Germany, Arendt, in reflecting on the totalitarian system reconstituted by the evidence in the Eichmann trial, talks of a whole nation indulging in "self-deception, lies, and stupidity" (47) while exuding an "aura of systematic mendacity" (47). The latter more accurately summarizes the overriding inflection of Vonnegut's novel.

Establishing that Campbell was brought up in Germany suggests another displaced echo of Vonnegut's own particular experience, reflecting the strong split in cultural identity Vonnegut experiences being part of a German American family, a fact he alludes to in his introduction to the first paperback edition. Given that identity there is an added poignancy to Vonnegut's explicit admission in this early prefatory piece that "If I'd been born in Germany, I suppose I would have been a Nazi, bopping Jews and gypsies and Poles around, leaving boots sticking out of snowbanks, warming my secretly virtuous insides. So it goes" (viii) According to Marvin, this risks naive readers "equating Vonnegut with the novel's American-Nazi protagonist" (232). And, as Marvin points out, despite this admission of the shaping forces of culture and history, in a later edition, Vonnegut felt he must further distance himself from the text by adding another device, an introduction that summarizes the moral position of the novel and warns against assuming a dangerous identity (231).

Campbell's disordered chronology not only reflects his evasiveness but significantly popularizes a strategy redolent of modernist writing in that it allows the past to be both immanent and yet diffused. Campbell's tone and his prewar subromantic kitsch fantasies both exemplify quite how he exists in a world that appears utterly mundane despite its monstrous core to the German Nazi apologists. Campbell achieves this by suppressing the visceral, sublimating any residual empathy. One sees this in his father-in-law who worries more over a valuable vase than a slave woman. In this world of Nazi moral indifference that they share, a fluctuating topography attempts to conceal the underlying evil. Moreover, Campbell may be culpable well beyond his propaganda, complicit in his artistic presence and taste, and his erotic obsession with his wife (the physicality replayed later in New York with Resi, her sister), for as Broch explains of the representation of evil, of conveying this abstract sense,

> This gratification of physical urges through finite and rational means, precisely this patheticizing of the finite to the infinite, this conscious working at "the Beautiful" gives kitsch that touch of mendacity behind which one senses the ethically evil. For the flight from death, which is not the annulment of death, this shaping of the world, which nonetheless leaves the world no further formed, is still just an apparent annulment of time: The goal of every value-system, the transformation of time into a simultaneous system, is likewise the goal of every imitation system, including kitsch. (36–37)

The latter also describes very precisely the structure of Campbell's abjection after his wife's death, particularly the years spent in Manhattan. During that time, and possibly from the period after the death of his German wife, Helga, an actress, Campbell exists as a ghost of his earlier self. His existence in Cold War America is largely bleak and friendless. Despite his sublimation of the past, he seems unconsciously haunted by it. In his later account, his memories reawakened by Kraft-Potapov, Campbell justifies his presence in prewar Germany, not simply by an appeal to his espionage undertaken on behalf of the allies during radio broadcasts, but by foregrounding the love for his wife in their "nation of two." Campbell's past crimes resurface in the realities of the subterranean American fascist following he has acquired after being "outed." Ironically, when the aging American neo-Nazi the Reverend Dr. David Jones reunites Campbell with his "wife"—who after her supposed "repatriation" to Dresden, in fact, proves to be Resi, his sister-in-law working as an agent for the Soviets—Jones tells him of his admirers: " 'For having the courage to tell the truth during the war,' said Jones, 'when everybody else was telling lies' " (55). In contrast to such earlier vitriolic propaganda, the sensibilities of his prose remain conversational, intimate, and populist. It incorporates and parodies many fictional subgenres, well beyond the "spy novel," which is identified by Bill Gholson in "Narrative, Self, and Morality in the Writing of Kurt Vonnegut" (154–55). As Kaufman states, Campbell finds himself in the company of other confidence men (158), not only Kraft, but Resi Noth, Dr. Lionel Jones, and the defrocked Father Keeley.

Through Wirtanen, who appears to rescue him from abduction by the Soviets (with more than a hint at cold war rivalries), Campbell learns of yet another confidence man, Bodovskov, a Russian soldier who has found Campbell's writing. Bodovskov recycles this sentimental romanticism, publishing his plays, one of which had become a favorite of Stalin. Bodovskov turns Campbell's personal erotic writing into an illicit yet condoned industry turning out a pornographic version of the originals in the Soviet bloc. Vonnegut's depiction of the war is at times peripheral to the pathos of the comedy of Campbell's self-deprecation, his admissions of the absurdity of war, the weakness of those implicated in Nazism, the admission that emerges with relation to the band of American fascists of the kinds of anti-Semitic and offensive propaganda he produced while working for Goebbels.

Campbell's explicit view is that the issue of evil is often tenuous and elusive, subsumed in the craziness of his situation. When Kraft and then Resi fracture the studied reclusiveness and anonymity that has allowed him to abjure any sense of guilt, that past begins to recur. Even in his recollections, finding the site of evil is problematic. Campbell admits of his wife's and his time in Germany as actress and playwright respectively as the time he recalls being almost reluctantly recruited as an American spy:

> It wasn't that Helga and I were crazy about Nazis. I can't say, on the other hand, that we hated them. They were a big enthusiastic part of our audience, important people in the society in which we lived.
>
> They were people.
>
> Only in retrospect can I think of them as trailing slime behind.

To be frank—I can't think of them as doing that even now. I knew them too well as people, worked too hard in my time for their trust and applause. (25)

To comprehend the dimensions of such events, as Broch indicates, would demand a palpable sense of evil, and yet in stubborn contradiction of this position, Campbell resists admitting their monstrous nature, foregrounding humanity and contingency. Campbell is not entirely wrong in this, for as Broch insists, when meditating on the contradictions of the cruel and malicious, "Radical evil is innate within the system and cannot be eradicated" (27). Marvin argues much of the novel's emphasis is to do with issues of identity, and it accordingly should "be read as a fable rather than as realistic fiction" (231) and as exhibiting a certain didacticism.

Despite the parallels with Eichmann and other Nazis tried for their crimes considered above, at another level, Campbell's experience of war typifies that of many fellow Americans, contiguous with that of Vonnegut's generation of men whose early adulthood was shaped by these historical forces. He was just on the wrong side, and Klinkowitz concludes that the novel combines elements of black humor, a certain bleak madness of "'criminals against humanity'" (158) with "all the stuff of middle class life" (158). As David Simmons says in *The Anti-Hero in the American Novel: From Joseph Heller to Kurt Vonnegut* (2008), "The Second World War...served to universalize an antiheroic sentiment that had long been implicit within American ideology" (11). In this sense, Campbell reflects many of the preoccupations and experiences of the males of his generation, retrospectively attempting to situate these experiences in an antiheroic world and in one where the absurdities of life are regarded in a comic vein. Hence, it is no accident that the narrative intercalates or juxtaposes the wartime past with the present of the late 1950s and the realities of the early 1960s, with an implicit normalization of certain cultural values that characterized the period, but concerning which Campbell seems either indifferent or immune. Life continues while he is in stasis, trapped in his unspoken sense of guilt, traumatized by his own malice. Around him are parades, families, political nutcases, but he wants to sustain his role as an outsider. As Broch comments, "In times of securely held values, it is easy to separate out evil from individual value-fields (easier than in the present age, which has declined into a value-anarchy), easier even though the tension between the poles of good and evil was considerably smaller" (7). This helps situate and understand the chaos that lies beneath the apparent conformist stability of the consumerist postwar America, which is much of the backdrop to Vonnegut's sense of life's absurdities.

Toward the end, a veritable cast of the characters from Campbell's narrative have either arrived to offer condemnation or support or have sent comments to be considered judicially. His fate is equivocal. Harold J. Sparrow's letter reveals him as Wirtanen, and suggests Campbell will be exonerated.

For his crimes legally judged, Eichmann was executed just before midnight on May 31, 1962, after the publication of Vonnegut's novel rooted in his predicament. In contrast, if judged, Campbell's execution will not be formal, but derived from a self-inflicted hanging that is intimated at the end of the text. Does this leave Vonnegut in equivocation, finding in Campbell only acquiescence, a moral vacuum, one that albeit risks an inevitability of conflict? Can one risk being relativistic about horrors such as those perpetrated by the Nazis? Is Vonnegut's only the conclusion that the contingency of evil derives from human nature itself, thriving in the banality encouraged by repressive ideologies?

One might argue that, ethically, Vonnegut's novel needs do no more than interrogate and thereby problematize Campbell's actions. How so? Well, as Paul Ricoeur elucidates in *The Conflict of Interpretations*, with the possibility and the problem of evil, one's ethical problem is "a double relationship, on the one hand the question of freedom and, on the other hand, with the question of obligation" (431). Campbell struggles throughout with the implications of his actions, contemplating whether his undercover role exonerates him from his political and social engagements with Nazism. Finally, his position appears to be one that results from his choice, an act of volition. Evil derives from free will, and as Ricoeur adds, "I am the author of evil. [...] There is no evil-being; there is only the evil-done-by-me" (431), rather than it being a matter of the structure of nature. However, in the novel there is also a profound sense of the weight of history, its irresistibility. Even here it is precisely the peculiar reciprocity between acknowledging freedom and a "reflection in the experience of evil" (432) that are difficulties for Vonnegut if one considers the position adopted by his text. From the experience of evil, one finds the paradoxical relation to obligation, "for in discovering the power to follow the law (or that which I consider as the law for myself) I discover also the *terrible* power of acting *against*" (433) and yet simultaneously discovering the arbitrariness of choice. Far from being simply biographical—although such an element is strongly present—this novel would appear to respond ethically, although with an emphasis on the overriding ambiguity of the situation. Arguably, rather than adopt a simplistic moral position, Vonnegut inscribes the arbitrariness of both choice and fate in the structures of *Mother Night*. Thus, perhaps very subtly, finally in a cumulative fashion, through myriad incongruities and contradictions, the novel manages to convey an emphatic sense of the lack of empathy in the Nazi period, allowing one to continue to recollect and understand the closed mentality that culturally allowed space in which the Nazis thrived, all focused through the prism of Campbell's life.

WORKS CITED

Arendt, Hannah. *Eichmann in Jerusalem: A Report of the Banality of Evil.* London: Faber, 1963.

Boon, Kevin Alexander, ed. *At Millennium's End: New Essays on the Work of Kurt Vonnegut.* New York: State U of New York P, 2001.

Broch, Hermann. "Evil in the Value-System of Art." *Geist and Zeitgeist: The Spiritual in an Unspiritual Age.* Ed. and trans. John Hargreaves. New York: Counterpoint, 2002. 3–39.

David, Todd F. *Kurt Vonnegut's Crusade or, How a Postmodern Harlequin Preached a New Kind of Humanism.* New York: State U of New York P, 2006.

Gholson, Bill. "Narrative, Self, and Morality in the Writing of Kurt Vonnegut." *At Millennium's End: New Essays on the Work of Kurt Vonnegut.* Ed. Kevin Alexander Boon. New York: State U of New York P, 2001. 135–47.

Hawthorne, Nathaniel. *The Scarlet Letter.* London/New York: Penguin, 2003.

Kaufman, Will. *The Comedian as Confidence Man: Studies in Irony Fatigue.* Detroit: Wayne UP, 1997.

Klinkowitz, Jerome. "Mother Night, Cat's Cradle, and the Crimes of Our Times." *Critical Essays on Kurt Vonnegut.* Ed. Robert Merrill. Boston: G. K. Hall, 1990. 82–93.

———. "Vonnegut the Essayist." *At Millennium's End: New Essays on the Work of Kurt Vonnegut.* Ed. Kevin Alexander Boon. New York: State U of New York P, 2001. 1–16.

Marvin, Tom. " 'Who Am I This Time?' Kurt Vonnegut and the Film *Mother Night.*" *Literature/Film Quarterly* 31.3 (2003): 231–36.

McInnis, Gilbert. "Evolutionary Mythology in the Writings of Kurt Vonnegut, Jr." *Critique* 46.4 (2005): 383–96.

Morse, Donald E. *The Novels of Kurt Vonnegut: Imagining Being an American.* Westport: Praeger, 2003.

Ricoeur, Paul. *The Conflict of Interpretations: Essays in Hermeneutics.* Ed. Don Ihde. London: Continuum, 1989.

Simmons, David. *The Anti-Hero in the American Novel: From Joseph Heller to Kurt Vonnegut.* New York: Palgrave Macmillan, 2008.

Veeder, William. "Technique as Recovery: *Lolita* and *Mother Night*." *Vonnegut in America: An Introduction to the Life and Work of Kurt Vonnegut*. Ed. Jerome Klinkowitz and Donald L. Lawler. New York: Delacorte, 1977. 97–132.

Vonnegut, Kurt. *Mother Night*. London: Vintage, 2000.

———. *Slaughterhouse-Five*. New York: Delta, 1969.

CHAPTER 3

"*No Damn Cat, and No Damn Cradle*": The Fundamental Flaws in Fundamentalism according to Vonnegut

Paul L. Thomas

" 'Might not we do without religion entirely?' " asked Kurt Vonnegut when he gave the commencement address at Hobart and William Smith Colleges in 1974 (*Palm Sunday* 181). Should we assume, simply by his raising the question, that Vonnegut believed humanity would be better off without any formal religion? If we consider that Vonnegut often claimed that he approached his work as a series of jokes, as he noted directly about *Cat's Cradle* (1963), we may feel even more inclined to accept that Vonnegut wished humans would evolve toward either secularism or atheism.

According to Chris Hedges, in both *American Fascists* (2007) and *I Don't Believe in Atheists* (2008), human discourse and thinking are driven by crisis rhetoric that is supported by our inherent utopian thinking. Both crisis rhetoric and utopian thinking contribute to our sense of disappointment, to our seeing failure at every turn; the world in reality simply can never fulfill our idealized hopes, thus leaving us always in crisis. This chapter will consider more fully this human propensity for oversimplification, for searching for that which confirms what we *assume* is true (or desirable) when reading the works of a writer as nuanced and challenging as Vonnegut. Even those of us who value the work of Vonnegut are at risk of the failures in such assumptions and misunderstandings (exemplified by Hattenhauer's discussion of "Harrison Bergeron," as I will consider later). Nothing easy or simple exists in the pages of Vonnegut's novels. As a result, there is much within his work that speaks to the human race in the twenty-first century.

If we believe Vonnegut still matters, and I do, what makes his work relevant today? Vonnegut offers contemporary readers universal considerations of the complexities inherent in the human condition (his persistent wrestling with free will, for example), and his works create numerous alternate universes that are essentially mirrors of our real world, focusing often on humans creating our own suffering because of our habitual weaknesses as humans. *Cat's Cradle*, for example, uncovers the frailties of the human heart within the family unit, and it examines a grand and sweeping exploration of humanity's ability to destroy ourselves—permanently—because of our enormous brains (also a central aspect of Vonnegut's *Galapagos* [1985]).

In the 127 chapters of *Cat's Cradle*, Vonnegut offers a complex and nuanced commentary on twentieth-century belief systems, creating a fictional world (that ends) and a fictional religion that mocks a specific aspect of faith (fundamentalism) without discounting the benefits of belief and morality. Instead, Vonnegut implores his readers to "make use of what has poisoned us, which is knowledge" and to embrace a "*heartfelt moral code*" (emphasis in original). He trusts fully his own humanism, his own life as a Free Thinker. In the commencement address, Vonnegut ends, " 'And now you have just heard an atheist thank God not once, but twice' " (*Palm Sunday* 182, 184, 191).

Such apparent contradictions uttered often by Vonnegut are his devices for forcing his readers and listeners to step back from their assumptions (about religion, morality, and ethics, for example) and reexamine essential truths. In many respects, Vonnegut bridges the modernist and postmodernist camps (ones that are often mischaracterized and oversimplified in popular discourse) without reducing such ideological debates to simply taking sides. Vonnegut is of many minds on the universe, on the nature of being human, and it appears that he wishes for all of us to join him as he wrestles for a better way.

Yet, Vonnegut is no ideologue. He is no voice for any dogma.

Vonnegut's work depends on paradox, a technique that makes *Cat's Cradle* an apt commentary on the flaws in fundamentalism. Today, fundamentalism has a powerful hold over humanity and can be felt in the influence of the Christian Right, the New Atheists within the neoconservative movement, and fundamentalist Islam. In addition, the dangers posed by fundamentalism are not unique to religion, as Vonnegut reveals in the world that ends (once again) in the pages of his novel. It is a fundamentalist view and the *practice* of science that lead to *ice-nine* and the end of humanity as we know it; we must not ignore that Vonnegut chooses science and *not* religion as the catalyst for the end of the world.

* * *

Vonnegut often wrote and spoke of his roots as a Free Thinker, born in Indiana and raised in a midwestern culture that he associated positively with his humanism. I, however, was born and raised in the Deep South of the United States, and I am a life-long resident and *teacher* in a religion that has fundamentalism as the default mindset for not just religion, but *living*. Fundamentalism is the norm in my world.

In my South, raising a question *is rejecting*—just as making a joke *is rejecting*. We, like Emily in William Faulkner's "A Rose for Emily," often cling to the rotting corpse of tradition simply because it is how we have always done things. Young people of the South in the twenty-first century wear the Confederate flag with *pride* and are quick to explain to you that the Civil War was about state's rights— *not* slavery. They bring this belief about history from their homes and families and are rarely persuaded otherwise within the classroom.

Evidence holds little weight against the fundamentalist mindset. Too often, the fundamentalist mind enters and leaves the classroom unchanged. It is a frozen mind.

For my entire life, a large percentage of the people in my world have been fervent about the Bible being the literal word of God. Most of these people say things that would stand as an example of broad comedy in a Vonnegut novel, but are stated with the deepest earnestness day-in and day-out: "It's God will"; "She's in a better place"; or "Have a blessed day."[1]

This world of mine is very much unlike the world that shaped Vonnegut, the foundation of a Free Thinker. And it is quite unlike the religious life of Chris Hedges, a graduate of Harvard Divinity School and an international correspondent who has recently begun to investigate and write about fundamentalism in U.S. culture:

> We were taught that those who claimed to speak for God, the self-appointed prophets who promised the Kingdom of God on earth, were dangerous. We had no ability to understand God's will. We

did the best we could. We trusted and had faith in the mystery, the unknown before us. . . . The Bible was not the literal word of God. It was not a self-help manual that could predict the future. (2)

Most people of my South would say with complete certainty that Hedges is no Christian. His nuanced religious ideals and moral grounding are heresy to a fundamentalist.

In the South, people are fervent about both their fundamental faith and their patriotism. They never hesitate in the face of the conflict between the dogmatism of their faith and the individual freedom at the heart of their country. Many of my students, many very *bright* students, have stated directly to me that they simply do not care that their philosophies defy logic when they persist in believing in free will *and* in an omniscient God. Such discussions grew from our reading and considering of Vonnegut's *Slaughterhouse-Five* (1969). These young people, by the way, live in homes where they hear, "Our troops are fighting for your right to free speech, so keep your mouth shut about the war!" Hedges captures these inconsistencies in his discussion of religious fundamentalism:

> The dominionist movement, like all totalitarian movements, seeks to appropriate not only our religious and patriotic language but also our stories, to deny the validity of stories other than their own, to deny that there are other acceptable ways of living and being. There becomes, in their rhetoric, only one way to be a Christian and only one way to be an American. (11)

Again, in a Vonnegut novel, these contradictions are often drawn in broad and humorous strokes, such as Dr. Felix Hoenikker who is characterized as both laughably childlike and the creator of the end of the world; but in my daily life as an educator, they are a reality. Increasingly, according to Hedges, these ways of thinking and living are the reality of the United States and the world, with real and catastrophic consequences.

BOKONONISM: WHEN METAPHOR MATTERS MORE THAN FACTS

Vonnegut's work and the messages that run throughout those works weave a tapestry of religion, science, and art—topics that carry the author's central concern for humanistic ideals. On one hand, Vonnegut is ironically grounded in the central ideals of the United States of America. These ideals have been voiced by humanists and

Free Thinkers, whom we continue to celebrate without mentioning their humanism or free thinking, and many of whom we simply ignore: "One of my favorite humans is Eugene Debs, from Terre Haute in my native state of Indiana," wrote Vonnegut, adding Debs ran for president five times for the Socialist Party ("Do You Know What a Twerp is ?" 96).

I add the caveat "ironically" above because, despite a solid argument that American thought is essentially humanistic and secular, the *popular* view of the founding of this country is clouded by a mischaracterization of our Founding Fathers as the monolithic voice of the country's genesis—a voice espousing the tenets of fundamentalist Christianity.[2] The rewriting of history has the voices of our Founding Fathers sounding like the people of the fundamentalist South, not Vonnegut's and not Hedge's (although their worldviews are much closer to the historical reality of the founding ideas of this nation).

A powerful and popular dynamic in the public discourse of the United States views questions and humor as *rejecting* the subject with which they engage. Many people open *Cat's Cradle* and see a book satirizing religion and religious people. Yet, as I will discuss here, it is more accurate to suggest that Vonnegut is not rejecting religion and not laughing at religious people. Indeed, it is not uncommon for people to jump to conclusions about Vonnegut's work. Hattenhauer, for example, has explained that many misinterpret and oversimplify Vonnegut's "Harrison Bergeron," primarily by misunderstanding the nature of Vonnegut's satire. *Cat's Cradle* and Vonnegut's complex approach to religion and science can be just as easily misinterpreted, I believe, because Vonnegut, throughout his career, has been discounted as merely a science fiction writer, as merely a comic writer ("Science Fiction," *Wampeters, Foma & Granfalloons* 1–5).

What then are Vonnegut's commentary and its significance, particularly in the twenty-first century when fundamentalist Christianity has unprecedented power in the political processes of the United States and fundamentalist Islam has a tremendous impact on the entire world? Here, my answer is that Vonnegut is not rejecting religion, is not being disrespectful of religious people, but is cautioning his readers about the fundamental flaws in fundamentalism, religious or otherwise. Fundamentalism threatens the fate of humanity (and readers must be careful here to note that Vonnegut places the fate of the universe in the hands of a fundamentalist who is *not* religious, but scientific).

Cat's Cradle explores much more than simply religion; but for me, the novel is primarily a cautionary work using many of the tropes of science fiction and the devices of satire in order to remove us as far as possible from the immediate details of our lives (all that become the norm of our existence—thus, what is right). This critical distance helps us open our eyes, remove our prejudices and assumptions about those issues and beliefs at the core of our being so that we can reexamine our own lives—even the religion, or lack of religion, that moves us.

* * *

And there is a religion. Bokononism.

Founded by Bokonon; this is not his real name, of course, which is Lionel Boyd Johnson. He is born into an affluent family and is well-educated. Should we be suspicious of the initials, L. B. J.? Should we pause that, like Gandhi, Bokonon has two lives—the materially rich and fortunate first life followed by the life as prophet?

The transformation was as follows:

> He was enchanted by the mystery of coming ashore naked on an unfamiliar island. He resolved to let the adventure run its full course, resolved to see just how far a man might go, emerging naked from salt water.
>
> It was a rebirth for him:
> Be like a baby,
> The Bible say, So I stay like a baby
> To this very day. (Vonnegut, *Cat's Cradle* 107–08)

Vonnegut performs a deft job, breathing fictional life into a religious messiah. Vonnegut's Bokononism reveals the power of legend and the intricate power of both a religion's structure and that religion's language.

Consider the use of a fictional language and a set of beliefs within the novel: A *karass* is a team of humans who "do God's will without ever discovering what they are doing" (*Cat's Cradle* 2). That team is brought together by some avenue, a *kan-kan*. And this is how the language of Bokononism goes: *sinookas* (the connections among people), *wampeter* (the crux of a *karass*), *vin-dit* (fate), *duprass* (soul mates), *granfalloon* (a fake karass), *boko-maru* (a ceremony for expressing love), *zah-mah-ki-bu* (destiny), *foma* (pacifying lies), *duffle* (destiny of those at the bidding of a *stuppa*, a clueless leader), *Pabu* (moon), *Borasisi* (sun), *saroon* (to embrace one's *vin-dit*), *sin-wat* (one who is possessive in loving), and *pool-pah* (tremendous mess).

These are just words, but words that represent powerful beliefs (although Vonnegut's religion openly combines deception with Truth). These are odd words for us, who are not accustomed to Bokononism—because it is a fabricated belief system invented by Vonnegut—but they are also humorous. And the religion acknowledges its literal untruth—*foma* and *granfalloon* (echoing "soma," *Brave New World*'s pacifying drug, and "balloon," a word in a verse from the Book of Bokonon).

* * *

In Richard Attenborough's movie rendition of Gandhi, one significant scene includes an Indian atop a train talking with a Christian minister. The Indian inquires about the minister drinking blood. There is a pause as the two stumble with trying to understand each other. Then the Indian clarifies—the blood of Christ. And they understand.

This scene always allowed me to pause the movie when showing it to my classes. I would ask the students what they knew about Hinduism. Nearly without failure, a student would offer hastily, "They worship cows." (Recently, I had a student in a college course characterize Mormonism and the LDS Church as, "Didn't someone talk to a lizard?") My students, like the Indian asking about Christians drinking blood, often fail to distinguish between the metaphorical and the literal.

And here we come to the central issue, the central flaw with fundamentalism: That what is True must also be literally true. When we allow ourselves to be trapped within fundamentalist assumptions, we also become trapped in the oversimplification of being human. For the fundamentalist, the metaphorical alone is not enough. Vonnegut uses Bokononism to pull us back far enough from our own religion, our own religious experiences and mythologies, so that we can see this fabricated religion being overtly honest about its dishonesty *and* yet still meaningful. Vonnegut is not laughing *at* Bokononism and its followers (or its myths, or its language, or its scripture); Vonnegut is laughing *with* his fictional religion.

He is asking his readers to do the same.

Throughout his career as an expert in mythology and comparative religion, Joseph Campbell argued often that it is entirely possible that several religions can be simultaneously contradictory in their details (the legends and myths, the prophets, the scripture, the language), while being simultaneously all *right*: "Every religion is true one way or another. It is true when understood metaphorically. But when it gets stuck in its own metaphors, interpreting them as facts, then you are in trouble" (56).

Is Vonnegut, then, laughing at us, at least those of us who dare to take either our belief or nonbelief seriously? No. If we read carefully Vonnegut's section on "Religion" in *Palm Sunday* (1981), we hear a man reverent of morality, a man seeking moral ground, but filled with disdain for the hypocrisy practiced in the name of religion (175–99). Now, if we hold Campbell's warning in mind, the work of Vonnegut, specifically *Cat's Cradle*, becomes a metaphorical plea for humans to avoid "get[ting] stuck in its own metaphors" by coming to terms with the fundamental flaws of fundamentalism.

The Opium of the People?—Stuck in the Metaphors

Karl Marx wrote, "Religious suffering is, at one and the same time, the expression of real suffering and a protest against real suffering. Religion is the sigh of the oppressed creature, the heart of a heartless world, and the soul of soulless conditions. It is the opium of the people." This was followed within a few decades by Emily Dickinson's "Narcotics cannot still the Tooth/That nibbles at the soul—" These parallel metaphors cast a distinct view of religion, but they are often misunderstood and oversimplified as broad condemnations of belief, when in fact they are, like in Vonnegut's work, commentaries on the corruption of belief in the name of religion.

"The moment a person forms a theory, his imagination sees, in every object, only the traits which favor that theory," Thomas Jefferson argued. With these distinct comments by Marx and Dickinson, as with *Cat's Cradle*, we often impose on powerful language a confirmation of our beliefs instead of seeing the intent of the writer.

Reality is far more complex than popular perception. Are Marx, Dickinson, and Vonnegut critical of organized religion and the inherent hypocrisy in those institutions? Yes. Is their criticism itself dogmatic and simple? No.

In the essay "Do You Know What a Twerp Is?" Vonnegut writes, "Christianity and socialism alike, in fact, prescribe a society dedicated to the proposition that all men, women, and children are created equal and shall not starve." Later in the same essay, Vonnegut quotes Marx's famous "opium" statement and then adds the following:

> Marx said that back in 1844, when opium and opium derivatives were the only effective painkillers anyone could take. Marx himself had

taken them. He was grateful for the temporary relief they had given him. He was simply noticing, *and surely not condemning* [emphasis added], the fact that religion could also be comforting to those in economic or social distress. It was a casual truism, not a dictum. (11, 12)

Vonnegut notes that Marx's comment during the mid-nineteenth century overlapped with the U.S. government and people, both allowing and even embracing slavery; then asks the reader: "Who do you imagine was more pleasing in the eyes of a merciful God back then, Karl Marx or the United States of America?" ("Do You Know What a Twerp is?" 12). For Vonnegut, the issues are about ethical and moral considerations—believing that Marx was taking a stronger ethical stand than the U.S. government in 1844—and not about ideological commitments. That the United States stood for democracy and freedom mattered little if the reality of some people's lives contradicted those ideals.

Vonnegut's life and work as an artist, if we freeze both in the early 1960s when *Cat's Cradle* was published, are grounded in a free-thinking tradition of the Midwest and a growing move toward fundamentalist thoughts, practiced in both religion and politics throughout the broader culture of the United States. Free Thinkers profoundly impacted the foundation of American thought during the nineteenth century. Many of the most revered minds of American history have been Deists, Socialists, Free Thinkers, and radicals of all stripes (names that crop up again and again in the works of Vonnegut, although the 1950s essentially erased that past and replaced it with a New American Myth[3]).

These were contradictory and complicated times.

Supreme Court rulings and the counterculture of the Beat Generation harkened change on the horizon throughout the 1950s and 1960s, and American Culture pulled back hard into an ironically single-minded conservative and fundamentalist view of the world. Mainstream Americans stood firm against the cartoonlike view created about Communism, Socialism, and Marxism—all reduced to forces as powerful and insidious as the pods of *Invasion of the Body Snatchers* (1955).

As a focus for the context of Vonnegut's life and work throughout the 1950s, let's return to his comment about "a merciful God" judging both Karl Marx and the United States in 1844. If Vonnegut could have made that statement in the 1930s, the *popular* reaction would have been profoundly different when compared to making it in the 1950s—and when compared to publishing it in the first decade of the twenty-first century. When Vonnegut passed from the planet in 2007, the *popular* views of Marx in the United States held about as much disdain as the Fox News on-air obituary of Vonnegut, a "fair and balanced" trashing of Vonnegut that characterized him as a minor author having become irrelevant (and rich) by the 1970s, as nothing more than a "liberal," and as a man whose only gift to his children was his pledge *not* to commit suicide.[4]

In the twenty-first century, Vonnegut's novel from 1963 is speaking to a world that stands in the middle of conflicting fundamentalist worldviews. For a temporary (and distorted-by-romanticism) moment in the 1960s, revolution took an upper hand. That era forced a free nation to acknowledge people as being created equal, nearly two centuries after radical Deists made that exact promise. The United States has become an increasingly conservative nation, increasingly represented by embodiments of rugged individualism *and* fundamentalist views of religion (recall that Bill Clinton and Al Gore promoted themselves as born-again Christians well before George W. Bush courted the Christian Right nationally, and the 2008 presidential election in the United States has included many references to Barack Obama as a "savior" and a "messiah").

A *founding* of a free people is quite different than *preserving* a free nation.

A fundamentalist worldview—whether Christian and American, or Islamic and Middle Eastern—is satirized by Vonnegut in *Cat's Cradle*, as the novelist calls for all humans to embrace a "*heartfelt moral code*," encouraging us to resist the urge to become stuck in the metaphors.

THE FUNDAMENTAL FLAWS OF FUNDAMENTALISM—THE TWENTY-FIRST CENTURY AND *CAT'S CRADLE*

In the first chapter of John Irving's *A Prayer for Owen Meany* (1989), when the reader is being introduced to the titular character, Owen makes a plea when the car he's a passenger in passes a church where a man is struggling with repairing the roof:

> "WE SHOULD STOP AND HELP THAT MAN," Owen observed....
> "WE MISSED DOING A GOOD DEED," Owen said morosely. "THAT MAN SHINGLING THE CHURCH—HE NEEDED HELP." (34, 35)

This scene, and the entire religious and moral theme running through Irving's novel, forms a commentary on living out the principles of faith regardless of the literal details of that faith. In that respect, Irving's novel is very much a war novel *and* a religious novel paralleling Vonnegut's works. I believe that because Irving avoids satire (and because Owen is a fundamentalist, but cast as a martyr), his commentary is apt to be received more positively and accurately than Vonnegut's.

We should, I believe, read *Cat's Cradle* as a case against fundamentalism, instead of a rejection of religion or people of faith, instead of a treatise by an atheistic ideologue as certain of his ideas as a True Believer. What *is* the difference between Madalyn Murray O'Hair (possibly the most recognized advocate of atheism in the twentieth century) and Pat Robertson (a powerful TV-evangelist who wielded his power on the U.S. political stage as well)?—we should ask ourselves. If we read this novel as a metaphor valuable to us today and tomorrow, we must begin with one of the central calypsos from the Books of Bokonon:

> I wanted all things
> To seem to make some sense,
> So we all could be happy, yes,
> Instead of tense.
> And I made up lies
> So that they all fit nice,
> And I made this sad world
> A par-a-dise. (127)

Vonnegut's opening quotes include "Nothing in this book is true" and a passage from the Books of Bokonon about *foma*, the harmless untruths of the faith. Immediately, the reader must consider the nature of "truth," distinguishing between the truths that are factual, such as "The name of the author of *Cat's Cradle* is Kurt Vonnegut," and Truths that are abstractions, such as "Thou shalt not kill." In our daily lives, we argue with far less energy about truths than about Truths—and that distinction is at the heart of fundamentalism.

For fundamentalists, regardless of religion or denomination, both the truth and Truth are sacred. The historical facts of a man named Jesus, having walked on water and risen from the dead, are as vital to a fundamentalist as the messages of love God and love your neighbor attributed to the Son of God. As Campbell and Vonnegut would argue, the fact that fundamentalists place the *same* significance on truth as Truth is a fundamental flaw of fundamentalism.

In Chapter 3, the narrator, quoting Bokonon, notes, "She was a fool, and so am I, so is anyone who thinks he sees what God is Doing" (5). Many throughout history, and we should heed this warning today, have noted that few people are as dangerous as those who believe themselves doing the will of God. From making political pronouncements on the sinful nature of gay marriage to the barbaric terrorist acts perpetuated in the name of Allah, the flaws in the thoughts and actions of fundamentalists face us daily in the twenty-first century. When Vonnegut holds up a mirror to us in his novel, it is for us to see more clearly how we persist in failing each other. Consider the ever-present and simultaneously never-present figure of Dr. Felix Hoenikker; Vonnegut persists in arguing the value of the extended family by emphasizing the failures within the Hoenikker family itself.

Dr. Felix Hoenikker enters the novel as a father of the atomic bomb, inventor of *ice-nine*, and personification of the division between science and morality:

> After the thing [atomic bomb] went off, after it was a sure thing that America could wipe out a city with just one bomb, a scientist turned to Father and said, "Science has now known sin." And do you know what Father said? He said, "What is sin?" (17)

Throughout many public schools in America today, the recurring battle over science and religion has raised its head again—as if the Scopes trial never occurred over eighty years ago. The tension today centers on evolution, again, but the new complaint comes from advocates for "Intelligent Design," a claim that a creator God can be proven scientifically through a rejection of evolution as "just a theory."[5]

The ID claim depends on fundamentalist thought; it depends on a mischaracterization of science, an oversimplification of evolution, and a distortion of the term "theory." Ironically, Vonnegut's *Cat's Cradle* satirizes nearly exactly the distorted view of scientists and science that the ID advocates want the American public to believe—and reject. The scientists in the novel have disdain for superstition and magic—ostensibly their view of religion—but the key aspect of science that Vonnegut challenges is the disjuncture between science and *morality*. Newt recognizes about his own father, the scientist: "People couldn't get at him because he just wasn't interested in people" (13–14). Science that proceeds as if there are no people is morally bankrupt.

A scientist invents *ice-nine* (a substance that instantly freezes all water and thus causes the end of the world)—and within the novel

Vonnegut reminds us that the Nobel Prize is named after the inventor of dynamite. Hoenikker appears to have no sense of morality, and he is occasionally childlike, the character in the novel depicted weaving the cat's cradle. The cat's cradle is, in many ways, the central image in the novel that deals with the distinctions between the literal and the metaphorical. Literally, the string is *just string*: " 'No wonder kids grow up crazy. A cat's cradle is nothing but a bunch of X's between somebody's hands, and little kids look and look and look at all those X's.... *No damn cat, and no damn cradle*' " (165–66).

Here, the reader confronts the essential worldviews that create the tensions of our lives today, tensions that are often dangerous. As this passage shows, children are often challenged by metaphor; the human brain must develop in order for people to manage abstractions, including metaphorical or sarcastic language. When a small child asks, "Daddy, can I stick my hand in the fire?" it is unwise to reply, "*Sure, go ahead.*" Note here that the scenario and my use of italics help us, as adult readers, understand that the reply is sarcastic, not literal. For the child, however, the literal words could lead to a serious burn.

Fundamentalist thought blurs the distinction between the literal and figurative, sometimes dangerously so, often in a childlike way. If we were to take the Christian Bible literally, for example, we would today put to death children who hit or swear at their parents (Exod. 21.15, 17). When fundamentalists call for literal and unwavering readings of biblical texts, they back themselves into a difficult corner. A central mantra of the conservative political movement is a rejection of choice related to abortion. Fundamentalists claim a biblical foundation for their commitment to the sacred nature of the fetus as a living being. Yet, Exodus 21:22 clearly acknowledges that an assault on a pregnant woman resulting in a miscarriage deserves no more than a fine; the loss of the fetus's potential life is not defined as murder. In most matters of certitude, in fact, fundamentalists are revealed to be adept at culling those literal passages that fulfill their agenda, while ignoring the inherent contradictions running throughout the Bible.

In the nineteenth-century South, sermons justifying slavery were preached weekly, again through biblical passage after passage. For fundamentalists, the language of slavery had to be literal.

In *Cat's Cradle*, Vonnegut offers a complex message on the consequences of such contradictions. Through Bokononism, we are admonished not to become stuck in our metaphors. But through Hoenikker, we are also admonished to be wary of science without morality. The scientist playing with string, calling a string of X's a "cat's cradle," is not a threat because of his childlike wonder, not a threat because he sees the likeness of a cat's cradle in a loop of string, but is dangerous because he fails to see the moral implications of his scientific actions—actions that lead to the catastrophic human consequences of *ice-nine*.

The fundamental flaw is that the religious fundamentalist is blinded by the literal. The fundamentalist as scientist is blinded by the science, unable to see the moral implications in all human endeavors. *Cat's Cradle* suggests that religion and science are joined in this flawed approach to the world by nationalism. For Vonnegut, "a false *karass*,...a seeming team that was meaningless in terms of the ways God gets things done, [is] a textbook example of what Bokonon calls a *granfalloon*." The narrator adds a list of *granfalloons*, including "any nation, anytime, anywhere" (91, 92).

In the middle of the novel, the reader is reminded of the McCarthy Era, a period of U.S. history marked by the manipulation of a rising fundamentalist view of the world. Vonnegut, in fact, weaves into his novel a discussion of Communist fears along with expanding his discussion of Bokononism—highlighting the Draconian demands placed on loyalty to Boknononism in San Lorenzo. In the first decade of the twenty-first century, we live in yet another perfect storm where fundamentalist thought converges to raise up *our* fundamental beliefs against the evil fundamental beliefs of the Other, to champion our country (and to shout down any who raise a voice in protest), and to reject science for a pseudoscience (that makes its case by trying to be accepted as a science).

It may be that the central flaw with fundamentalism, as revealed in Vonnegut's novel, is blindness, an inability to see, or a refusal to see. Vonnegut continues considering the failures of nations, of governments, blending Bokononism with Christianity. Bokonon "paraphrase[s]" Jesus' "'Render therefore unto Caesar the things which are Caesar's'" as "'Pay no attention to Caesar. Caesar doesn't have the slightest idea what's *really* going on'" (101). We must see not only the moral implications within science, but also the distinction between our commitments to human law and moral law.

Bokonon creates a morality play within San Lorenzo, the fictional home of the religion in the novel, and his fabricated religion: "It was the belief of Bokonon that good societies could be built only by pitting good against evil, and by keeping the tension between the two high at all times" (102). Writing throughout the 1950s, Vonnegut lived and watched as the morality play of the McCarthy Era exploded before him; readers today can see the parallel between the antagonisms of the cold war (Communists as evil empire to good cap-italistic Americans) and the much more explosive War on Terrorism. As Bokonon professes, when the tension is high between good and evil, societies are good—in the sense of being compliant. (Many today filled with nationalist zeal admonish those who protest the war in Iraq for emboldening the terrorists.) Doesn't any entity with power benefit if those over which it has power are always *looking the other way*? Blind, in effect? If we in the twenty-first century keep our eyes focused on the ever-present threat of terrorism (and remain silent), do we see the cracks in our government, our leaders, our faith, our church?

Science, church, and state are corrupted by the narrowness of fun-damentalist thought, the blindness of fundamentalism. So too the corrupting influence of materialism on matters of the heart.

Again, if we as humans focus our attention on the details, we lose sight of the enduring. When the narrator of *Cat's Cradle* falls in love with Mona, he exposes the flaw in his own corrupted view of love after the *boko-maru*, "the mingling of awareness..., the foot ceremony." Later, the narrator discovers that Mona "adored her promiscuity," because love in Bokononism is universal while the narrator's love is possessive. The narrator discovers he is a *sin-wat*, " '[a] man who wants all of somebody's love. That's very bad' " (158, 207, 208).

To see this world as consisting of either possessions or potential possessions is a fundamental flaw of fundamentalism, as it manifests itself in capitalism, according to Vonnegut. Materialism and consum-erism are corrupting and blinding. Like the narrator, many today are willing to die and to kill in order to establish or maintain property. While the terrorist act of flying jets into the twin towers on 9/11 is deplorable for the loss of life, it was also a statement, a symbolic gesture on the supposed value of buildings. The United States has been driven to retaliate and to launch preemptive strikes primarily because the acts of terrorism occurred on U.S. soil—somehow imply-ing that the same taking of innocent lives is *less* tragic if occurring somewhere else. Vonnegut would ask us to value humanity regardless of property—either the ownership of it or the ground upon which any human stands.

Vonnegut's targets within the novel, however, are not as simple as a religion, a government, or even a declaration of free love. While the novel and the religion of Bokononism force the reader to consider the tension between the literal and the metaphorical, it also gives us pause about the nature of ignoring the physical and the material through metaphor: "All else was shaped by Mona herself. Her breasts were like pomegranates or what you will, but like nothing so much as a young woman's breasts" (203).

Here, the narration of the novel emphasizes not just the flaw of being stuck in the metaphor but the urge of the poet to raise all things of this world to poetry, to metaphor. There may be something to the simple beauty in the object; it doesn't need to be raised to any higher level by comparison. This is significant because Vonnegut waits until late in the novel to reveal the sacred nature of humans in Bokononism:

> "What *is* sacred to Bokononists?" I asked after a while....
> "Man," said Frank. "That's all. Just man." (211)

Vonnegut's plea for a religion not trapped by the flaws of fundamentalism demonstrates a sense of faith in the human, in the potential humanity in all humans. It is to love God *by* loving humans—a simplification of Jesus' plea for humans to love God *and* love each other.

Utopian Thinking—The Final Fatal Flaw

In her "Writing Utopia," Margaret Atwood muses about her own novel, *The Handmaid's Tale* (1985), and the concern for the genre identifying that work: Is it science fiction? Is her work in the utopia/dystopia tradition? She settles on the term "speculative fiction," but her discussion of the utopia/dystopia tradition parallel many of Vonnegut's own arguments regarding critics' desire to label him and his work. Atwood's definitions are also appropriate for the tradition within which *Cat's Cradle* sits:

> Utopias are often satirical, the satire being directed at whatever society the writer is currently living in—that is, the superior arrangements of the Utopians reflect badly on *us*. Dystopias are often more like dire warnings than satires, dark shadows cast by the present into the future. They are what will happen to us if we don't pull up our socks. (94)

The end of the world, this time in Vonnegut's universe, comes at the hands of scientists. Dr. Hoenikker, inventor of *ice-nine*, and thus the end of the world, is revealed to the reader as a scientist oblivious to morality; but other scientists and portrayals of attitudes by scientists pervade this novel. These are the most biting moments in the work—not his often saccharin characterizations of Bokononism. Scientists, not the Bokononists, are portrayed as blind to their own folly; when

Dr. Hoenikker misses a commencement speech, Dr. Breed delivers it instead, explains Sandra:

> "The trouble with the world was," she continued hesitatingly, "that people were still superstitious instead of scientific. He said if everybody would study science more, there wouldn't be all the trouble there was." (24)

This claim, of course, is utopian, thus unrealistic, thinking, no more valuable to humans than superstition itself.

As I end this discussion and make a final argument that *Cat's Cradle* is relevant today—possibly even more so than when Vonnegut wrote and published it—I want to consider these portrayals of scientists in the novel, ones that breath fundamentalist life into those who blindly end humanity:

> "Science is magic that *works*."
> ... "I am a very bad scientist. I will do anything to make a human being feel better, even if it's unscientific. No scientist worthy of the name could say such a thing." (218, 219)

The scientists of Vonnegut's novel are blind to moral groundings, blinded by their own faith in science as "magic that *works*" and in science as an ideology higher than respecting the dignity of any human.

If *Cat's Cradle* as a dystopian novel offers, as Atwood states, "a dire warning," that warning concerns fundamentalist scientists—ones similar to those identified by Hedges in *I Don't Believe in Atheists*:

> The blustering televangelists, and the atheists who rant about the evils of religion, are little more than carnival barkers. They are in show business, and those in show business know complexity does not sell. ... These antagonists each claim to have discovered an absolute truth. They trade absurdity for absurdity. They show that the danger is not religion or science. The danger is *fundamentalism itself.* (32)

And this is the danger Vonnegut's *Cat's Cradle* suggests that we face in the contemporary era.

In the wider public discourse of the twenty-first century, Americans are still easily drawn to a simplistic battle between religious and scientific fundamentalists clothed as both religious and scientific. Ben Stein's movie *Expelled: No Intelligence Allowed* (2008) caters to this false dichotomy, but the weakness of the documentary is far less important than the reality it captures, as expressed by Hedges in a much broader context:

> The battle under way in America is not a battle between religion and science; it is a battle between religious and secular fundamentalists. It is a battle between two groups intoxicated with the utopian and magical belief that humankind can master its destiny. (10)

We might imagine that Vonnegut would say "So it goes," about such a battle of worldviews, his patience and the optimism of a Free Thinker wearing thin at the many ways we humans persist in denying who we are by always seeking something *beyond* the human, by keeping our focus on the simplistic instead of the True.

NOTES

1. See Tyson.
2. See Jacoby's discussion of the mid–twentieth-century shift to viewing the Founding Fathers as fundamentalist Christians.
3. See Jacoby 292–347.
4. A video commentary on the Fox News coverage is available online: <http://www.youtube.com/watch?v=1SiVasR2Gzo>.
5. Scott and Branch.

WORKS CITED

Atwood, Margaret. "Writing Utopia." *Writing with Intent: Essays, Reviews, Personal Prose: 1983–2005.* New York: Carroll, 2005.

Campbell, Joseph, and Bill Moyers. *The Power of Myth.* New York: Doubleday, 1988.

Dickinson, Emily. "This World is Not Conclusion" [501]. *The Complete Poems of Emily Dickinson.* Ed. Thomas H. Johnson. New York: Back Bay, 1960. 241.

Faulkner, William. *A Rose for Emily.* London: Harcourt, 2000.

Hattenhauer, Darryl. "The Politics of Kurt Vonnegut's 'Harrison Bergeron.'" *Studies in Short Fiction* 35.4 (1998): 387–92.

Hedges, Chris. *American Fascists: The Christian Right and the War on America.* New York: Free, 2006.

———. *I Don't Believe in Atheists.* New York: Free, 2008.

Hill, Sam. "Fundamentalism in Recent Southern Culture: Has it Done What the Civil Rights Movement Couldn't Do?" *The Journal of Southern Religion* 1.1 (1998). 5 May 2008 <http://jsr.fsu.edu/essay.htm>.

Huxley, Aldous. *Brave New World.* New York: HarperCollins, 1998.

Irving, John. *A Prayer for Owen Meany.* New York: William Morrow, 1989.

Jacoby, Susan. *Freethinkers: A History of American Secularism.* New York: Metropolitan, 2004.

Jefferson, Thomas. "On Politics and Government." *Thomas Jefferson on Politics and Government.* The University of Virginia. 5 May 2009 <http://etext.lib.virginia.edu/jefferson/quotations/jeff0750.htm>.

Marx, Karl. "Contribution to the Critique of Hegel's *Philosophy of Right.*" *Reading Greats and Doing Philosophy: Scott H. Moore's Virtual Office.* Baylor University. Feb. 1984. 5 May 2009 <http://bearspace.baylor.edu/Scott_Moore/www/texts/Marx_Contr_Crit.html>.

Roszak, Theodore. *The Making of a Counter Culture: Reflections on the Technocratic Society and Its Youthful Opposition.* Garden City: Doubleday, 1969.

Scott, Eugenie C., and Glenn Branch. "Evolution: Just Teach It." *USA Today* 14 Aug. 2005. 5 May 2008 <http://www.usatoday.com/news/opinion/editorials/2005-08-14-evolution-teach_x.htm>.

Thomas, P. L. *Reading, Learning, Teaching Kurt Vonnegut.* New York: Peter Lang, 2006.

Tyson, Timothy B. *Blood Done Sign My Name.* New York: Three Rivers, 2004.

Vonnegut, Kurt. *Cat's Cradle.* New York: Dell, 1998.

———. "*Christian Century* Interview." *Vonnegutweb.com* 1976. 5 May 2008 <http://www.vonnegutweb.com/vonnegutia/interviews/int_xiancentury.html>.

———. "Do You Know What a Twerp is ?" *A Man without a Country.* New York: Seven Stories, 2005. 7–22.

———. *Galapagos.* New York: Dell, 1985.

———. *Palm Sunday: An Autobiographical Collage.* New York: Dell, 1999.

———. *Slaughterhouse-Five.* New York: Delta, 1969.

———. *Wampeters, Foma & Granfalloons.* New York: Dell, 1999.

CHAPTER 4

"God Damn It, You've Got to Be Kind": War and Altruism in the Works of Kurt Vonnegut

Rachel McCoppin

World War II is a central component in many of Kurt Vonnegut's novels; he uses the topic of war to advocate altruism. As stated in *Slaughterhouse-Five* (1969), Vonnegut understands that it is pointless to write an antiwar book because wars are "as easy to stop as glaciers," yet, arguably, many of his novels still impart an antiwar message.

Many post–World War II authors, including Thomas Pynchon, Norman Mailer, Joseph Heller, and Vonnegut, were wary of the military. Writers of the 1960s were concerned with "what...brutalizing war meant for human goodness" (Wagner-Martin 110). Wagner-Martin explains, "After the atomic bomb...a great many writers chose a humor of ironic understatement as a basis for their philosophy" (118). Vonnegut uses the topic of war and his black humor to advocate the existential component of individual responsibility for one's actions in the modern and postmodern world; " 'I beg you to believe in the most ridiculous superstition of all: that humanity is at the center of the universe....If you can believe that and make others believe it, human beings might stop treating each other like garbage' " (qtd. in Schulz 60–61).

Vonnegut's message of personal responsibility and altruism in the face of violence is an important one for modern and contemporary audiences. Vonnegut's works have straddled modernism and postmodernism for years. Many of the postmodern techniques he uses are connected to science fiction, but it seems, as Jerome Klinkowitz and

Donald L. Lawler point out, that his use of science fiction inevitably has modernist aims: "science fiction in Vonnegut's hands enables us to distance ourselves from ourselves, to face problems we cannot otherwise face directly. To enable himself and his readers to cope with the slaughter of innocents" (93). Even Vonnegut has the central character of *God Bless You Mr. Rosewater* (1965) declare of science fiction writers, "You're the only ones with guts enough to *really* care about the future, who *really* notice what machines do to us, what wars do to us" (18).

R. D. Laing in *The Politics of Experience* (1967) offers an existential conception of accepting personal responsibility for one's own involvement in the violence of the modern era. Laing believes that society only serves to propel violence; one is forced at an early age to repress oneself into accepting false beliefs, like fate and God, and this then serves to take responsibility away from the individual. Subsequently, violence is the result, because we are led to believe that everyone else is of lesser importance than ourselves. Humanity either turns a blind eye to injustice or feels that what it does does not matter. Laing states that "We seem to seek death and destruction as much as life and happiness.... If we can stop destroying ourselves we may stop destroying others. We have to begin by admitting and even accepting our violence" (49).

Vonnegut's revolt against war in the four novels discussed in this chapter is for the benefit of the community of mankind. His form of revolt in these novels is to have his characters embrace altruism. Through altruism in a time of war, his characters arguably attain self actualization.

As Vonnegut stated in *Conversations with Kurt Vonnegut* (1988), there are two recurring themes throughout his works: "The first is Be Kind; the second is God doesn't care if you are or not," and in *Mother Night* (1961) Vonnegut introduces a third message: "We are what we pretend to be, so we must be careful what we pretend to be" (*Conversations* 5). Vonnegut repeatedly stresses the importance of personal responsibility in a time of war.

This chapter examines Vonnegut's "war" novels—*Mother Night, God Bless You Mr. Rosewater, Slaughterhouse-Five,* and *Bluebeard* (1987)—and their engagement with the idea of personal accountability in times of violence. In *Mother Night* Howard W. Campbell, Jr., pretends to be a Nazi, though he is really an American spy, and realizes that what he pretended to be made him partially accountable for the Holocaust. Eliot Rosewater in *God Bless You Mr. Rosewater* suffers so much guilt from his war memories that he gives his life over to endlessly helping those in need. In *Slaughterhouse-Five* Billy Pilgrim travels through time in order to see his own personal accountability; though he believed he was detached from the war, he experiences a moment that finally makes him cry when he realizes that he was responsible for the mistreatment of horses after the bombing of Dresden. Finally, Rabo Karabekian shows an ultimate act of forgiveness by painting in *Bluebeard* his vision of all the survivors at the end of the war.

Though it is not entirely certain that Vonnegut draws from his own life experiences for his novels, it seems likely. In 1944 Vonnegut was a prisoner of war in Dresden where he witnessed the slaughter of "135,000 civilian inhabitants—the largest massacre in European history. Vonnegut and his fellow prisoners were drafted as corpse-miners, taking the dead Germans from their shelters and stacking them in funeral pyres across the ravaged city" (*Vonnegut in America* 13). Indeed, it is accepted critical knowledge that Vonnegut frequently mentions Dresden in his novels.

Moreover, in many personal interviews, Vonnegut's beliefs on war are revealed. When speaking about Vietnam, he speaks honestly, condemning both society and the government: "Our 45,000 white crosses in Vietnam were the children of lower class families....War was hell for them, and...highly paid executives are coming back saying, 'Yes, it's a wonderful business'" (*Conversations* 96).

Vonnegut undoubtedly looks keenly at the sad and horrific side of existence, but he still holds onto the belief that mankind can choose to treat others with kindness:

> Any sadness I feel now grows out of frustration, because I think there is so much we can do....I just know that there are plenty of people who are in terrible trouble and can't get out. And I'm so impatient with those who think it's easy for people to get out of trouble; I think there are some people who really need a lot of help. (*Conversations* 88–89)

Vonnegut makes it clear that he believes life is a series of constant choices, but he consistently states that the most important choice is to treat others with dignity.

Chances Lost in *Mother Night*

Vonnegut's *Mother Night* is important because it deals with a central character that fails to reach the levels of altruism that Billy

Pilgrim in *Slaughterhouse-Five* and Eliot Rosewater in *God Bless You Mr. Rosewater* achieve. This novel tells the story of Howard W. Campbell, Jr., who works as a spy for America during World War II. Campbell pretends to serve the Nazis in a radio program slandering Jews and praising Hitler, while in reality he is helping reveal coded information to the Americans. But, as times passes, his father-in-law, a German officer, reveals that, in actuality, Howard served the Nazis better than he ever served the Americans:

> "do you know why I don't care now if you were a spy or not?...Because you could never have served the enemy as well as you served us....I realized that almost all the ideas that I hold now, that make me unashamed of anything I may have felt or done as a Nazi, came not from Hitler, not from Goebbels, not from Himmler—but from you." (99)

Vonnegut explicitly states his moral to this novel in the first sentence: "We are what we pretend to be, so we must be careful about what we pretend to be" (v).

Campbell's fatal flaw is that he is an idealistic romantic when he chooses to be an American spy, and the postwar world is not the place for idealism. Initially, he is a famous American playwright living in Germany, whose only concern is creating a separate "Nation of Two" with his German wife, Helga. He is approached by a man he later calls his Blue Fairy Godmother, who asks him to give up everything to be a spy in the upcoming war. Campbell at first refuses by claiming, "'I'm not a soldier, not a political man. I'm an artist....If war comes, it will find me still working at my peaceful trade'" (38). But his Blue Fairy Godmother counters: "'I wish you all the luck in the world, Mr. Campbell...but this war isn't going to let anybody stay in a peaceful trade'" (38). The existentialist, Sartre, believed that all men were responsible for all actions. If one were drafted to fight in a war, there were always choices to be made: one could desert or commit suicide. Campbell is definitely faced with a hard decision. Vonnegut makes it clear that there are no easy answers, but he also makes it clear that Campbell chooses a decision that goes on to ruin his life.

Campbell's Blue Fairy Godmother knows that Campbell is an idealist: "'I think there's a chance I've made it attractive to you...you admire pure hearts and heroes...you love good and hate evil...you believe in romance'" (39). Campbell agrees to do something that appears to make him altruistic, giving up his civilian life to be an American spy; but in reality, Vonnegut's message is clear. Campbell admits, "I *did* fool everybody. I began to strut like Hitler's right-hand man, and nobody saw the honest me I hid so deep inside" (39). Vonnegut implies that all action that has to do with perpetuating war is wrong. There is no "right" side to fight for; there are no chosen people to win. All that matters are the concrete actions one performs toward others, and Campbell, to the whole world, even to his wife, was a Nazi supporter. The novel centers on the importance of individual responsibility. Campbell is eventually driven to suicide because of his initial inability to understand the importance of his actions. By dismissing his wartime exploits as being the necessary result of his undercover persona, Campbell ignores the role he has himself played in propagating the atrocities of the Nazis:

> I would prefer to dedicate it [*Mother Night*] to one familiar person, male or female, widely known to have done evil while saying to himself, "A very good me, the real me, a me made in heaven, is hidden deep inside."...Let me honor myself in that fashion. This book is rededicated to Howard W. Campbell, Jr., a man who served evil openly and good too secretly, the crime of his times. (xiii)

Throughout the novel, the reader sees Campbell as a sad, lonely man, who loses his wife in the war, loses his fame as a painter, and must now hide away in a small apartment in New York to avoid recrimination. He is given the chance to love again when Helga's sister, Resi, comes to him pretending to be Helga, but his life is doomed because of his wartime involvement. Resi turns out to be working for the Soviets and trying to capture him, and though she truly falls in love with him and denies her Communist involvement, proposing to escape with him to Mexico, she is shot by men hunting Campbell down. Campbell is not allowed to live in the romantic world he so badly wants to live in. After Resi dies, he is arrested but is again set free by his Blue Fairy Godmother. However, at this ostensibly happy moment Campbell freezes: "What froze me was the fact that I had absolutely no reason to move in any direction" (232). While it is true that Campbell is a victim of the processes of war, he still makes the decision to become a spy. Vonnegut depicts the character as someone who is indifferent to life. Indeed, life has no meaning for Campbell until the man that initially captured him at the end of World War II, Bernard B. O'Hare, finds him again after a lifetime of searching.

O'Hare tells Campbell, " 'I was born to take you apart, right here and now' " (249). But Campbell reveals the truth of his own life, and seemingly the moral of the novel, which is the importance of accepting one's own personal responsibility. In *Mother Night* Vonnegut promotes kindness toward others. To believe that any human is pure evil perpetuates violence, because it ignores one's own personal responsibility in turbulent times. Campbell reiterates O'Hare's beliefs, which shows that he finally understands his own involvement and responsibility for the violence that occurred during wartime:

> "I'm not your destiny, or the Devil, either!...Where's evil? It's that large part of every man that wants to hate without limit, that wants to hate with God on its side.... It's that part of an imbecile...that punishes and vilifies and makes war gladly.... If you want to be a soldier in the Legions of God so much...try the Salvation Army." (251–52)

Campbell has recognized that kindness toward others is more important than superficially being a good person.

This realization of personal culpability is explored further when Campbell remembers the time when Helga and he went below ground to escape more bombing. A man, woman, and their three children were also down there with them. The woman started yelling at God, so her husband knocked her unconscious and explained to a Nazi vice-admiral that she was simply "hysterical." The admiral "gave the man absolution" (242). Her husband "marveled at a system that could forgive weakness" (242). At this point, Vonnegut reveals his ironic tone through Campbell's thoughts. More bombs go off, and the couple's three children do not "bat an eye. Nor, I thought, would they ever. Nor, I thought, would I. Ever Again" (242). These last lines are important because they show a process whereby humanity does not develop the courage to do what is right. In the bomb shelter, during wartime, at least six people witnessed a destructive process of violence that, as Campbell states, would be their attitude throughout the entire war. The woman who acted out, perhaps rightly, is immediately stifled, and the others not only allow it but learn to continue the cycle of violence from their reactions to this act.

At the end of the novel, directly after talking to O'Hare, Campbell turns himself in to be tried for his past actions. He goes to the apartment of a young Jewish doctor and his mother, who experienced the concentration camps first hand. Extraordinarily, the Jewish characters, upon learning who he is, fight their feelings of rage and treat him with kindness, allowing him to come into their home to be treated: "When I did not move, did not reply, did not even blink, did not even seem to breathe, he begun to understand that I was a medical problem after all. 'Of, for Christ's sake!' he lamented. Like a friendly Robot, I let him lead me inside. He took me back into the kitchen area of his flat, sat me down at a table there" (256). Campbell then asks them to call the authorities, who could then put him on trial, because he finally understands his own culpability for his actions in the war; he notes how the doctor's mother

> understood my illness immediately, that it was my world rather than myself that was diseased. "This is not the first time you've seen eyes like that," she said to her son in German, "not the first man you've seen who could not move.... You saw thousands of them at Auschwitz.... as one who remembers...let me say that what he asks for he should have. Call someone." (256)

Although she recognizes the injustice of the world, the injustice of the situation that Campbell was placed in, the mother also believes that he is still responsible for his actions.

At the end of the book, Vonnegut presents us with a picture of a very indifferent, cruel world. Campbell commits suicide because he realizes that pretending to be a Nazi made him a Nazi in the end: "I think tonight is the night I will hang Howard W. Campbell, Jr., for crimes against himself" (268). Campbell's final statement reveals not only his sense of personal fault but Vonnegut's own belief that we must all recognize our own personal responsibility for the violence in the world around us if we are ever to eradicate, or at least lessen, man's inhumanity to man. Vonnegut understands that each person has a role to play in contemporary violence, which is explicitly stated when he tells his sons in *Slaughterhouse-Five* that "they are not under any circumstances to take part in massacres, and that the news of massacres of enemies is not to fill them with satisfaction or glee" (24); they are also not to work for companies that manufacture "massacre machinery." Jerome Klinkowitz and Donald L. Lawler comment on Vonnegut's theme of personal responsibility: "we in our daily simplifications assume that we are not all killers.... Through Vonnegut's technique we eschew such righteous simplicity and recognize...that any one of us...can victimize any one of us" (114).

Eliot Rosewater's Sacrificial Guilt in *God Bless You Mr. Rosewater*

Eliot Rosewater, the protagonist of *God Bless You Mr. Rosewater*, embraces the importance of kindness. At the start of the novel he has few friends and has purposely alienated himself from his extremely rich family. As the sole inheritor of his father's millions, Eliot chooses to reject his father's constant pursuit of making more millions. Instead, Eliot moves to the home of his ancestors, Rosewater, Indiana, to "care about the people there. . . . *That is* going to be my work of art" (44). This novel is an important text in relation to Vonnegut's commentary on war because Eliot's life choices are a direct result of his sense of guilt concerning his actions in World War II.

It is apparent early on in the novel that Eliot is altruistic. He gives up his inheritance and lifestyle in order to help other people. In Rosewater, Indiana, he sets up an extremely modest office, with almost nothing but a phone with a big red light for people to call whenever, day or night, they feel that they need something from him. Eliot chooses to live in poverty while helping the people of Rosewater, Indiana; a sick woman who Eliot visits states: " 'you could have been so high and mighty in this world, that when you looked down on the plain, dumb, ordinary people of poor old Rosewater County, we would look like bugs. . . . You gave up everything a man is supposed to want, just to help the little people, and the little people know it. God bless you, Mr. Rosewater' " (79). Eliot states that "There's only one rule that I know of, babies—: 'God damn it, you've got to be kind' " (129); this quote is important to the novel because it seems to be Eliot's mantra. He strives to not judge others while giving them all that he has to give.

Eliot undergoes a process that is well-defined in Jonathan Baumbach's *The Landscape of Nightmare* (1965). Baumbach's book studies American modernism from an affirmative, existential stance: "Though generally not religious in a traditional sense, a large number of our recent novels are almost paradigms of the existential possibilities (and impossibilities) of sainthood" (3). Baumbach states that modernism "at its best goes beneath the particular social evil to the fact of evil itself and dramatizes the extent and implications of personal culpability in a self-destroying civilization" (6). Baumbach believes there is a path that characters in modern novels consistently follow that progresses from innocence, to guilt, to redemption.

Baumbach suggests that in the postwar devastation of the twentieth century, characters feel guilt over the destruction of the present era. Modern characters feel that it is their responsibility to correct some of the contemporary wrongs of society. This idea of guilt is very important in connecting existentialism to modern novels because it shows that out of the devastation caused by World Wars I and II, characters learn to embrace altruism. The lesson, according to Baumbach, is that the characters generally accept a certain amount of responsibility for the evils of society, regardless of whether they could realistically be held accountable in any way.

According to Baumbach, once the characters have accepted their own responsibility, they move on to pursue redemption, either for themselves or for others, even though many times the effort to redeem is a failure. Eliot's guilt originates from one particular act that he committed during World War II, where as a soldier he killed three Germans with a grenade, not knowing that they were firemen:

> It was true: Eliot had killed three unarmed firemen. . . . When the medics got the masks off the three Eliot had killed, they proved to be two old men and a boy. The boy was the one Eliot had bayoneted. He didn't look more than fourteen. Eliot seemed reasonably well after that. And then he calmly lay down in front of a moving truck. (83–84)

After this, Eliot has a nervous breakdown and chooses to change his life to become a savior to all he can reach. Baumbach's study is specifically relevant to Vonnegut's works, because individual guilt and societal redemption are direct issues in his works. Vonnegut is preoccupied with accepting individual responsibility in order to help humanity on a personal level.

The feelings of guilt that Eliot experiences are directly tied to the three innocent lives that he took, and it is this sense of guilt that enables him to become altruistic. He wishes to make up for not only his wrongs but for all the injustices of life that he can connect with on a personal level.

Later in the novel, Eliot experiences a moment of epiphany:

> He's stopped working. He's all calmed down. . . . You look in his eyes, and the secrets are gone. . . . He goes back to work, but he'll never be the same. That thing that bothered him so will never click on again. It's dead, it's *dead*. And that part of that man's life where he had to be a certain crazy way, that's done! (237)

Eliot explains that he feels " 'as though some marvelous new phase of my life were about to begin' " (238–39).

Eliot leaves the people who have grown to depend on him in Rosewater, Indiana. While leaving, he sees an enormous firestorm swallowing up the entire city, after he reads about firestorms in a book about the bombing in Dresden. This obvious connection to Vonnegut's personal experience is important; Eliot's guilt at killing three innocent firemen is also connected. Clearly, returning to scenes of pain or guilt is important for the personal development of Eliot, and perhaps for Vonnegut himself. The firestorm that Eliot sees is imagined, but out of it, a spiritual experience occurs: "Within the boundaries, helixes of dull red embers turned in stately harmony about an inner core of white. The white seemed holy" (253). Eliot wakes up in an insane asylum.

With the firestorm, Eliot's strong sense of personal guilt is gone; he has forgiven himself. The "poo-tee-weet?" that recurs at the end of *Slaughterhouse-Five* is the first thing he hears upon awakening. The first words he sees are carved into a fountain: "Pretend to be good always, and even God will be fooled" (255). Something happens to Eliot by witnessing the firestorm; he replaces his personal guilt with acceptance: "'*Poo-tee-weet?*' Eliot looked up at the bird and all the green leaves, understood that this garden...could not have survived the fire he saw. So there had been no fire. He accepted this peacefully....it was Eliot's feeling that he had nothing of significance to say or give" (256–57). Instead, Eliot accepts life the way that it is.

Many months pass before Eliot consciously awakens and everyone becomes convinced that he is finally sane, yet Eliot is not yet consciously awake. When he does come back into consciousness, he appears as a simple man who has forgiven himself for his own past. In this manner, he resembles Billy Pilgrim in Vonnegut's *Slaughterhouse-Five*.

Eliot's father brings Kilgore Trout, a science fiction writer who appears in many of Vonnegut's novels, to the asylum, because Eliot tells him that Trout will be able to explain everything he did in Rosewater, Indiana. And Trout has an answer:

> "What you did in Rosewater County was far from insane. It was possibly the most important social experiment of our time....The problem is this: How to love people who have no use....So—if we can't find reasons and methods for treasuring human beings because they are *human beings,* then we might as well, as has so often been suggested, rub them out....We must find a cure. Your devotion to volunteer fire departments is very sane, too, Eliot, for they are, when the alarm goes off, almost the only examples of enthusiastic unselfishness to be seen in this land....So from this we must learn." (264–66)

Though Eliot does not return to Rosewater County, he maintains his desire to help people. It seems he becomes more altruistic because he accepts a certain amount of anonymity in his final act of sacrifice. Eliot's father proposes that the people who Eliot helped will "'take you for everything they can get'" (268). However, Kilgore Trout refutes Eliot's father by stating that "'The main lesson Eliot learned is that people can use all the uncritical love they can get'" (268). This is a powerful statement because though people may not appreciate or invite altruism, Eliot is a character who gives it freely; Eliot looks up into the trees and hears the birds again "*Poo-tee-weet?*" And he suddenly remembers everything about his experience during his blackout: "the fight with the bus driver, the strait jacket, the shock treatments, the suicide attempts, all the tennis, all the strategy meetings about the sanity hearing" (272). Eliot gets the doctors and lawyers to declare that he is now sane, and then he signs over his entire inheritance to fifty-eight mothers who have accused Eliot of being the father of their babies: "'Let them all have full rights of inheritance as my sons and daughters....Let their names be Rosewater from this moment on. And tell them that their father loves them, no matter what they may turn out to be. And tell them....to be fruitful and multiply'" (275).

Eliot becomes more altruistic as the novel progresses because he not only forgives himself but learns that he will never be able to change human nature; Eliot can only change himself. Eliot accepts the people of Rosewater for who they are; they accuse him of lies and constantly want as much as they can get, but Eliot still gives them all of the money he has because he views everyone as worthwhile: "The key solution to the human problem, Vonnegut kept insisting, is to find human dignity for all human beings—even those who seem to least deserve it" (*Vonnegut in America* 31). Eliot gave all he had to save himself; through his sense of personal responsibility toward his community, he experiences his own self-actualization. At the close of the novel, Eliot seems to have been reborn; he overcomes his past by giving up his millions. Eliot's example is what lives on; perhaps "his" babies will carry forth his mission:

> It's news that a man was able to *give* that kind of love over a period of time. If one man can do it, perhaps others can do it, too. It means that our hatred of useless human beings and the cruelties we inflict upon them for their own good need not be parts of human nature. Thanks to the example of Eliot Rosewater, millions upon millions of people may learn to love and help whomever they see. (268)

SLAUGHTERHOUSE-FIVE AND INTERGALACTIC ALTRUISM

Vonnegut's *Slaughterhouse-Five* begins with a chapter that is in part autobiographical about the author's true-life experience of surviving the bombing of Dresden. Vonnegut states that he understands fully that to write this "antiwar" novel will not put a stop to war: "there would always be wars…they were as easy to stop as glaciers" (4). So, knowing this, why does Vonnegut write this novel? Richard Giannone suggests that

> Vonnegut, the witness, acts as a moral scout, smuggling himself across battle lines to reach the front of consciousness where he hopes to find final resistance to killing. His moral awareness accounts for the uncommon affection for a cherished city of the declared enemy and for the German people themselves. They are presented as fellow human beings struggling against their own propensity for violence.…Both political sides lost in the struggle for human decency. (87)

It is clear that Vonnegut is antiwar in sentiment, as it is clear that he feels it is his responsibility to write a novel against war; Vonnegut states that " 'Military science is probably right about the contempt-ibility of man in the vastness of the universe. Still—I deny that contemptibility, and I beg you to deny it' " (qtd. in Merrill and Scholl 142).

Vonnegut knows that *Slaughterhouse-Five* will be unlikely to insti-gate much social or political change, yet the novel does its best to promote the idea that we are responsible for our actions and that a greater acknowledgment of this culpability may influence the future for the better. When Mary O'Hare accuses Vonnegut of writing a novel that will popularize war, the traditional purpose of war novels is criticized: " 'You'll pretend you were men instead of babies.…And war will just look wonderful, so we'll have a lot more of them. And they'll be fought by babies like the babies upstairs.' … She didn't want her babies or anybody else's babies killed in wars" (18–19). In order to address these accusations, Vonnegut states that his novel will be antiwar, recognizing the human cost of violence in its subtitle: " 'The Children's Crusade' " (19).

Slaughterhouse Five appears bleak in nature: "It is so short and jumbled and jangled…because there is nothing intelligent to say about a massacre. Everybody is supposed to be dead, to never say any-thing or want anything ever again" (24). Yet, it offers hope, but this sense of hope is only brought about by the protagonist Billy Pilgrim, an individual who doubts popular opinion, thinks independently, and accepts personal responsibility in an otherwise desperate, indifferent world.

Billy Pilgrim is depicted as extremely different from the other sol-diers in the novel. He is not in the war to fight; we are told that he is a "valet to a preacher [and] bore no arms" (38). Billy seems to be against violence throughout the war; in fact, the absurdity of Billy's appearance and actions makes the people who care about the "honorable cause" of war, like Roland Weary, appear absurd. Perhaps most importantly, Billy is depicted as different because he is a time traveler. Aliens, called the Tralfamadorians, teach Billy how to time travel, and this ability serves to show the reader Billy's unique way of looking at life—choosing to focus, mostly, on the positive moments of life rather than the negative ones: "That's one thing Earthlings might learn to do, if they tried hard enough: Ignore the awful times, and concentrate on the good ones" (150).

Billy's conscious concern for others makes him stand out, as is evident by the strange way he dresses. As mentioned earlier, Billy's attire makes some laugh in the midst of war. Eight Dresden soldiers, who are apprehensive about having the hundred American prisoners see them in their dilapidated condition, see Billy and laugh. Billy brings out the fact that both opposing sides in the war are composed of individual human beings: "Their terror evaporated. There was nothing to be afraid of. Here were more crippled human beings, more fools like themselves" (191).

When Billy is captured, he serves to reveal that war is often only about prejudice. The Germans who capture Billy and the soldier he is with are farmers; they are "sick of war," wounded multiple times and sent continuously back to fight. Staring into the corporal's golden boots, Billy thinks of Adam and Eve, how they were "naked...so innocent, so vulnerable....Billy Pilgrim loved them" (68). He looks up into the face of another one of his captors and discovers that it is the face of a fifteen year old boy; he sees it as an angel's face: "the boy was as beautiful as Eve" (68). There is no hatred here; even at the moment of his capture by the supposed "enemy," he is able to see them as worthy individuals. Billy is the main character of this antiwar novel because he chooses to see differently.

Later in the novel, Billy is the sole survivor in an airplane crash. When Billy's son, now a soldier, shows up at his hospital bed, Billy realizes the never-ending nature of war: "he was decorated with a Purple Heart and a Silver Star and a Bronze Star with two clusters...and he was a leader of men....Billy Pilgrim closed his eyes again" (242).

Throughout the novel, Billy commits many altruistic acts. When he is working in the syrup factory in Dresden, he chooses to hand Edgar Derby, the man condemned to die, a spoonful of vitamin-enriched syrup though it was illegal to do so because Billy knows that Derby is as malnourished as he is: "A moment passed, and then

Derby burst into tears" (205). Billy is also quite altruistic in his desire to teach the people of the world what he has learned from his experiences with the Tralfamadorians:

> The cockles of Billy's heart…were glowing coals. What made them so hot was Billy's belief that he was going to comfort so many people with the truth about time.…So many of those souls were lost and wretched, Billy believed, because they could not see as well as his little green friends on Tralfamadore. (35–36)

After all he has experienced, Billy wants to help others. He wants to show others how to manage in this hard world, and he believes teaching others about the Tralfamadorian philosophy will help people to cope. It appears that Vonnegut sums up his view of the novel's function with this quote: "If what Billy Pilgrim learned from the Tralfamadorians is true, that we will all live forever, no matter how dead we sometimes seem to be, I am not overjoyed. Still—if I am going to spend eternity visiting this moment and that, I'm grateful that so many of those moments are nice" (269). Vonnegut speaks out about the destruction and despair of this world, but he also offers hope through the ability of people to choose to view the positive moments in life.

Perhaps the most telling scene in the novel reveals Billy crying for the first time during his war experience while he is driving a horse-drawn wagon, searching for corpses after the bombing of Dresden: "He burst into tears" after seeing the condition that the two horses pulling the wagon were in: "he hadn't cried about anything else in the war" (252). In many ways this scene is the thematic climax of the novel. It is possible to suggest that the horses represent innocence, serving as a metaphor for all the living beings that were used to the point of death because of the inhumanity of men during wartime. Billy at this moment feels his personal accountability for this incident. Throughout the entire war, he is a man who floats in and out of consciousness and realities; but at this one moment, Billy realizes his own blame. He feels that he could have cared for the horses more than he did. This scene imparts a message of the importance of personal responsibility in all situations. From this point onwards, Billy is no longer aloof; instead of continuing to be a victim of circumstance, he learns the importance of altruism from this one incident. To constantly strive to be kind in the face of such sadness forms a kind of salvation for Billy: "Many survived the war; Billy survived with his tender concern for others intact" (Giannone 89).

Vonnegut states in the closing chapter of the novel that one of the nicest moments of his personal life is going back to Dresden with his old war buddy Bernard V. O'Hare, which is in itself a scene about seeking the good in a bad situation. In Dresden, he reads "key facts about the world," how 10,000 people die a day of starvation, 123,000 die for other reasons, and yet 324,000 new babies are born each day. By the year 2000 the population was predicted to be 7,000,000,000; he concludes melancholically by stating, that "'I suppose they will all want dignity'" (270–71).

Vonnegut has written that, as an author, it is his duty to reveal injustice: "'I continue to believe that artists—all artists—should be treasured as alarm systems'" (qtd. in Merrill and Scholl 143). The sociopolitical role that Vonnegut believes authors should fulfill is further exemplified in Vonnegut's affirmation of the Communist belief in the social function of literature. Vonnegut says that he "'agree[s] with Stalin and Mussolini that the writer should serve his society. I differ with dictators as to *how* writers should serve. Mainly, I think they should be—and biologically *have* to be—agents of change'" (Merrill and Scholl 143). *Slaughterhouse-Five* arguably fulfils this criterion, offering a message of pacifism in opposition to America's proclivity toward militarism.

RABO KARABEKIAN'S GIFT TO THE WORLD IN *BLUEBEARD*

In Vonnegut's *Bluebeard*, the protagonist, Rabo Karabekian, differs from the type of altruistic figure seen in *Slaughterhouse-Five* or *God Bless You Mr. Rosewater*, nor is he the doomed Howard W. Campbell, Jr., of *Mother Night*. Instead, Rabo falls somewhere in between these two poles. Vonnegut writes *Bluebeard* as if it were the memoir of Rabo. Rabo was a soldier in World War II; he lost an eye in the only battle he ever fought in, and directly after the battle, he was taken prisoner: "I was forced to fight at last on the border of Germany, and was wounded and captured without having fired a shot" (220). He served instead as an art collector for the Americans. After the war, he became a friend, and peer, of modern American expressionist painters, such as Jackson Pollack, Mark Rothko, and Terry Kitchen.

Bluebeard centers, as do many of Vonnegut's novels, on the violence and hardship that often exist in modern society. Rabo's parents are amongst the few survivors of an Armenian massacre. His father hid in the bathroom of a schoolhouse when the inhabitants of his village were gathered to be assassinated. His mother survived the attack by falling and pretending to be dead. As she lay there, she looked next to her, and in the mouth of an old, dead woman, there were jewels spilling out. Rabo's mother used the jewels to escape with his father to America, where they had Rabo.

Rabo grew up during the Depression and then went to work as an apprentice for an illustrator, who was famous for creating intensely realistic representations of items and scenes for many popular magazines. He fought in World War II, came home, got married, had two children, and attempted to become a famous painter; although his career was successful for a time, his paintings eventually faded to nothing. He also failed as a husband and a father. He saw most of his friends, the modern painters, commit suicide. He became a hermit, living in a potato barn behind the home of a rich woman, named Edith. Rabo states that he has been lonely all his life: "I actually went looking for loneliness and found it. I was a hermit for eight years. How is that for a full-time job for a wounded vet?" (10). Edith saves him, invites him to move in with her, and becomes his second wife. She later dies, and he inherits her mansion.

Rabo fails as a father and husband because of his experience in the war; he witnessed too much violence in the war to be able to live a conventional life. He tries to be an artist to forget his pain. He is intoxicated most of the time. His wife begs him to become a family man and to give up trying to be a famous artist. He learns that she was right. His choice not to be kind to his own family is his greatest regret: "Of all the things I have to be ashamed of, the most troublesome of this old heart of mine is my failure as a husband of the good and brave Dorothy, and the consequent alienation of my own flesh and blood, Henri and Terry, from me, their Dad" (258).

Despite all the tragedy Rabo and those close to him have experienced, there are many small instances of kindness throughout the novel. In fact, a quote, written by Vonnegut's son, opens the book, which suggests the importance of kindness toward others in a pain-filled world: "'We are here to help each other get through this thing, whatever it is.'" Rabo's second wife, Edith, shows him the value of kindness. She goes out into the potato barn and rescues him as if he were an injured animal. After he moves in with her, she asks him if he could be happy in such an old-fashioned house; he tells her not to change a thing, but she transforms the house into a modern gallery for Rabo because she knows that art may be his only salvation.

Another moment that is important for Rabo happens directly after he is set free. Thousands of people are led to an area of countryside on the border of what is now East Germany and Czechoslovakia on the day that World War II ends:

> There may have been as many as ten thousand people below us—concentration camp survivors…captured officers and enlisted men from every Army that had fought the Germans. What a *sight*!…the very last remains of Hitler's armies, their uniforms in tatters but their killing machines still in working order were also there. Unforgettable! (221)

The importance of this incident is revealed at the end of the novel. Throughout the book, Rabo has been hiding something in the potato barn where he used to live. The reader discovers that Rabo's secret is an incredibly detailed painting of the scene he saw on that last day of the war: "On an average, there are ten clearly drawn World War II survivors to each square foot of the painting.…There is a war story to go with every figure in the picture, no matter how small. I made a story, and then painted the person it had happened to" (300). Rabo himself is also in the painting, telling a dying Canadian bombardier who asks him if they're home, " 'Yes! We're home! We're home!' " (301).

It is significant that the gigantic canvas that Rabo uses for the picture is recycled from his most famous piece of work, a painting that had previously hung in the lobby of the GEFFCo headquarters, but had been returned to him because all the paint had faded until there was nothing but a perfectly blank canvas.

Instead of his former desire to make paintings that will last and carry forth his name to future generations, Rabo realizes that all that matters in life is giving something to others. That is what he proclaims his new painting is: "it is the last thing I have to give to the world" (296). Rabo opens his barn to the public in an act of sharing: "I at first made myself available in the barn to tell anyone who asked what the story was of this person or that one, but soon gave up in exhaustion: 'Make up your own war stories as you look at the whatchamacallit,' I tell people" (239). This adds to his newfound understanding of the importance of sharing, as Rabo allows the people that view the painting to make up their own stories for each individual rather than prescribing a single narrative.

Rabo learns to accept who he is and what he did. Just as the Tralfamadorians teach Billy Pilgrim to do in *Slaughterhouse Five*, he chooses to view life in positive terms. He is like Sisyphus in Camus's "The Myth of Sisyphus," who, despite being cursed to roll a rock uphill for eternity, still takes the time to enjoy the moment in which he arrives at the top of the mountain: "Sisyphus teaches the higher fidelity that negates the gods and raises rocks. He too concludes that all is well. This universe henceforth seems to him neither sterile nor futile.... The struggle itself toward the heights is enough to fill a man's heart. One must imagine Sisyphus happy" (Camus 123). Sisyphus, like Rabo, finds moments in life in which he is conscious of a good and purely beautiful quality to existence. Like Rabo's "non-epiphany" with Marilee, in which he is finally allowed to be human, so too was his miraculous experience at the end of the war. He was a part of the "Peaceable Kingdom," the title Marilee gives Rabo's experience at the end of the war, for a moment. The fact that he painted, in such detail, this experience, is a form of giving. He not only captures his experience, but that of his mother's, as well as the thousands more that he portrays. As Jerome Klinkowitz and Donald L. Lawler suggest,

> Driven to defend his painting, Karabekian says that it "shows everything about life which truly matters, with nothing left out." This accords exactly with what Vonnegut has said about his own intentions... "I would write about life. Every person would be exactly as important as any other.... Recognizing that within each individual being...lives...the 'sacredness' of that being." Here Vonnegut perhaps approaches [existentialist] Iris Murdoch, who frequently has her characters struggle through solipsism toward a love which she defines as an "imaginative recognition of, that is respect for, the otherness of another person."...This recognition thus becomes a key to behaving towards others with humaneness. (165–66)

Rabo does not offer commentary about what the scene means; instead, he lets the simple truth of this moment's historical existence speak for itself. He shares an important moment in his life with many other people.

For decades, Vonnegut continued to promote altruism in a modern and postmodern world, and it is for this that he should be remembered and valued as essential to the American canon. Vonnegut's novels condemn war. Though it is evident in his writing that he felt war would continue, Vonnegut spent his life teaching millions of readers to "Be Kind"; he writes to " 'catch people before they become generals and Senators and Presidents, and [...] Encourage them to make a better world' " (qtd. in *Conversations* 5). Vonnegut's novels have a humanist aim. He revolts against war by teaching his readers to value altruism. His characters learn self-actualization by respecting and valuing others. Vonnegut's novels force readers to reevaluate personal responsibility. In a time of war, Vonnegut asks his readers to maintain a position of pacifistic altruism.

Works Cited

Baumbach, Jonathan. *The Landscape of Nightmare*. New York: New York UP, 1965.

Camus, Albert. *The Myth of Sisyphus and Other Essays*. Trans. Justin O'Brien. 1942. New York: Vintage, 1991.

Giannone, Richard. *Vonnegut: A Preface to His Novels*. New York: Kennikat, 1977.

Hanna, Thomas L. "Albert Camus and the Christian Faith." *Camus: A Collection of Critical Essays*. Ed. Germaine Bree Englewood Cliffs: Prentice-Hall, 1962. 48–58.

Klinkowitz, Jerome, and Donald L. Lawler, eds. *Vonnegut in America: An Introduction to the Life and Work of Kurt Vonnegut*. New York: Delacorte, 1977.

Laing, R. D. *The Politics of Experience*. New York: Pantheon, 1967.

Mayo, Clark. *Kurt Vonnegut: The Gospel from Outer Space: (Or, Yes We Have No Nirvanas)*. San Bernardino: Borgo, 1977.

Merrill, Robert, and Peter A. Scholl. "Vonnegut's *Slaughterhouse-Five*: The Requirement of Chaos." *Critical Essays on Kurt Vonnegut*. Ed. Robert Merrill. Boston: G. K. Hall, 1990. 145–51.

Schultz, Max F. *Black Humor Fiction of the Sixties: A Pluralistic Definition of Man and His World*. Athens: Ohio UP, 1974.

Simmons, David. *The Anti-Hero in the American Novel: From Joseph Heller to Kurt Vonnegut*. New York: Palgrave Macmillan, 2008.

Vonnegut, Kurt. *Bluebeard*. New York: Delta, 1987.

———. *Conversations with Kurt Vonnegut*. Ed. William Rodney Allen. Jackson: UP of Mississippi, 1988.

———. *God Bless You, Mr.Rosewater*. New York: Delta, 1965.

———. *Mother Night*. New York: Delta, 1961.

———. *Slaughterhouse-Five*. New York: Delta, 1969.

Wagner-Martin, Linda, ed. *The Mid-Century American Novel: 1935–1965*. New York: Twayne, 1997.

CHAPTER 5

The Journey Home in Kurt Vonnegut's World War II Novels

Elizabeth Abele

In the first chapter of his cult classic *Slaughterhouse-Five or The Children's Crusade* (1969), Kurt Vonnegut explains why it took him two decades to articulate his World War II experience:

> And somewhere in there a nice man named Seymour Lawrence gave me a three-book contract, and I said, "O.K., the first of the three will be my famous book about Dresden." . . . It is so short and jumbled and jangled, Sam, because there is nothing intelligent to say about a massacre. Everybody is supposed to be dead, to never say anything or want anything ever again. Everything is supposed to be very quiet after a massacre, and it always is, except for the birds. (18–19)

Between VE Day and the publication of *Slaughterhouse-Five*, Vonnegut lived a normal life, suppressing his identity as a veteran—and perhaps his own feelings of guilt. Joseph Heller's classic *Catch-22* likewise was not published until 1961. In writing about Vonnegut, Heller, and their peers, Leslie Fiedler noted the irony that World War II (unlike World War I) was fought against "brutal and reactionary states despised by all men of goodwill," yet the most highly regarded novels about it "deliberately [subvert] values of heroism and combat heroism" (390–91). As is evident from Vonnegut's brief explanation, heroism is not central to his memories of Dresden—whether or not Vonnegut deliberately subverts heroism, it is clear that he resists heroic portraits of World War II veterans.

It actually took Vonnegut four sequential and interconnected, novels to express his personal response to the violent reality of World War II—*Mother Night* (1962); *Cat's Cradle* (1963); *God Bless You, Mr. Rosewater* (1965); and finally *Slaughterhouse-Five* (1969). These novels share certain settings and characters, in addition to having as a key subtext the horrors committed by the Allied Forces. Their focus is on the unintentional results of war: not only the killing of civilians but, just as importantly, the aftereffects that follow the veteran home; the particular manner in which those left behind are nonetheless infected by war. Though the majority of his civilian characters suffer in silence, Mary O'Hare in *Slaughterhouse-Five* is direct in her condemnation of war and its glorification: "It was war that made her so angry. She didn't want her babies or anybody else's babies killed in wars. And she thought wars were partly encouraged by books and movies" (15). Not coincidentally, Vonnegut dedicated the novel to her.

Vonnegut's war novels are also significant for their quasi-autobiographical nature, which works to bring reality to the more fantastic elements of the narratives, as well as confirms the author's intimate relationship to the work. Vonnegut denies his audience the pleasure of "over there," because the majority of the action of these novels takes place in the United States. George M. Cohan's popular song "Over There" encapsulates how the American experience and vision of the world wars were so divergent from that of Europeans: since the war never touched American soil or civilians, we could assume that the war only affected the combatants—and that it was "over" the moment that they returned home or "here." Instead, Vonnegut's World War II novels present an overlapping, sometimes fictional, world that refuses to allow the author or audience the comfortable distance of physical or emotional deniability.

Though most critical attention has focused on Dresden as the central issue of Vonnegut's World War II experience, the aforementioned novels—as well as later works like *Palm Sunday* (1981) and *Timequake* (1997)—reveal that Vonnegut's German American identity and his mother's suicide are intimately entwined with his war trauma. As these novels obsessively return to World War II, they likewise circle the issues of family legacies and our responsibility to those who love us.

This chapter will work to untangle the threads that run through these personal novels, examining how they attempt to disrupt the ideal of a noble war that serves to preserve a democratic society. Instead, their protagonists assume personal responsibility for how violence on foreign soil disrupts true intimacy and belonging at home—where it appears the real dance of duty takes place.

Hiding behind White Picket Fences

"Show me a hero and I'll show you a villain with good excuses" (Cumbow 155). Though Robert Cumbow articulated this maxim in a book about the Spaghetti Westerns of the 1970s, the sentiment was an important unspoken question after World War II: were Americans truly the heroes that we thought we were, or had our military forces committed horrors in Asia and Europe, only with "good excuses?" The national secret was that peacetime prosperity had been purchased with a horrendous victory. Americans were proud of their country's triumphs and military superiority—but do warriors have a place behind picket fences? Is it possible to comfortably enjoy the fruits of war living in a country that had not seen war firsthand in almost a hundred years?

Despite the portrayal of the manliness of this "greatest generation" that returned home after World War II, beneath the surface often lay their failure to provide properly for the people who counted on them the most. Cultural critics have noted the disjunction between the postwar American triumph and a less confident subtext in American film and literature of the period.

In select films like *Lost Weekend* (Billy Wilder, 1945), *Pride of the Marines* (Delmer Daves, 1945), *State Fair* (Walter Lang, 1945), and *The Best Years of Our Lives* (William Wyler, 1946), Kaja Silverman notes that male impotence is portrayed with unusual candor, with the supporting female characters taking over the scopic and narrative control of these films. This unabashed vulnerability is particularly apparent in *The Best Years of Our Lives*, which portrays the obstacles that a group of World War II veterans face in returning home, in sharp contrast to the strength of the female characters. Silverman describes the film's marked shift to a female-identified gaze: "it repeatedly calls upon her to look acceptingly at his lack—to acknowledge and embrace male castration" (69). It is ironic that these films presented returning veterans as castrated, as somehow less masculine, despite the ostensibly tremendous triumph of World War II. This view of World War II veterans is reminiscent of the returning soldiers in Vonnegut's *Slaughterhouse-Five* and *Mother Night*. When *Mother Night*'s Howard Campbell meets decorated veteran Bernard V. O'Hare again, he is no longer the man Campbell knew during the war: "he looked unhealthy—pale and stringy and hot-eyed. He had become less wolf than coyote, I thought. His post-war years had not been years of merry blooming" (245).

Amy Lawrence similarly explores this conundrum of the repatriated warrior, focusing on the persona of actor James Stewart, a decorated veteran who specified in his postwar contract that he would not appear in war films. Even so, Stewart did not return to the frothy romantic comedies of his prewar films such as *You Can't Take it with You* (Frank Capra, 1938), *Shop Around the Corner* (Ernst Lubitsch, 1940), and *Philadelphia Story* (George Cukor, 1940). Instead, Lawrence sees Stewart's after-war career as exemplifying the secret struggles of the "happy days" of postwar America, when the country tried to forget about war and focus on the domestic bliss of suburbs and new kitchen appliances:

> There was a lingering ambivalence about the massive destruction it had taken to win the war....As a combat veteran Stewart was trapped by a contradiction which, in the wake of the officially sanctioned postwar euphoria, produced psychological turmoil veterans were left to negotiate alone. Consequently, nearly all of Stewart's postwar roles are haunted by an undercurrent of confusion, guilt, and shame that is historically specific but can never be articulated. (70)

Though Stewart refused to handle a gun in a war film, he handled many in Westerns—a timeless setting, removed from contemporary history, where perhaps American triumph could be enjoyed with fewer qualms. However, the guilt that Lawrence notes is still evident: *Broken Arrow* (Delmar Daves, 1950) and *Winchester 73* (Anthony Mann, 1950) both present complex portraits of the tired warrior. However, in the contemporary, urban thriller *Rope* (Alfred Hitchcock, 1948), Stewart's character is forced to directly confront the murderous implications of his flippant ideals, because his former students have killed a man in cold blood following his lectures.

As part of America's recuperation from the shame and defeat of the Vietnam Era, the 1990s saw an intense interest in remembering and memorializing the intense sacrifices and losses of World War II. Since images of World War II abound in Steven Spielberg's earlier films (from *Jaws* and the *Indiana Jones* films onward) it is not surprising that he should choose World War II as the subject for his move to "serious" films: *Schindler's List* (1993) and *Saving Private Ryan* (1998). Marcia Landy discusses *Schindler's List*'s process of remembering:

> By perpetuating the salvation scenario, [*Schindler's List*] participates in discourses that have been identified with popular models of narration.

The films is a text that relies on common sense to dramatize its relation to the history of the Holocaust—in its highlighting of the drama
of survival to work, in its reenactment of the ritual of mourning, and
in its recourse to an elegiac style that mimes mourning. (256)

Both *Schindler's List* and *Saving Private Ryan* end by celebrating
survivors and their descendants who, in turn, perform an elegy for
the heroes responsible for their being alive. Like Tom Brokaw's *The
Greatest Generation* or the Tom Hanks-produced miniseries "Band
of Brothers," Spielberg's films acknowledge the "unpayable debt"
that the present has to the participants of World War II—as well as
boomers' regret that they were not similarly tested, in a battle against
true evil.

World War II veteran and author, Kurt Vonnegut, Jr., reflected a
response in his writing more akin to James Stewart than either Tom
Brokaw, Steven Spielberg, or Tom Hanks. Unlike Landy's description
of witnessing as "related to the need to lament, to mourn, and to
restore dignity to the victims and to the survivors" (250), Vonnegut's
witnessing refuses to mourn or to believe that dignity is a possible,
or even a worthwhile, goal. Likewise, Vonnegut never documents the
"true evil" of the Nazis or the Japanese, but merely the arrogant, careless evils of the Allies. Vonnegut's obsessive remembering of World
War II and Dresden bares more similarities to Stewart's "confusion,
guilt, and shame." As he commented in a recent joint interview with
Joseph Heller, "Only one person came home from World War Two
who was treated like a hero and that was Audie Murphy. Everybody
knew he was the only hero" (Mallory).

Ironically, though Vonnegut spent so much time writing about the
events in Dresden, it is possible to suggest that he might still accept
Brokaw's appellation of belonging to "The Greatest Generation."
Part of Vonnegut's own confusion is that though *Slaughterhouse-Five*
is commonly characterized as an antiwar novel, the author felt genuine pride to have served in the military. In describing himself in his
self-interview for the *Paris Review* in 1977, he wrote, "He is a veteran
and a family man, large-boned, loose-jointed at ease" (qtd. in *Palm
Sunday* 83). It is apparent that "veteran" is given equal weight with
his identity as a "family man," with "writer" nowhere to be seen. In
the same interview, he admitted (albeit ambiguously) that he'd like
a military funeral: "It will be a way of achieving what I've always
wanted more than anything—something I could have had, if only I'd
managed to get myself killed in war . . . the unqualified approval of my
community" (84).

As reflected in interviews and other commentaries, Vonnegut felt particularly connected to fellow World War II veteran-authors Heller, Norman Mailer, William Styron, James Jones, and Irwin Shaw. In *Palm Sunday* Vonnegut recounted Jones's disinterest in his publisher's offer to introduce him to Ernest Hemingway, because Jones did not consider Hemingway a true "veteran": "Real soldiers, according to Jones, damn well had to stay where they were told, or go where they were told, and eat swill, and take the worst the enemy had to throw at them day after day, week after week" (3). Even in the last interview before his death, Vonnegut expressed no regret for his military service: "This should have been a great country. But we are despised all over the world now. I was hoping to build a country and add to its literature. That's why I served in World War II and that's why I wrote books" (qtd. in Rentilly). Again, it is significant that Vonnegut presents his war service and his writing as equally valid contributions to society. From these comments, it would seem that Vonnegut, like Jones, did not regret that he did what his country *told* him to—however, he did appear to regret what *had to* be done and *had to* be lived through.

There are several explanations for Vonnegut's unresolved ambivalence toward World War II. Vonnegut's war service was in the infantry; however, the destruction of Dresden came from the air, an example of what Eduoardo Mendieta terms "urbicide," which he defines as violence toward cities with little military significance. In a speech for the Smithsonian in 1990, Vonnegut similarly differentiated between military airstrikes against Hamburg and Hiroshima, targets with military value and therefore justifiable, and airstrikes against Dresden, Nagasaki, and Panama—largely civilian areas and therefore not justifiable (Klinkowitz 25). In his book on World War II, Max Hastings described the difference between the war fought on the ground and that fought in the air:

> It was a policy quite at odds with the spirit in which the Americans and the British otherwise conducted their war effort. The remoteness of bombing rendered tolerable in the eyes of Western political leaders and military commanders, not to mention their aircrew, actions which would have seemed repugnant and probably unbearable had the Allies confronted the consequences at close quarters. (308)

James Stewart and Joseph Heller both flew bombing missions like these. Since Heller referred to his missions as "milk runs," his view from the air might explain the detached quality of *Catch-22* and the reason why Heller himself had the personal detachment to leave World War II behind in his subsequent novels in the 1970s and 1980s, only returning to the subject at the end of his career. Vonnegut does not appear to share Heller's detachment. In *Slaughterhouse-Five* Vonnegut includes the advice he gave to his sons to never participate in massacres nor to ever rejoice in the massacres of enemies (19). Vonnegut's work takes particular umbrage with the dehumanizing processes of war.

Vonnegut not only explained why he felt it was so vital to report what he witnessed on the ground at Dresden but also stated that he realized that his countrymen who dropped the bombs had been honorable men, with "no more fury and angry vigor than would" any man on "an automobile assembly line" (qtd. in Mendieta). However, though these pilots and their commanders were not guilty, they may have been culpable. What Vonnegut realized through his experience on the ground in Dresden was, as Mendieta noted, "technology makes it both necessary and easy to destroy without having to confront the consequences of one's acts of destruction."

One element that connects Vonnegut's 1960s' novels is his protagonists' commitment to face the consequences of their acts of destruction, no matter how unintended these acts were. Though Vonnegut had nothing to do with the bombing of Dresden, his obsessive return to the same narratives and themes reveals the responsibility that he felt for his indirect acts of destruction, which he found as difficult to chronicle as Dresden. Through his fiction, he appears to use writing as a means of atonement, both for his time as a German American soldier and also for his perceived failures as a son, brother, and husband.

Truth through/despite Fiction

In 1989 Vonnegut proposed a new genre for his anthology Palm Sunday: "blivit," work that combines fiction, nonfiction, and journalism (he stole the term from an adolescent expression for two pounds of shit in a one pound bag). Retrospectively, this term could be applied to many of his novels—in particular *Slaughterhouse-Five*. However, this need to implicate himself in his work is not driven merely by a narcissistic need to work out his personal issues; as Klinkowitz suggests, "never is mere confession or simple autobiography his method; rather, his way is to engage this personal self in larger issues" (24). These larger issues include remembering World War II and its full implications on the domestic front.

Vonnegut presents his position as a witness in a more direct fashion than is typical for a work of fiction. Vonnegut himself surfaces in these novels, not as an omniscient narrator or an objective journalist, but as a character, "Vonnegut," who is as fallible as any of the other characters: "not many words come now [about Dresden], either, when I have become an old fart with his memories and his Pall Malls, with his sons full grown" (*Slaughterhouse-Five* 2). Klinkowitz sees Vonnegut's style as integrated with his public speaking and nonfiction work:

> Indeed because more literary approaches have proven not to work, Vonnegut must speak to his audience and readership directly—personally, and yet wearing the mantle of an otherwise unspeakable experience in a way that makes his achievement a shared occasion. (18)

Vietnam veteran and author Tim O'Brien similarly describes the challenges of writing about the experience of war and how these difficulties have necessitated the methods he developed:

> The looping aspect of my writing is important. To tell stories in a linear way would be deceitful. The trauma doesn't end, it comes back in memory, returns and returns, often with a different take on the original event; horror, outrage, disbelief. War and trauma don't end in a literally sense, they reverberate across time, and my repetitions are a way to get at this psychological truth.

Not only is looping evident in the narrative of *Slaughterhouse-Five* itself but also in the way that Vonnegut's personal war-narrative loops throughout his entire oeuvre, from *Mother Night* to *A Man without a Country* (2005). Vonnegut's war trauma reverberated across his entire life, and so through his fiction and autobiographical writings, he tried to find the psychological truth of his experience. Not coincidentally, Vonnegut created two novels where the flow of time is directly altered, *Slaughterhouse-Five* and *Timequake*, which also, not coincidentally, are the novels in which "Vonnegut" most intrudes into the fictional narrative.

In much of his writing, Vonnegut directly calls attention to the blurred line between fiction and reality, even in terms of his own personal "reality." Throughout his work, Vonnegut deliberately weaves truth into his fiction, without privileging one over the other. For example, Vonnegut announces his personal connection to the content of *Slaughterhouse-Five* with a unique title page that does not differentiate between the "truth" of Dresden and the "fiction" of Tralfamodore:

> *Slaughterhouse-Five or The Children's Crusade. A Duty-Dance with Death.* By Kurt Vonnegut, a fourth-generation German-American now living in easy circumstances on Cape Cod and smoking too much, who, as an American infantry scout *hors de combat,* as a prisoner of war, witnessed the fire-bombing of Dresden, Germany, "The Florence of the Elbe," a long time ago, and survived to tell the tale. This is a novel somewhat in the telegraphic schizophrenic manner of tales of the planet Tralfamodore, where the flying saucers come from. Peace.

In the "Editor's Note" to *Mother Night,* Vonnegut similarly establishes his relationship with truth and fiction: "I will risk the opinion that lies told for the sake of artistic effect…can be, in a higher sense, the most beguiling forms of truth" (ix). Artistic "lies" are essential to his truth telling, as his personal "truth" is essential to his fiction.

While Vonnegut's identity as an actual witness to Dresden forms an integral part of his World War II writing, the author's classification of himself as German American plays an equally significant role in these novels. As German American, Vonnegut feels linked both to the deaths of Holocaust victims and Allied Forces. In his introduction to *Welcome to the Monkey House,* Vonnegut states, "When I write I simply become what I seemingly must become" (ix). Such a statement blurs the line between his lived experience and the experience of his imagined protagonists.

A secondary theme that connects these novels is suicide—both as a deliberate act and as a passive refusal to survive. In his preface to *Welcome to the Monkey House* (1968), Vonnegut described his smoking as a form of suicide to a woman at a cocktail party: "She thought that was reasonably funny. I didn't. I thought it was hideous that I should scorn life that much, sucking away on cancer sticks" (x). Vonnegut was deeply affected by his mother's suicide as well as his sister's welcoming of her death by cancer. Therefore, for him to choose a slow death when he is "now living in easy circumstances" is disrespectful to all those who did not choose death, during or after the war.

The other significant suicide that Vonnegut witnessed as part of his war experience was that of Joe Crone, the model for *Slaughterhouse-Five*'s Billy Pilgrim. Klinkowitz tells us that in the prisoner-of-war camp, Joe Crone despaired of surviving and gave away his food rations; he "virtually willed himself to death, four weeks before the war would end" (7). Perhaps since Vonnegut could not convince his fellow POW to continue living, he created Billy as unstuck in time so that Billy could see the life he had ahead and save him from the despair that Crone experienced. Vonnegut confirmed the impact of Joe Crone's suicide when he visited Crone's grave in Rochester on the fiftieth anniversary of his death: "I was deeply moved, and it finally closed out the Second World War for me completely" (Klinkowitz 26). In this comment, Vonnegut confirms how much World War II had been a part of his life for fifty years—however, whether he actually did close it out at that point is debatable.

Joe Crone's suicide connects him with Vonnegut's mother. Over the course of his writing, Vonnegut presented several reasons for his mother's suicide; the one that resonates most as a subtext in his 1960s' novels is that she was upset by his war service. Edith Vonnegut committed suicide when her son was home on leave before shipping overseas. Since she was still in contact with relatives in Germany, Vonnegut surmised that she could not face either his being killed or his killing Germans. Not coincidentally, his protagonists in *Slaughterhouse-Five* and *Mother Night* both have parents die during their war service. So while for most people suicide and war are unconnected issues, it might be surmised that Vonnegut experienced the deaths of his mother and Joe Crone as casualties of war.

Vonnegut's specific position in World War II, as a soldier who passively witnessed a massacre as well as the suicides of his mother and friend, is foundational to the four novels that he published in the 1960s. Not only does he not allow the protagonists of these novels an easy pardon for their direct or indirect sins, by weaving himself into these narratives, he refuses to allow himself to let himself get "off so light" (qtd. in Leeds and Reed ix).

The War "Novels"

Vonnegut's struggle with World War II and the boundaries between life and fiction begins with his novel *Mother Night,* whose first edition appeared in 1962. *Mother Night* is the fictional memoir of Howard W. Campbell, Jr., an American-born playwright, whose success in the German theater saw him recruited to deliver covert messages to the Allies during his ostensibly anti-American radio broadcasts. After years living underground in America, Campbell must personally confront whether he was actually an American spy or, in fact, became a highly effective Nazi propagandist.

The novel contains two prologues: an "Editor's Note," describing the editor's relationship to the "memoirs" of Howard W. Campbell, Jr., signed "Kurt Vonnegut, Jr."; and an introduction, added in 1966, describing the author's personal experiences in Dresden, unsigned. In this prefatory material, Vonnegut gives us both a "true" autobiographical account and a "false" "Editor's Note," which asserts that the novel is actually the edited autobiography of Campbell. The Dresden essay makes the "Editor's Note" spoof even more unsettling. It appears that Vonnegut does not want to allow us the comfort of dismissing Campbell's character as fictional, nor does Vonnegut want to dismiss the care and respect he took in "editing" Campbell's work: "My duties as an editor are in no sense polemic. They are simply to pass on, in the most satisfactory style, the confessions of Campbell. As for my own tinkerings with the text, they are few" (x).

It seems strange that Vonnegut felt the need to add the Dresden introduction to this novel, because many of these details can be found in *Slaughterhouse-Five*, which he was writing almost simultaneously. Furthermore, Vonnegut would go on to write the story of the Dresden firebombing again, when, in 1977, he conducted a self-interview for the *Paris Review* (reprinted in *Palm Sunday*). He asked himself about surviving the Dresden firestorm and replied with almost the same details that he related in the introduction to *Mother Night* and in the body of *Slaughterhouse-Five*. His need to repeat the story of Dresden speaks to Vonnegut's obsession, whether due to the American public's continued lack of knowledge of Dresden (as compared to Hiroshima or Auschwitz) or possibly his own inability to come to terms with the event.

Following *Mother Night*, Vonnegut continued to complicate the concept of reality in his writing. While Vonnegut claims that "all of this happened" (1) in *Slaughterhouse-Five*, the opening of *Cat's Cradle* states that "Nothing in this book is true." For *God Bless You, Mr. Rosewater* he uses the epigraph "All persons, living and dead, are purely coincidental and should not be construed," which for *Timequake* he shortens to "All persons, living and dead, are purely coincidental." As Michelle Persell writes,

> His success is grounded in posing the problem of veracity in fictions of the self—both at the level of subject matter, via the portrayal of would-be creative producers, and at the level of discourse, the fragmented structure and narrational stance of the plots themselves. (50)

Persell's comments above directly relate to Vonnegut's excuses for the "jumbled and jangled" nature of *Slaughterhouse-Five* but can be applied to much of his fiction as well as the "blivits," *Palm Sunday*, and *Timequake*. He presents the fragments of his life and his art as a mosaic, not as a coherent picture. These fractures in his autobiographical narrative seem to have begun with Dresden and *Mother Night*.

Dresden is not the only connection between *Mother Night* and *Slaughterhouse-Five*. Howard W. Campbell, Jr., makes several appearances in *Slaughterhouse-Five* as a Nazi villain (our most complete sample of Campbell's propaganda appears in *Slaughterhouse-Five*, not *Mother Night*). The "truth" about Campbell is made more unstable by these appearances; though we know of his "innocence" from the earlier novel *Mother Night*, he is presented solely as a traitorous villain in *Slaughterhouse-Five*.

A particularly strange fictional/actual overlap between the two novels is that in *Slaughterhouse-Five* Bernard V. O'Hare is Vonnegut's "actual" war buddy and a successful district attorney (this information is verifiable outside of the novel); in *Mother Night* Bernard B. O'Hare is the hotdog lieutenant who captures Howard W. Campbell, Jr., at the end of the war, and later becomes a miserably married, failed salesman and maniac—the opposite of everything that Mary and Bernard V. O'Hare stand for. Though Vonnegut claims not to be the author of Campbell's memoirs in the "Editor's Note," he does admit to christening the character "O'Hare," saying that he changed the names of specific characters from Campbell's "original." Adding to the inappropriateness of the character's name is that, according to Chapter 1 of *Slaughterhouse-Five*, Vonnegut had been out of contact with O'Hare until 1964, *after* the original publication of *Mother Night*. Perhaps at the time of writing *Mother Night*, Bernard B. is who Vonnegut was afraid that his friend might have become—and maybe what he himself could have become after his war experience.

As his first World War II novel, *Mother Night* contains many of the seeds for Vonnegut's later novels. Though Howard Campbell, Jr., is officially exonerated for his crimes against humanity, he "executes" himself because he understands that, though he may not be guilty, he is responsible:

> So I am about to be a free man again, to wander where I please.
> I find the proposal nauseating.
> I think that tonight is the night I will hang Howard Campbell Jr. for crimes against himself. (288)

By being false to himself, Campbell fueled the hatred of countless Germans and Americans. As his Nazi father-in-law explained,

> "...you could never have served the enemy as well as you served us," he said, "I realized that almost all the ideas that I have now, that make me unashamed of anything I may have felt or done as a Nazi, came not from Hitler, not from Goebbels, not from Himmler—but from you." (99)

In addition, Campbell's position as a double agent indirectly leads to the deaths of his parents, his beloved wife, and his sister-in-law.

Unlike in *Mother Night*, World War II is only a backstory in *God Bless You, Mr. Rosewater*. Whereas Campbell was on trial for war crimes, Eliot is on trial merely for his sanity, after abandoning his life of privilege, comfort, and wealth to minister to the lives of the citizens of Rosewater, Indiana.

God Bless You, Mr. Rosewater may appear to be the least autobiographical of Vonnegut's war novels; however, Vonnegut creates clear connections between himself and three different characters in the novel, starting with the title character. We are told that Eliot Rosewater did serve in the World War II infantry, but unlike Vonnegut and Billy Pilgrim, he was a decorated officer. In addition, Rosewater is not a German American but the scion of a prominent WASP family. Nonetheless, there remain echoes between Vonnegut and Rosewater. Both share guilt for the deaths of their mothers: Mrs. Rosewater died in a sailing accident with Eliot at the helm; Edith Vonnegut committed suicide right before Kurt shipped off to Europe to fight her relatives. Similarly, Eliot is burdened by guilt for the accidental deaths of German firemen, an event that echoes the civilians killed in the Dresden firestorm. Lastly, the Rosewaters' money and family estate are in Indiana; though Vonnegut's family lost most of their money by the time he was a teenager, both his mother and father came from prominent Indiana families who could likewise trace their fortunes and their standing back to the Reconstruction.

The other key autobiographical connection between Vonnegut and *God Bless You, Mr. Rosewater* is the introduction of the character Kilgore Trout, a recurring figure in the Vonnegut oeuvre, often seen as Vonnegut's alter ego. Kilgore Trout is a science fiction writer, whose work is largely out of print and accidentally distributed as porn. Vonnegut was likewise dismissed as an obscene science fiction writer, with all of his novels being out of print at the time of *Slaughterhouse-Five*'s writing. As Peter Reed suggests, the bedraggled Kilgore Trout functions for Vonnegut as "a self-mocking parody of himself, an embodiment of his worst fears of becoming a denigrated science fiction writer, and a voice for some of his own most impish and inventive ideas" (67).

Vonnegut may actually have a third doppelganger in *God Bless You, Mr. Rosewater*: Fred Rosewater, Eliot's distant cousin who is suing for control of the Rosewater Foundation. While the death of Eliot's mother was accidental, Fred's father actually committed suicide, allowing Vonnegut to write of the legacy of parental suicide:

> Sons of suicides rarely do well.
>
> Characteristically, they find life lacking a certain *zing*. They tend to feel more squeamish than most, even in a notoriously rootless nation. They are squeamishly incurious about the past and numbly certain about the future to this extent: they suspect that they, too, will probably kill themselves. (144)

In addition to this link, Fred Rosewater is a New England insurance salesman. As Klinkowitz writes, "Through story after story, Vonnegut's narrators feel compelled to speak…most often in the guise of what the real Kurt Vonnegut was during the 1950s, a salesman working out his home" (28) in New England.

Though it is possible to read the character of Fred as an extrapolation of who Vonnegut fears he may be—a mediocre salesman and a potential suicide—Eliot may represent who Vonnegut would like to be, a man committed to achieving personal atonement and improving the world. Eliot carries with him the triple burden of matricide, the accidental murder of German civilians (firemen, a category Vonnegut held in particular regard), and the undeserved good luck of a great fortune—which parallels Vonnegut's "living in easy circumstance" (*Slaughterhouse-Five* title page). Fred Rosewater's lawsuit against Eliot is largely based on his humbling himself to serve the residents of Rosewater, Indiana, a people who received none of the good fortune that his family did from the town. Eliot's actual nervous breakdown is tied to his reading about the Dresden firestorm, with Vonnegut reprinting a passage from Hans *Rumpf*'s *The Bombing of Germany* (1963) (because *Mother Night*'s preface was not added until 1967, this is actually Vonnegut's first account of Dresden). Eliot's hallucination of a firestorm in Indianapolis connects his personal war trauma with Vonnegut's trauma of Dresden.

Through Vonnegut's connections to Eliot, Fred, and Trout, he presents the possibility of negotiating between his various selves to achieve both atonement and a sense of wholeness. Eliot Rosewater, as advised by Kilgore Trout, creates a fiction that allows him not only to defeat his cousin Fred—but, more importantly, to take responsibility for the future of people who count on him, as a means to atone for his past, divesting himself of his fortune in the same way that Campbell divests himself of his life.

While Vonnegut claims that there is no truth in his next novel, *Cat's Cradle*, he undercuts this distancing disclaimer by again choosing to use and maintain a first-person narrative throughout. Vonnegut creates connections between himself and his unnamed narrator in the novel. The narrator of *Cat's Cradle* is a journalist-author, who, like the Vonnegut of *Slaughterhouse-Five*, is struggling with a book project about World War II. In researching the children of an atom bomb scientist, the narrator is drawn into the tangled mess of these damaged siblings' lives, damage that eventually has catastrophic consequences for the entire world.

The most telling autobiographical element of *Cat's Cradle* occurs while the narrator is researching the Hoenikker family in Ilium, New York (hometown also of Billy Pilgrim), and visits a local cemetery. The narrator finds a stone angel commissioned generations ago by a German immigrant, for his wife who died of small pox. The great-grandson of the original sculptor comments, "There's a screwy name for you.... If that immigrant had any descendants, I expect they Americanized the name. They're probably Jones or Black or Thompson now." But the narrator corrects him: "The name was my last name, too" (67). By not directly naming the "screwy" German surname, Vonnegut introduces the possibility that the name on the stone is "Vonnegut," a screwy German name.

The plausibility of this assumption is confirmed by the fact that Vonnegut originally planned to name the narrator "Vonnegut," but his editor talked him out of it (Klinkowitz 41). Kurt's compromise was to never state his narrator's name, again removing deniability. Though Vonnegut may use fewer autobiographical elements in *Cat's Cradle* than his other World War II novels, he most fully places himself—an author named Vonnegut—at the center of the story.

The narrator is not the only German American in the novel. As Fiedler notes,

The Hoenikkers, father and children, like Vonnegut bear a name which memorializes their connection with a European people who made soap of dead Jews and were themselves roasted, boiled, turned to tinder by bombs from American planes. And before those Germans he

feels the fascinated repulsion all of us Americans experience confronting the particular people abroad from whose midst our ancestors fled,
but who persist still in our flesh, our dreams; and with whom therefore
we die a little, when we come to bomb them. (14)

Cat's Cradle is the only one of Vonnegut's 1960s' novels to feature
German surnames, though Howard Campbell is German by residence
and marriage. While not marked by a German surname, Billy Pilgrim
does encounter his German cousin, Werner Gluck, in Dresden—
though neither is aware of the relationship. His blivit *Palm Sunday*
fully reveals Vonnegut's complicated feelings toward his heritage: not
only is *Palm Sunday* dedicated to his German relatives ("For my cous-
ins the de St. Andres everywhere. Who has the castle now?") but several chapters specifically address being German American during the
twentieth century. He comments that the negative associations with
his surname lead him to be funny as soon as possible.

Cat's Cradle also develops themes that appear in the other novels,
most specifically the personal damage caused by participating in massacres. In the novel, the world is destroyed not through a deliberate
act of war, but through the careless handling of a military discovery,
ice-nine. However, what has made *ice-nine* more dangerous than it
need be is Dr. Hoenikker's failure to properly father his children. By
putting the development of weapons of mass destruction before his
family, he leaves his children so emotionally starved that they barter
their share of this deadly crystal to anyone who promises them love
and a sense of belonging. However, with little experience of love, the
Hoenikkers choose poorly. As in *Mother Night*, Vonnegut illustrates
the danger of putting service to one's country above love and honesty
to one's family: "crimes against himself" (288).

Vonnegut's presence is most evident in the novel that is the most
overtly concerned with the bombing of Dresden. The first chapter of
Slaughterhouse-Five relates in first person how "Vonnegut" began to
write the novel, opening with "All this happened, more or less. The
war parts, anyway, are pretty much true" (1). Vonnegut then talks
about his family and his postwar career as a police reporter and a public relations official for General Electric. Most importantly, he talks
about his visit to Bernard V. O'Hare as inspiration for his "Dresden
novel," and his cold reception from Mary O'Hare. She assumed that
he would imagine them both as heroic figures, like John Wayne or
Frank Sinatra, rather than as the pitiful "babies" they were: "And war
will look just wonderful, so we'll have a lot more of them. And they'll
be fought by babies like the babies upstairs" (14). Within this first

chapter, he promises her that he will not glorify their experiences and will in fact subtitle the novel "The Children's Crusade."

A more typical introduction or foreword might create a more definite barrier between autobiography and fiction. As in his extended title, Vonnegut does not differentiate or privilege the factual over the fictional, or even the fantastical; they are all building blocks for constructing his narrative. Though the author's approach has often been categorized as postmodern, this does not quite capture the earnestness of Vonnegut's comic fable—his storytelling extends his lived experience into fantasy, and his lived reality grounds his fantasies. His goal may be to approximate his description of the novels produced by Tralfamodores, who see all time at once: "There is no beginning, no middle, no suspense, no moral, no causes, no effects. What we love in our books are the depths of many marvelous moments seen all at one time" (88).

Chapter 2 of the novel begins the story of Billy Pilgrim, a fictional character in the same prisoner-of-war unit as the author; this device allows the author to interrupt the narrative to point himself out in the background: "I was there. So was my old war buddy Bernard V. O'Hare" (67). True to his word to Mary, there is nothing reminiscent of John Wayne about Billy; based on a member of Vonnegut's unit who died of starvation, after losing all hope and giving away his rations, Billy is a pitiable character. The only two members of Vonnegut's prisoner-of-war unit that died (the other is the middle-aged teacher executed for stealing a clock) are both fictionalized in *Slaughterhouse-Five*. However, though they are preserved through Vonnegut's remembering, they are neither mourned, elegized, nor have their dignity restored. Morehead Wright sees Billy Pilgrim as deliberately moving away from the adventurers of earlier American war novels: "The marginality of [Billy's] role [as chaplain's assistant] is associated with a sense of control by the trivial, the accidental, the degradingly unheroic, despite the preservation of such emblems of the noble as a red badge" (103). Indeed, it is telling that the doomed schoolteacher Edgar Derby reads *The Red Badge of Courage*. Yet, Edgar fails to find the heroic adventure he expected from his enlistment, while Billy exhibits no agency or heroism in his "adventures" in Germany, through time or in Tralfamodore.

Even once Chapter 2 officially begins the fictional narrative, "Vonnegut" continues to interrupt the narrative throughout the novel to highlight "factual" details or to add comments, from noting that Dresden was the first city he'd seen besides Indianapolis to recalling a soldier with severe diarrhea shouting, "There they go. There they go."

He meant his brains. That was I. That was me. That was the author of this book (125). Some critics deal with these intrusions as nonauthorial, belonging instead to a postmodern character, "Vonnegut." However, Vonnegut in his essays and speeches has never disavowed the thoughts that he has expressed as "Vonnegut"—any more than he has disavowed the insights of Kilgore Trout of the Tralfamodorans. What is definite is that in *Slaughterhouse-Five* Vonnegut kept his word to Mary O'Hare, portraying the soldiers as "babies," not heroes.

Significantly, of all the horrors of World War II, the one atrocity that *Slaughterhouse-Five*'s Billy Pilgrim "undoes" is the bombing of Europe; by using his unstuck-in-time position to view a documentary backwards, the Allied air strikes become a healing rather than a destructive event:

> The formation flew backwards over a German city that was in flames. The bombers opened their bomb bay doors, exerted a miraculous magnetism which shrunk the fires, gathered them into cylindrical steel containers, and lifted the containers into the bellies of the planes. (74)

It is the impersonality of technologically-led massacre that Vonnegut seems to find the most unsettling.

The final chapter of *Slaughterhouse-Five* moves back and forth between finishing the narrative of "Billy Pilgrim," remarking on the dramatic events of the summer of 1968, and relating "Vonnegut's" return to Dresden with Bernard V. O'Hare. True events and feelings from Vonnegut's life are woven into this fictionalized World War II novel. Jerome Klinkowitz suggests,

> Vonnegut's message was a simple one, its testimony an act of witness. The novel's speaking voice is plain and simple, suiting its message that one had best be kind and unhurtful because "Death is coming for all of us anyway, and it is better to be Lot's wife looking back through salty eyes than the Deity that destroyed those cities of the plain in order to save them." (Quoting Robert Scholes in *NY Times Book Review* 12)

Klinkowitz and Scholes's comments refer indirectly to Vonnegut's refrain of "So it goes," which follows *each* death announced in the novel—whether in the war or otherwise. Those who died "over there" are accorded no more or less respect than those who have or will die "over here." Most war novels tend to either glorify wartime deaths as meaningful or decry deaths as meaningless and tragic. Vonnegut portrays all deaths, in war or in peace, as equally meaningful/meaningless.

Because the Tralfamodores see all time at once, they choose to focus on all the moments when the person was alive rather than the ones where he or she happens to be dead. In Vonnegut's novels, it is what you do with your life that matters—not how you die.

* * *

Together, these 1960s' novels represent Kurt Vonnegut's attempt to record his various experiences as a World War II soldier, prisoner of war, firestorm survivor, German American, and returning veteran. In these four novels, Vonnegut witnesses the aftereffects of World War II as Howard Campbell, Eliot Rosewater, *Cat's Cradle's* unnamed journalist, and Billy Pilgrim. Only Eliot Rosewater survives the novel's end, and only Billy Pilgrim produces children. Responsibility and kindness are given more weight than survival or legacies.

The other significant difference in Vonnegut's way of remembering World War II and understanding its legacy is that the majority of the action of these novels takes place stateside after the war. The "war crimes" considered the most serious are actually domestic. Howard Campbell, Jr., betrayed the "Nation of Two" that he had created with his wife, Helga, when he became both a Nazi propagandist and an American spy; it feels more than a coincidence that her death was also political. His sister-in-law, Resi, is likewise pulled into his Nazi persona, and her suicide is triggered by the intrigue that surrounds him. Eliot may be directly haunted by the death of firemen, but his compulsive philanthropy is equally compelled by his family's robber-baron disdain for the backs on which his family fortune is built; it is to the citizens of Rosewater, Indiana, that he makes his final amends. In *Cat's Cradle* Hoenikker's work on weapons of mass destruction leaves his children the doubly lethal legacy of emotional abandonment and *ice-nine*, a dangerous combination that nearly destroys not only the Hoenikkers but the whole world. Billy Pilgrim's ineptness as a soldier is only matched by his ineptness as a husband and father, yet his kindness and good luck built him a better life than he could have expected. Together, these novels urge the reader to stop looking at the enemy and to focus on their own more personal responsibilities.

Though the line between autobiography and fiction may be blurred in these novels, there is evidence to suggest that the two may have been blurred in the author's life itself. In his 1966 introduction to *Mother Night*, Vonnegut wrote on reflection that he considered the novel to be his only book for which he knew the moral: "We are what we pretend to be, so we must be careful about what we pretend to be" (v). Though we can't know how careful Vonnegut has been, it appears that he believes that he is what he has pretended to be. He is not only Eliot Rosewater, Howard Campbell (the patriot), the narrator "Jonah," Kilgore Trout, and Billy Pilgrim, but he is also Fred Rosewater, Howard Campbell (the traitor), Bernard B. O'Hare, and all the versions of "Kurt Vonnegut" that appear in his work.

Through his looping narratives, he acknowledges the worst aspects of these characters/his character and hopes to promote the best. Kilgore Trout explains what makes the alcoholic Eliot Rosewater a vital example to the world:

> [Rosewater] dealt on a very small scale with a problem whose queasy horrors will eventually be made world-wide by the sophistication of machines. This problem is this: How to love people who have no use?...if we can't find reasons and methods for treasuring human beings because they are human beings , then we might as well, as has been suggested, rub them out. (264–65)

Perhaps, through Rosewater, the only protagonist to survive any of the World War II novels, Vonnegut indirectly endorses the attempt to make amends. Eliot's final act goes even further than the confession/execution of Howard Campbell or the witnessing of Billy Pilgrim, *Cat's Cradle*'s narrator or Vonnegut himself: he adopts the children of Rosewater, Indiana, making them his family and his legal responsibility: "And tell them their father loves them, no matter what they may turn out to be" (275). For Vonnegut, the personal is truly political, with the potential to be transformative. Throughout his writing, Vonnegut expresses his unconditional love for his own children—four of whom he adopted.

Vonnegut ends his introduction to *Mother Night* by presenting two more morals: "When you're dead you're dead" and "Make love when you can" (viii). In a similar vein, Vonnegut often repeated the advice given to him by his uncle, Alex, that when life is going well, we should *notice* it and mark those occasions by saying out loud, "If this isn't nice, what is?" (*Timequake* 14). In *Slaughterhouse-Five* similar advice is offered by a Tralfamodoran: because nothing can be done to change the horrible moments, these aliens "spend eternity looking at pleasant moment—like today at the zoo" (117). Together, these are the simple solutions Vonnegut offers to try to avoid future massacres.

While *Slaughterhouse-Five* ends with the forlorn sound "Poo-tee-weet?," the last novel of this World War II veteran, *Timequake*, ends with the fantasy of a clambake surrounded by doppelgangers of all those whom Vonnegut has loved and have died, with an acknowledgment of the vibrancy of his family. The antidote to a massacre may be to hold in memory and to celebrate those good moments of life—particularly those moments marked by the love of friends and family.

WORKS CITED

Cumbow, Robert C. *Once Upon a Time: The Films of Sergio Leone.* New York: Scarecrow, 1987.

Fiedler, Leslie A. "The Divine Stupidity of Kurt Vonnegut: Portrait of the Novelist as Bridge over Troubled Water." *Kurt Vonnegut: Images and Representations.* Ed. Marc Leeds and Peter J. Reed. Westport: Greenwood, 2000. 5–18.

Hastings, Max. *Armageddon: The Battle for Germany 1944–1945.* New York: Knopf, 2004.

Heller, Joseph. *Catch-22.* London: Vintage, 1994.

Klinkowitz, Jerome. *Vonnegut in Fact: The Public Spokesmanship of Personal Fiction.* Columbia: U of South Carolina P, 1998.

Landy, Marcia. *Cinematic Uses of the Past.* Minneapolis: U of Minnesota P, 1996.

Lawrence, Amy. "American Shame: Rope, James Stewart, and the Postwar Crisis in American Masculinity." *Hitchcock's America.* Ed. Jonathan Freedman and Richard Millington. New York: Oxford UP, 1999. 55–76.

Mallory, Carole. "The Joe & Kurt Show." *Playboy* 39.5 May 1992. 12 Dec. 2008 <http://www.vonnegutweb.com/vonnegutia/interviews/int_heller.html>.

Mendieta, Eduardo. "The Literature of Urbicide: Friedrich, Nossack, Sebald, and Vonnegut." *Theory & Event* 10.2 (2007). *Project Muse.* 15 June 2008 <http://ezproxy.ncc.edu>.

O'Brien, Tim. Personal interview. Conducted by Zoe Trodd. 12 July 2005.

Persell, Michelle. "It's All Play-Acting: Authorship and Identity in the Novels of Kurt Vonnegut." *Kurt Vonnegut: Images and Representations.* Ed. Marc Leeds and Peter J. Reed. Westport: Greenwood, 2000. 39–50.

Reed, Peter J. "Kurt Vonnegut's Bitter Fool: Kilgore Trout." *Kurt Vonnegut: Images and Representations.* Ed. Marc Leeds and Peter J. Reed. Westport: Greenwood, 2000. 67–80.

Rentilly, J. "Kurt Vonnegut: The Last Interview." *Writer's Report* 13 Dec. 2007. 26 May 2008 <http://writersreport.wordpress.com/2007/12/13/kurt-vonnegut-the-last-interview>.

Rumpf, Hans. *The Bombing of Germany.* London: White Lion, 1963.

Silverman, Kaja. "Historical Trauma and Male Subjectivity." *Psychoanalysis and Cinema.* Ed. E. Ann Kaplan. New York: Routledge, 1990. 110–27.

Simenson, Eric. "Pilgrim's Process." *Kurt Vonnegut: Images and Representations.* Ed. Marc Leeds and Peter J. Reed. Westport: Greenwood, 2000. 131–34.

Vonnegut, Kurt. *A Man without a Country.* New York: Seven Stories, 2005.

———. *Cat's Cradle.* New York: Dell, 1963.

———. Foreword. *Kurt Vonnegut: Images and Representations.* Ed. Marc Leeds and Peter J. Reed. Westport: Greenwood, 2000. ix–x.

———. *God Bless You, Mr. Rosewater.* New York: Dell, 1998.

———. *Mother Night.* New York: Dell, 1999.

———. *Palm Sunday: An Autobiographical Collage.* New York: Delacorte, 1981.

———. *Slaughterhouse-Five or The Children's Crusade: A Duty Dance with Death.* New York: Dell, 1991.

———. *Timequake.* New York: Dell, 1997.

———. *Welcome to the Monkey House.* New York: Dell, 1988.

Wright, Moorhead. "The Existential Adventurer and War: Three Case Studies from American Fiction." *American Thinking about Peace and War: New Essays on American Thought and Attitudes.* Ed. Ken Booth and Moorhead Wright. New York: Rowman, 1978. 101–10.

PART II

Vonnegut's Later Writing (1970–2005)

CHAPTER 6

Art, Domesticity, and Vonnegut's Women

Susan E. Farrell

Artists are people who say, "I can't fix my country or my state or my city, or even my marriage. But by golly, I can make this square of canvas, or this eight-and-a-half-by-eleven piece of paper, or this lump of clay, or these twelve bars of music, exactly what they ought to be!"

(Vonnegut, Timequake *162)*

Kurt Vonnegut's novels and stories are peopled by artists and failed utopian dreamers who try to make the world a better place, at least for a little while. Most of these artist figures are male—religious prophet and scribe Bokonon of *Cat's Cradle*, who invents a new religion so that a group of downtrodden Caribbean islanders become like actors "employed full time…in a play they understood" (174–75); hapless millionaire Eliot Rosewater, who experiments with being kind to everyone he meets; abstract painter Rabo Karabekian, whose ridiculously overpriced painting of an orange stripe against a green background restores Vonnegut's own faith in human nature; and even ubiquitous science fiction writer and Vonnegut's alter ego Kilgore Trout, whose ludicrous stories nevertheless point out flaws in human behavior and imagine "impossibly hospitable" (*God Bless You* 21) new worlds. Although overlooked in most criticism of his work, Vonnegut also includes women artists and utopian dreamers in many of his stories and novels. This chapter examines Vonnegut's depiction of these women. It argues that, along with other social issues that concern him throughout his career—war and violence, racism, environmental degradation—he is also interested in the role of women in American society, specifically in the relationship between gender issues and artistic practices. His writing, I argue, reflects larger cultural conversations about gender and art that were taking place as his work was published.

In his 1950s' and 1960s' short magazine stories, Vonnegut questions the relegation of women to the domestic sphere. In these early stories, he often depicts women who, like his male characters, express artistic aspirations, yet he also shows how these aspirations are frequently circumscribed by the traditional gender views of midcentury America. He especially critiques overly idealized notions of romantic love, exposing how love is increasingly commodified in the rising consumerist culture of the 1950s and 1960s. Next, I examine Vonnegut's breakthrough novel, *Slaughterhouse-Five*, in which he imagines women characters who challenge traditional views of masculinity and femininity, particularly in relation to war and violence, perhaps the leading political issues of the late 1960s, a period that witnessed intense protest against American escalation of the war in Vietnam. His women characters in *Slaughterhouse-Five* lead Vonnegut to question his own artistic rendering of his wartime experiences. Finally, I focus on the work in which Vonnegut most fully elaborates his views about gender and art: the 1987 novel *Bluebeard*. In this book, artist Rabo Karabekian experiences numerous rebirths, prompted by his relationships with women characters who teach him to question male privilege both in the domestic and the artistic realm. In *Bluebeard* Vonnegut participates in a larger critical reevaluation of women's writing and painting, particularly of sentimental and domestic art, taking place among critics during the 1980s.

EARLY MAGAZINE FICTION

"More Stately Mansions," a short story published in *Collier's Magazine* in December of 1951, is narrated by a man who moves with his wife into a small New England village where they meet a neighboring couple, George and his wife, Grace McClellan. Grace talks endlessly about her plans for improving her own home, gives her neighbors reams of advice about decorating, and subscribes to numerous home magazines, which she seems to have nearly memorized. Advising the new couple to cover a whole wall with bottle-green curtains, Grace points out that the effect would be "almost exactly like that problem living room in the February *Better House and Garden*" (134). The unnamed male narrator of the story wryly points out that the current month is August. This narrator, whose job is buying and selling office furniture, is professionally allied with the workplace rather than the domestic sphere. It would have been easy for Vonnegut to use the narrator, who finds his neighbor difficult to be around because of her single-minded obsession, to mock Grace's interest in home decorating as pedestrian, silly, and stereotypically feminine, yet the story asks readers to view Grace more complexly. Grace's husband, George, to the narrator's surprise, is not condescending toward his wife. George upsets the narrator's expectations when he gives Grace a glance that is "affectionate and possessive" (137) after she makes a disparaging remark about the lack of artistic temperament displayed by men. In addition, the narrator notes that when George is among friends whom he knows will not bait his wife, he "did nothing to discourage or disparage her dreaming" (143). And the story reveals that Grace's home plans are just that—dreams. Much to the astonishment of the new arrivals in the village, when they visit the McClellans in their home, they do not see the beautifully decorated, stylish showcase they expect. The house is actually dirty, decrepit, and bare. Yet, despite the seeming strangeness of this couple, the narrator observes that each provides the other uncritical support. George appreciates Grace's upbeat tendency to live in the future. In return, she never reproaches him for the very little money he earns in his leather goods shop, which prevents her from buying the kind of home furnishings she would like.

Grace McClellan fits the definition of an artist that Vonnegut will develop in later works such as his novel *Bluebeard*, where abstract artist Terry Kitchen equates sexual ecstasy to losing one's self in artistic pursuits: both involve moments of "non-epiphany," when the outside world drops away and "God almighty lets go of the scruff of your neck and lets you be human for a little while" (184). Grace, like the abstract expressionists Kitchen describes, loses herself completely in her artistic pursuits, forgetting the outside world as she ponders furniture styles and color patterns. At the story's end, it becomes clear that Grace, like other utopian dreamers in Vonnegut works, has retreated completely into her imagination. When his wife comes down with a viral infection that requires hospitalization, George McClellan, having inherited a small legacy from a relative he'd never met, decides to use the money to completely redo their house while Grace is away. He even subscribes the help of the narrator and his wife, Anne, who throw themselves into the project. By the time Grace is released from the hospital, the house is perfect, done up exactly according to the plans she'd outlined in such specific detail. The friends anticipate Grace's reaction with glee, but when she actually arrives home, she takes the changes completely in stride. Readers are left to surmise that Grace believes the house has always been decorated this way and that George has simply kept things clean and well-ordered while she's been gone. Not much different from later Vonnegut characters like Howard W. Campbell, Jr., with his invented "Universe of Two" or like Billy Pilgrim and his Tralfamadorian fantasies, Grace McClellan imaginatively invents a world that is more amenable to her than the real one she lives in. Although Grace McClellan's palette is the home, one of the few outlets for creativity available to ordinary housewives in the early 1950s, Vonnegut takes her artistic ambitions seriously. The story suggests that such ambitions can make life worth living.

These early stories also critique idealized notions of romantic love and marriage that tend to turn women into objects rather than agents. "Custom-Made Bride," published a little more than two years after "More Stately Mansions," satirizes a male artist who tries to turn his wife into a work of art. In this story, Vonnegut again comments on women's relegation to the domestic sphere in the 1950s, exposing the emptiness of a woman whose only function is to serve as a beautiful object rather than as an individual in her own right. The story is narrated by an advisor from an investment counseling firm who is sent to the home of famous designer and artist Otto Krummbein to straighten out his finances, since Krummbein has never paid income tax on his lavish earnings. Krummbein's home is extremely modern in design. Krummbein's wife, Falloleen, dressed in a leopard-print leotard, with silver hair and one huge hoop earring, is beautiful, sleek, and ultramodern as well. Before long, readers discover that Otto views Falloleen as one of his creations. He has transformed the plain, mousy Kitty Cahoun, the girl he originally married, into the glamorous Falloleen, a woman whose status as just another decorative object is made clear when Otto praises his wife as being the only famous beauty among his women acquaintances "who doesn't look like a piece of 1920-vintage overstuffed furniture" (138). Instead, Falloleen is "designed for contemporary living" (137). But Otto's transformation of his wife creates a vicious cycle. After molding plain Kitty into glamorous Falloleen, Otto feels trapped by his creation, falling prey to stereotypes about grasping, shallow, materialistic women. When the narrator first proposes putting Otto on an allowance, the eccentric artist is worried mainly about Falloleen's reaction, arguing that "Entertaining Falloleen on an allowance is like running a Mercedes on Pepsi-Cola" (140). The marriage is reduced to a consumer exchange.

The narrator soon discovers that Kitty, rather than desiring more clothes, jewelry, or material goods, is unhappy because she recognizes that a life dedicated solely to style creates a woman who is "dull and shallow, scared and lost, unhappy and unloved" (147). But even more, Vonnegut shows that reducing women to such ornamental roles will not produce happiness in the husband either. Otto admits that he "lived in terror of being left alone" with Falloleen, who "was a crashing bore when she wasn't striking a pose or making a dramatic entrance or exit" (148). Otto insists that he never meant to remake Kitty's soul, which is one of "only four things on earth that don't scream for redesigning" (148). Yet, Otto, and perhaps Vonnegut himself, is not willing to give up the notion that women should still be beautiful to look at, even while being individuals on the inside. The other three things that Otto says need no improvement are the egg, the Model-T Ford, and "the exterior of Falloleen" (148). The story closes with the couple agreeing that Falloleen will remain, though she will be only the exterior Mrs. Krummbein while Kitty Cahoun lives as the woman inside the glamorous body. While "Custom-Made Bride" criticizes the propensity for the male artist to create a female subject that is artificial and unrealistic, the story nevertheless stops short at the end, somehow wishing that women could be both thinking individuals and beautiful objects who satisfy the male gaze.

Vonnegut again explores inaccurate male perceptions of women in "Miss Temptation," a story that first appeared in the *Saturday Evening Post* in April of 1956. Reminiscent of Ernest Hemingway's well-known 1925 short story "Soldier's Home," about Harold Krebs, a returning World War I soldier who no longer fits into the small-town life he left to go to war and who has a particular problem with the changes the town's girls have gone through while he's been gone, "Miss Temptation" depicts the return of Corporal Norman Fuller to his small New England hometown after serving eighteen months in Korea. It is summer, and a nineteen-year-old "bit-part actress" (75) from New York City named Susanna, who is working in summer theater and renting a room over the village fire station, has captivated the local men with her black eyes and hair, hoop earrings, and belled ankle bracelets. Another Vonnegut woman with artistic aspirations, the free-spirited Susanna unwittingly offends Fuller, who has a deeply Puritanical streak, when she appears in the local drugstore early one afternoon to pick up the New York papers. He loudly and publicly humiliates the young actress, shaming her for the sexualized way she walks and dresses. Vonnegut, unlike Hemingway, however, is more interested in condemning the zealous bigotry of its main character than in showing the malaise of the damaged and alienated soldier. He presents Fuller's humiliation of Susanna as a throwback to the New England witch hunts, writing that "the wraith of a Puritan ancestor, stiff-necked, dressed in black, took possession of Fuller's tongue" and that the young man speaks with "the voice of a witch hanger...redolent with frustration, self-righteousness, and doom" (81). Like his Puritan forebears, Fuller operates according to a very narrow definition of gender roles—Susanna is a woman who defies the demure modesty demanded of young unmarried women by small-town 1950s' social norms, and Fuller's reaction seems to be fearful as well as self-righteous, again much like his Puritan ancestors' reactions to women who defied gender norms. The late–seventeenth-century Puritan witch trials occurred largely because of the patriarchal belief that women were naturally more lustful than men and more likely to be tempted by the devil, and the women initially accused of witchcraft lived lives outside the normal sphere of acceptable female behavior—women who were old, widowed, poor, did not regularly attend church services, or who outspokenly expressed skepticism about the accusations. Fuller's fear of Susanna's openly expressed sexuality as well as her unconventional, bohemian lifestyle link him to these earlier, patriarchal views of women.

In the army, Fuller was confronted by glamorized, consumerist images of women he calls "professional temptresses" (80). These actresses and pinup girls, in Fuller's own words, "had beckoned" to him "from makeshift bed-sheet movie screens, from curling pinups on damp tent walls," and from "ragged magazines in sandbagged pits" (80). In fact, when Fuller speaks to Susanna late in the story, he finds himself wishing that "she were in black and white, a thousandth of an inch thick on a magazine page" (86). It would be easier for Fuller to deal with the flat stereotypes of women he has internalized than the real-life human being he meets when he actually speaks with the young actress. Like Otto Krummbein, Norman Fuller is used to thinking of women as artistic objects, not as potential artists themselves. Susanna, however, insists to Fuller that she indeed has "a soul" (86) and that high school boys like him were quick to condemn her without even speaking to her. "I'm not Yellowstone Park!" she tells him angrily, "I'm not supported by taxes! I don't belong to everybody! You don't have any right to say anything about the way I look!" (86). During this confrontation, Susanna appears "appallingly human" (86) to Fuller, no longer the flat image on a magazine page he had earlier imagined her to be. Susanna is a free-spirited artist who defies traditional gender roles by demanding to be treated as a human being rather than a stereotype.

While his 1950s' stories frequently explored the "ornamental" role housewives were expected to play, Vonnegut's 1963 story, "Lovers Anonymous," responds specifically to a large, cultural conversation taking place about the role of women in America in the early 1960s. Prompted by the publication of Betty Friedan's *The Feminine Mystique*, which argued that American housewives often felt worthless and unfulfilled because they were expected to find their identity through their husbands and children, this conversation would erupt a few years later into the women's liberation movement of the late 1960s and early 1970s. Vonnegut's story, published the same year as *The Feminine Mystique* and appearing in *Redbook*, a women's magazine, reacts very specifically to Friedan. Set in North Crawford, New Hampshire, and narrated by a storm window salesman, "Lovers Anonymous" tells the story of Sheila Hinckley White, a very pretty and intelligent local girl whom all the young men in the town wanted to marry when they were in their early twenties. Much to their surprise, however, Sheila dropped out of the University of Vermont in her junior year to marry bookkeeper Herb White. On the evening of Sheila's wedding day, a group of drunken young men formed the club "Lovers Anonymous" to commemorate their feelings for Sheila. When the story opens, it is ten years later, and rumors are going around that trouble is brewing between Sheila and Herb. Herb has moved into the ell of his home, where he has set up a mattress and kerosene stove and is keeping house for himself. Soon Sheila is seen turning a big red book called *Woman, the Wasted Sex*, or *The Swindle of Housewifery* in to the library, clearly a mock version of Friedan's influential book.

While Vonnegut's attitude toward Friedan and the emergent women's movement is somewhat difficult to discern in the story, he does not simply satirize or undercut the idea of women longing for lives richer than those lived as middle-class housewives. Sheila White is treated with respect by the story's narrator. Although she begins as a love object for the men in town, they nevertheless have high expectations for her. When she writes in her high school yearbook that she hoped that she would discover a new planet or serve on the Supreme Court or become president of a company, the narrator adds that "she was kidding, of course, but everybody—including Sheila…had the idea that she could be anything she set her heart on being" (330). Yet, at her wedding, when she speaks with the narrator about her previous ambitions to run a company, Sheila seems to have swallowed the dominant 1950s' view about the role of women. She tells him, "I'm taking on a job a thousand times as important—keeping a good man healthy and happy, and raising his young" (330). When he asks her about her future seat on the Supreme Court, she replies, "The happiest seat for me, and for any woman worthy of the name of woman…is a seat in a cozy kitchen, with children at my feet" (331). Asked about discovering planets, Sheila says, "Planets are stones, stone-dead stones….What I want to discover are my husband, my children, and through them, myself" (331). These platitudes suggest that Vonnegut is spoofing ideas about women's destiny being completely tied up with their domestic roles; he suggests that women can and should strive to be more.

In addition, Sheila is not the only person affected by reading *Woman, the Wasted Sex,* or *The Swindle of Housewifery.* Both Sheila's husband Herb and the narrator, who checks the book out of the library to read for himself, are changed as a result of the text. The narrator seems persuaded by the author's argument that women have been mistreated over the years, and Herb begins to feel terribly guilty that Sheila has not used her intelligence in a more productive manner. Yet, perhaps the most interesting part of the story occurs when the narrator comes to the house to install the storm windows on Herb's ell. To the narrator's surprise, Sheila tells him to report back to the group Lovers Anonymous that she and Herb "have never been this happy before" (336). But it is not her own liberation from housewifery that Sheila is pleased about so much as it is Herb's newfound freedom. When she sees Herb sleeping happily on his mattress in the ell the first morning he moves out there, she tells the narrator that she realizes "he'd been a slave all his life, doing things he hated in order to support his mother, and then me, and then me and the girls. His first night out here was probably the first night in his life that he went to sleep wondering who he might be, what he might have become, what he still might be" (336). As he does in "Custom-Made Bride," Vonnegut suggests here that a reexamination of stereotypical male and female gender roles can be a liberating exercise for *both* sexes. The story ends with the narrator giving his own wife *The Swindle of Housewifery.* Yet, as is often the case in his work, Vonnegut mitigates the social critique somewhat with a joke at the end. When the other men in Lovers Anonymous warn that, after reading the book, the narrator's wife will "walk out on" him and their kids to "become a rear admiral" (337), the narrator claims to have prevented that possibility with the "magic bookmark" (338) he inserted into the volume—his wife's old high school report card. While concerned about gender issues at this stage in his career, and careful to show women with artistic and intellectual aspirations who are limited by their domestic roles, Vonnegut nevertheless still undercuts much of his social criticism with joking or pat endings, a characteristic that he came to control more effectively as his career advanced.

SLAUGHTERHOUSE-FIVE

Although *Slaughterhouse-Five* is certainly the most critically acclaimed and studied of Vonnegut's works, very little has been done to explore the presentation of gender in the novel. Dale Hearell is perhaps the sole critic to directly address this topic, arguing that *Slaughterhouse-Five*, along with the rest of Vonnegut's pre-1973 work, presents women characters negatively, "either as pro-authority anti-individualists or as helpless or male-manipulated victims who never 'grow' in either a personal or literary sense" (27). While Hearell makes some convincing points about Vonnegut's first novel, *Player Piano*, he oversimplifies Vonnegut's depiction of gender in *Slaughterhouse-Five*, especially since the only character he considers from that novel is Valencia Merble Pilgrim, wife of Billy Pilgrim. Hearell overlooks that the novel is dedicated to an intelligent, caring woman, Mary O'Hare, who also appears as a character in the opening chapter, and that it concludes with another smart, concerned woman, a German obstetrician who worries about the condition of the horses pulling Billy Pilgrim's cart after the firebombing of Dresden. Both of these women draw attention to the suffering caused by war: they each ask that a male character open his eyes to see the world more realistically; and they work to contrast the more cartoonish women in the novel: Valencia Merble and Montana Wildhack.

In the opening chapter of *Slaughterhouse-Five*, Vonnegut writes of his trip to visit his old war-buddy Bernard V. O'Hare in the hopes that O'Hare will help stimulate his wartime memories. Vonnegut initially imagines a cozy scene for the remembrances to take place in: "two leather chairs near a fire in a paneled room, where two old soldiers could drink and talk" (12–13). But just as Vonnegut undercut notions of idealized romance in his early magazine stories, in 1968, as he was working on *Slaughterhouse-Five* at the height of American involvement in the Vietnam War, he satirizes as well the romantic, nostalgic notions of war that the armchairs, paneling, and fireplace evoke. O'Hare's wife, Mary, does not create the warm, comforting stage initially imagined by Vonnegut. Instead she sets the two men up to talk at a kitchen table with a white porcelain top that reflects light from a 200-watt overhead bulb. Vonnegut describes this scene as an "operating room" (13), and readers discover as well that Mary is a trained nurse. The imagery in this scene is rich and evocative—the glaring overhead light suggests that Mary will help the two men see their past more clearly; the operating table hints at the human toll, the death and injury, caused by war. And Mary, as a nurse, serves as Vonnegut's assistant in the dissection of the Dresden bombing that will become the book itself.

Mary's fear that Vonnegut will write a book that glorifies war—that can be turned into a movie with roles for Frank Sinatra and John Wayne—while frequently noted by critics, is not often discussed in terms of gender politics. But Mary specifically associates war with conventional macho heroics, calling the participants in such films "glamorous, war-loving, dirty old men" (14). Interestingly, Vonnegut himself claims not to have been immune from the glamorizing of war experience that Mary O'Hare deplores. In a 1977 *Paris Review* interview, he says that he began thinking about writing his war story soon after his return home from Dresden in 1945: "All my friends were home; they'd had wonderful adventures, too" (qtd. in Allen 175). He also speaks about being envious of Andy Rooney, whose book *Air Gunner* made it into print very early, referring to Rooney's wartime experience as a "classy adventure" (qtd. in Allen 175). Later in the interview, Vonnegut credits the real-life Mary O'Hare with refocusing his thinking, with turning him away from the idea of writing an exciting adventure story:

> I would try to write my war story, whether it was interesting or not, and try to make something out of it. I describe that process a little in the beginning of *Slaughterhouse-Five*; I saw it as starring John Wayne and Frank Sinatra. Finally, a girl called Mary O'Hare, the wife of a friend of mine who'd been there with me, said, "You were just children then. It's not fair to pretend that you were men like Wayne and Sinatra and it's not fair to future generations because you're going to make war look good." That was a very important clue to me. (qtd. in Allen 175)

Vonnegut credits Mary O'Hare, then, with instigating the aesthetic choices he made in his famous Dresden novel. By helping him to see more realistically, Mary, ironically, encouraged Vonnegut to adopt his nonrealistic style—the nonlinear time frame, cartoonish characters, trips on flying saucers, etc.—devices that undercut the form of the conventional war novel.

Mary O'Hare, in fact, can be considered one of the people that Vonnegut, in later works, calls "secular saints." These saints are compassionate, unselfish human beings who help others and who, as he explains in his novel *Timequake*, make "being alive almost worthwhile" (239). Throughout Vonnegut's body of work, readers meet many examples of these secular saints, who are most often doctors and nurses: the physician friend he describes in *Timequake* who works at Bellevue Hospital is one, as is the obstetrics nurse whose influence keeps her son from dropping the third atomic bomb in the Kilgore Trout story "No Laughing Matter." Another is Dr. Ignaz Semmelweis, whom Vonnegut describes in *A Man Without a Country* as a nineteenth-century Hungarian obstetrician who greatly reduced maternal death when he insisted that physicians wash their hands before performing examinations. In *Slaughterhouse-Five*, Vonnegut introduces two more of these secular saints near the very end of Billy Pilgrim's story: the German obstetricians who croon lyrically to the injured horses pulling the coffin-shaped green wagon that Billy and five fellow soldiers recline in after their release as prisoners of war.

This couple is in the business of saving lives rather than taking lives. The woman, a well-educated, worldly professional (she and her husband "had nine languages between them" [196]), contrasts with the clownish, obese Valencia Merble, who simplemindedly "associate[s] sex and glamour with war" (*Slaughterhouse-Five* 121), and with the sex kittenish ex-porn star Montana Wildhack, much as her husband, a doctor as well, contrasts with the buffoonish Billy Pilgrim or the war-hungry history professor Bertrand Copeland Rumfoord. The obstetricians urge Billy to see realistically the devastation and trauma of war. Before they point it out to him, Billy had not noticed that "the horses' mouths were bleeding, gashed by the bits, that the horses' hooves were broken, so that every step meant agony, that the horses were insane with thirst" (196). When Billy finally sees the condition of the horses, he bursts into tears, even though he had not cried about anything else in the war.

As his very last wartime experience, the doctors' admonitions to Billy perhaps prompt his later aesthetic response to the war. This response, much like Vonnegut's reaction to Mary O'Hare, is an attempt to disrupt traditional narrative form, which Billy does through his Tralfamadorian adventures. Critics have written extensively about the Tralfamadorian sections of the book. While a few, most notably Kevin Boon, argue that the Tralfamadorian events are to be taken at face value, that Billy really is kidnapped by a flying saucer, put into a zoo with Montana Wildhack, the consensus of the rest is that these scenes are Billy's fantasies, whether conscious or subconscious. Most critics read Billy's Tralfamadorian fantasies as a coping device, though they disagree about the moral value of coping in such a way. Some, such as Robert Merrill and Peter Scholl, or Josh Simpson, argue that Billy makes a harmful retreat into utter passivity; others, like Susanne Vees-Gulani, view the fantasies as a lifesaving method of dealing with war trauma. But another way of reading Billy Pilgrim is to see him as an *artist*. Tralfamadore is an imagined, created world, inspired by a piece of Kilgore Trout literature, but fleshed out and authored by Billy who, like a long series of Vonnegut artists, beginning with his early magazine stories, tries to invent for himself a more hospitable world than the one he lives in. Tralfamadore is comforting to Billy because the alien philosophy does away with conventional human time, and thus with death. If death is only one moment on an endless loop of time that has no beginning and no end, both the finality and the gravity of death are greatly diminished. Billy takes these reassuring ideas and works them into his theory of literary art, which he claims to have learned from Tralfamadorian books, in which linear narrative is completely done away with: "There is no beginning, no middle, no end, no suspense, no moral, no causes, no effects" (88). Instead, Tralfamadorian literature supplies a series of urgent messages that, when seen all together, "Produce an image of life that is beautiful and surprising and deep" (88). Billy has invented a new aesthetic, and it is one that Vonnegut himself adopts in the structure of *Slaughterhouse-Five*.

At the height of the Vietnam War, then, Vonnegut invents women characters who challenge traditional gender roles—particularly the expectations of a heroic type of masculinity that perpetuates violent conflict. The two women who frame Vonnegut's Dresden story, Mary O'Hare and the German obstetrician, work directly against the glamorizing of war. Furthermore, these women help male characters to *see*, honestly and realistically, the suffering of war and even to make artistic choices that attempt to disrupt old ways of thinking and talking and writing about war. While not artists themselves, they inspire a new brand of art.

BLUEBEARD

Bluebeard is presented as the autobiography of abstract expressionist artist Rabo Karabekian, a character Vonnegut readers first met in the author's 1973 novel, *Breakfast of Champions*. Karabekian is writing his memoirs in 1987, at the age of seventy-one, at the urging of Circe

Berman, a brassy, voluptuous widow he recently met on the beach, who invited herself to live as a guest in his beachfront home in East Hampton, Long Island. Karabekian's beloved second wife, Edith Taft Karabekian, died two years previously, and since that time, Karabekian has been rattling around his mansion, lonely and depressed. The first of Vonnegut's novels to explicitly incorporate gender disparity as a major theme, *Bluebeard* follows Rabo Karabekian's relationships with a series of women who challenge his thinking about both domestic relationships and artistic expression, especially the sexism of the male-dominated art world he moves in.

The child of parents who meet as they are fleeing a genocide— the Turkish massacre of Armenians in 1915—Rabo's childhood is an unhappy one. He is the son of a bitter, distant father who is trapped by his memories of the friends and relatives he lost in the carnage and who, therefore, has given up on life itself. Rabo's mother, who actually had a worse experience during the Turkish brutality, having to play dead among the corpses, remains fairly optimistic. But she dies of a tetanus infection when Rabo is only twelve years old, leaving him motherless like so many of Vonnegut's characters, including Eliot Rosewater in *God Bless You, Mr. Rosewater*, the Hoenniker children in *Cat's Cradle*, Bunny Hoover in *Breakfast of Champions*, and Leon Trout in *Galapagos*. All the missing mothers in Vonnegut's fiction may serve as a testament to the suicide of Vonnegut's own mother when he was twenty-one years old. In *Breakfast of Champions* Vonnegut recalls that Thomas Wolfe's editor told the famous American novelist to keep in mind the unifying idea of a hero's search for a father as he wrote. Vonnegut, however, argues that it may be more important for authors to search for mothers, because he believes they are more influential in the lives of their children. In *Bluebeard* Rabo Karabekian's search for a mother suggests his longing for more balanced and nurturing human relationships. Such relationships will eventually lead Rabo to an art that is neither morally repressive nor elitist, an art that is socially engaged and emotionally meaningful.

The first woman in the novel who shapes Rabo's artistic vision is Marilee Kemp, mistress and assistant to the world famous artist and illustrator Dan Gregory in New York City. When Rabo shows remarkable artistic talent as a young boy in California, he writes letters to Gregory, never realizing that it is Marilee Kemp who writes back and who, after many years of correspondence, encourages him to move to New York at the age of seventeen to become Dan Gregory's apprentice. "So I went to New York City to be born again," Rabo writes (72). He describes his mind as being "as blank as an embryo's" as he crosses the continent in "womblike Pullman cars," and writes that, when the train plunges into a tunnel under New York City, he is "out of the womb and into the birth canal," to be "born" ten minutes later in Grand Central Station (72). Part of Rabo's rebirth in New York will involve the loss of his earlier naiveté. He will awaken to the fact that Dan Gregory cares nothing about him, and he will also witness Dan Gregory's physical and psychological cruelty to Marilee, noting that when Gregory talks about his mistress, "he never mentioned her name again. She simply became 'women'" (151). And in his diatribes against women, Gregory argues that men and women have separate, distinct roles. Sounding much like the brainwashed Sheila Hinckley White in "Lovers Anonymous," he tells Rabo that "no woman could succeed in the arts or sciences or politics or industry, since her basic job was to have children and encourage men and take care of the housework" (152). While the young Rabo politely agrees with Dan Gregory at this point, he will later be able to move beyond and criticize Gregory's sexist thinking.

Once in New York, Rabo is also introduced to the fundamental artistic debate in the novel. Dan Gregory is an entirely realistic artist, an illustrator, whose ability to mimic the real world in his paintings is the root of his fame. In fact, Gregory views all modern art as "the work of swindlers and lunatics and degenerates" (147). He also associates modern art with dangerously democratic principles, pointing out to the young Rabo that if Gregory's hero, Benito Mussolini, took over America, he would "burn down the Museum of Modern Art and outlaw the word *democracy*" (147). Gregory, in his abhorrence of democracy, has an overinflated view of the importance of artists in the world, seeing them as gods on earth: "Painters—and storytellers, including poets and playwrights and historians," he tells Rabo, "are the justices of the Supreme Court of Good and Evil, of which I am now a member, and to which you may belong someday" (150). The older Rabo, writing his memoirs, follows this comment with one of his own: "How was *that* for delusions of moral grandeur!" (150). Partly as a reaction to the fascist and cruel Dan Gregory, Rabo will reject realistic art completely, blaming people like Gregory for causing a great deal of "senseless bloodshed" (150).

Marilee and Rabo, against Gregory's express orders, begin to visit the New York Museum of Modern Art together, where Rabo's appreciation of abstract expressionism will emerge. While he believes that Gregory's delusions of moral grandeur cause bloodshed and suffering, abstract art, Rabo explains, refuses to present a moral stance on the world. He tells readers that the abstract expressionist paintings in his collection at his home on Long Island "are about absolutely nothing but themselves" (9). Later, in Florence, readers see that Marilee Kemp agrees with Rabo's views about the dangers of realistic art. She tells Rabo she had considered hiring women and children to paint the blank spaces on her rotunda with "murals of the death camps and the bombing of Hiroshima and the planting of land mines, and maybe the burning of witches and the feeding of Christians to wild animals in olden times" (255). Yet, she decides not to do this, arguing that "that sort of thing, on some level, just eggs men on to be even more destructive and cruel, makes them think: 'Ha! We are as powerful as gods!' " (255). This indictment of realism echoes, in many ways, Vonnegut's criticism of traditional storytelling in *Breakfast of Champions*, the work where readers first met Rabo Karabekian. In that novel, Vonnegut explained that it was "innocent and natural" for people to behave "abominably" because they're simply doing their best "to live like people in story books" (*Breakfast* 215). Rabo's refusal to assign artists an elevated moral position also reflects Vonnegut's debunking of literary art in the opening chapter of *Slaughterhouse-Five*, where Bernard O'Hare speaks of Vonnegut's writing as his "trade" (5) and where Vonnegut refers to himself not as an arbiter of morality but simply as a "trafficker in climaxes and thrills and characterization..." (5). In *Bluebeard* both Marilee's and Rabo's dedication to modern art suggests a rejection of the pretensions to moral authority by egotistical and sexist artists like Dan Gregory.

Gregory's belief in his own godlike stature is exemplified when he catches his mistress and his apprentice coming out of the museum they have been forbidden to enter: "Your loving Papa asked just one thing of you as an expression of your loyalty: 'Never go into the Museum of Modern Art,' " he seethes (175). Gregory behaves here like God castigating Adam and Eve for eating the apple in Eden. The parallel is made especially clear when Rabo describes his and Marilee's walk home later that afternoon: "the supposition was that we would be leaving the Garden of Eden together, and would cleave to one another in the wilderness through thick and thin," he writes (180). Yet, in their rebellion against the tyrannical Gregory, Rabo and Marilee create a new Eden of their own making. Rabo writes that they "were about to do the one thing other than eat and drink and sleep which our bodies said we were on Earth to do," and further, "there was no vengeance or defiance or defilement in it" (181). The two make love for three hours, Marilee initiating the not-yet-twenty-year-old Rabo into the mysteries and pleasures of sexual ecstasy. And, in fact, Rabo will connect this "brainless lovemaking" with abstract expressionist painting when he says that it, too, "was about absolutely nothing but itself" (181). While realistic art and storytelling offer moments of epiphany, in which divine beings reveal themselves or spiritual insight is achieved, abstract art eschews such moments, refusing to be "about" anything at all, and thus releasing people from the burdens of spiritual insight.

Any remaining innocence Rabo carries from his childhood disappears completely when Marilee informs him that their lovemaking doesn't mean that the two will move into the future together, "smiling bravely and holding hands" (192). Marilee, abused horribly by Gregory, nevertheless realizes that the great illustrator is her meal ticket and that she must return to him. The women who nurture Rabo throughout the book are decidedly practical and unromantic. Telling Rabo that he is "still a little boy" (193), Marilee parts ways with him, a parting that will set the stage for the next key relationship in Rabo's life, his marriage to his first wife, Dorothy. While Marilee introduced Rabo to the artistic world of New York City, Dorothy tries very hard to remove Rabo from that world. Dorothy, a trained nurse, is a sensible woman, concerned that Rabo should provide for his growing family. Thus, the two make plans that Rabo will give up his artistic endeavors and become a businessman. If his dream with Marilee was to become a great painter, Rabo's dream with Dorothy is to be a "good father" (85). Yet, Rabo, as he's writing his memoirs, will see himself as a failure in both roles. He neglects Dorothy and his young sons, preferring instead to drink in bars with a group of abstract expressionist artists he's met in New York City. When, in later life, Rabo's cook, Allison White, will berate him for not treating her as a full-fledged human being, for not even knowing her name, Rabo is reminded of his relationship with Dorothy: "This was dismayingly close to what my first wife Dorothy had said to me," Rabo writes, "that I often treated her as though I didn't even care what her name was, as though she really weren't there" (140). Rabo's failings as a husband and father cause him much anguish: "Of all the things I have to be ashamed of," he writes, "the most troublesome of this old heart of mine is my failure as a husband of the good and brave Dorothy, and the consequent alienation of my own flesh and blood, Henri and Terry" (258). Before Rabo can become the great artist he'd always dreamed of being, he must first learn to love and appreciate women.

This process will begin when Rabo remeets Marilee Kemp in Florence, Italy. As the Contessa Portomaggiore, Marilee has transformed herself from a victim, a woman abused by her lover, Dan

Gregory, into an outspoken feminist. Offended by the crude remarks Rabo makes on the telephone, Marilee, when she sees Rabo in person, rages against men, against war, and against the effects of both on women. She tells Rabo that the real war is "always men against women, with the men only pretending to fight among themselves" (238). When Rabo replies that men can "pretend pretty hard" sometimes, Marilee argues that the men who pretend the hardest "get their pictures in the paper and medals afterward" (239). While Rabo has received medals for saving fellow soldiers and for suffering injuries, women like Marilee's servant Lucrezia, who lost both an eye and a leg after stepping on a mine while trying to do a kind act for a neighbor, received nothing. Marilee, in fact, has turned her Palazzo into a kind of home for women injured and abused during the war. She defends her sex vigorously, berating Rabo for his assumption that women are "useless and unimaginative" (239). While Marilee's views on the differences between the sexes might be exaggerated and might tend to romanticize women, she nevertheless makes Rabo think in a new way. For the first time, he must examine his own status as a privileged member of society as well as his own earlier attitudes about women and their roles.

After this meeting with Marilee, Rabo is able to begin again in a new marriage, this time with Edith Taft, a kind, generous woman who doesn't try to change Rabo, but allows him to be what he is. Described in Rabo's autobiography as an "Earth Mother" who fills their home with "love and merriment" (7), Edith allows Rabo to redeem himself as a husband. His relationship with Edith also allows Rabo to cope with the great disaster that strikes his abstract paintings— having used a bogus "postwar miracle" (21) product called Sateen Dura-Luxe to paint his canvases, all his pictures are now cracking and peeling, and, in fact, disappearing, returning to blank canvases. This phenomenon suggests that Rabo, now happy in his life, has also started over as a blank canvas. When a curator at the Guggenheim Museum returns the remains of his famous "Windsor Blue Number Seventeen" to him, Rabo works hard to remove all traces of "faithless Sateen Dura-Luxe" from them, restretching and repriming the canvases. He explains to Edith that this "eccentric project" is "an exorcism of an unhappy past, a symbolic repairing of all the damage" Rabo had done to himself and others during his "brief career as a painter" (292). Yet, even amidst the seeming Eden Rabo is able to create with Edith, sorrow inevitably creeps in when she dies unexpectedly of a heart attack twenty years into their marriage. Rabo's grief for Edith causes him to paint his final masterpiece, the huge, elaborate canvas he locks in the potato barn behind his mansion. He tells his friend, the novelist Paul Slazinger, that what he's hidden in the barn is "the emptiest and yet the fullest of all human messages.... Good-bye" (211). The painting is his good-bye to Edith, but Rabo expects it to be his good-bye to the larger world as well. For two years after Edith's death, Rabo himself is like the walking dead, his Long Island mansion having become a mausoleum.

Unexpectedly, however, yet another rebirth is in store for Rabo Karabekian. When he meets Circe Berman on the beach, Rabo's life, as well as his artistic vision, takes another dramatic turn. Although the two clash, disagreeing about nearly everything, including the role and purpose of art, Rabo realizes that he wants "someone as vivid as [Circe] to keep [him] alive" (146). Mrs. Berman calls Rabo her "Lazarus," arguing that she has brought him "back to life" (137), and she also guides Rabo to a newfound appreciation for representational art and the fact that art can, in fact, *say* something about the contemporary world. Circe Berman's views on art provide a necessary balance and corrective to the artistic vision embraced by Rabo Karabekian. In the guise of wildly popular young-adult novelist Polly Madison, Circe looks unflinchingly at the problems facing contemporary teenagers, writing smart and realistic books that mean a great deal to ordinary people. Rabo, on the other hand, tends to be elitist in his views of art. He often wallows in the past, using his conversations with Celeste, his cook's fifteen-year-old daughter, to bemoan the lack of knowledge he sees in contemporary teens. He belittles the artistic taste of Celeste's mother, Allison White, by selling the only painting in his collection she really liked: a magazine illustration of two black boys and two white boys painted by Dan Gregory. Allison points out that she is uneducated and that the abstract paintings in Rabo's collection simply don't "*mean* anything" to her (142). Finally, Rabo jeers at the chromos of children on swings that Circe hangs in his foyer, arguing that "anybody with half a grain of sense about art" would see these pictures as "a *negation* of art," as "black holes from which no intelligence or skill can ever escape" (136). He calls Circe's pictures "kitsch," in fact, condescendingly asking the widow if she knows the meaning of the word. We see that Rabo's artistic snobbery is also tied up with feelings of gender superiority when Circe replies that she wrote a book called *Kitsch*, and Celeste explains that "it's about a girl whose boyfriend tried to make her think she has bad taste, which she does—but it doesn't matter much" (138).

While Rabo Karabekian's embracing of abstract expressionism is a corrective to the dangerously fascist artistic views of Dan Gregory,

Circe Berman teaches Rabo to revalue representational, even sentimental, art. Feminist literary critics, such as Nina Baym, Sandra Gilbert and Susan Gubar, and Jane Tompkins, beginning in the late 1970s and 1980s, similarly challenged a literary canon that devalued women's work, particularly sentimental and domestic writing. While Vonnegut may or may not have been aware of such critiques, he was certainly responding to a cultural zeitgeist. In *Palm Sunday*, an essay collection published in 1981, Vonnegut notes ruefully that most literature deemed "great" ignores domestic experience. Yet, he writes of the importance of such experience in his own life: "The most meaningful and often harrowing adventures which I and many like me have experienced have had to do with the rearing of children" (*Palm Sunday* 143). Circe Berman in *Bluebeard* defends her pictures of little girls on swings by arguing that their value lies in the very fact that they *are* about something: "Try thinking what the Victorians thought when they looked at them," she tells Rabo, "which was how sick or unhappy so many of these happy, innocent little girls would be in just a little while—diptheria, pneumonia, smallpox, miscarriages, violent husbands, poverty, widowhood, prostitution" (138). Realistic art, which makes a specific connection to the world, can attempt to change that world for the better. Rabo himself uses this same defense of the sentimental pictures when three writers from the Soviet Union come to tour his collection, and the men leave the house unanimously "agreeing that these were the most important pictures" they had seen (166).

But that's not to say that Vonnegut believes Rabo should completely reject abstract expressionism in favor of realistic art. Both types of art, Vonnegut seems to argue, can coexist alongside one another. As critic David Rampton points out, Rabo, at the very end of the novel, turns his mansion into a museum that comments on the history of art. Visitors begin in the foyer, viewing the sentimental pictures of little girls on swings, then move on to the works of the first abstract expressionists, before finishing their tour with what Vonnegut describes as "the perfectly tremendous watchamacallit in the potato barn" (299). Rabo's gigantic painting that he has locked in the barn all these years, titled "Now It's the Women's Turn," suggests the culmination of art. Every square inch of the painting is "encrusted with the most gorgeous jewelry" (297). The jewelry is humanity itself in all its motley and teeming glory. Although an impossible feat in the real world, Vonnegut has imagined a painting that depicts *all* of life, that is somehow equivalent to life itself. The painting, in its depiction of the moment "when the sun came up the day the Second World War ended in Europe" (298), suggests great sorrow, the suffering caused by World War II as well as Rabo's grief over Edith's death, yet it is also a testament to the human will to survive and points to the possibility of rebirth after tragedy. The novel ends with Circe Berman, a dedicated and successful artist in her own right, teaching Rabo to look at his hands with "love and gratitude," and to say out loud, "Thank you, Meat," for the wonderful work they have accomplished (318). Circe has brought Rabo back to life, and in finally showing her his painting, Rabo has offered a new beginning both to Circe Berman and to the world at large. The painting depicts the world poised on the brink of a rebirth, turned over to women, who will now take their chances with it.

Although Vonnegut is a novelist sometimes criticized for stereotypical portrayals of women characters, it seems to me that he is a writer who has taken gender issues seriously throughout his career, condemning sexism alongside other social ills he satirizes. Cartoonish characters are a hallmark of Vonnegut's fiction, and they appear in both genders throughout his work. Yet, Vonnegut is nevertheless deeply concerned about ethically responsible artistic expression, and he realizes that a type of art that excludes half the human population can never be morally viable. From aspiring artists imprisoned by 1950s' domestic ideology to caregivers whose abhorrence of war and violence shape new narrative forms, to female art lovers who question elitism and sexism in the male art world, Vonnegut's female characters have consistently shown the impact of gender on the artistic imagination.

Works Cited

Allen, William Rodney, ed. *Conversations with Kurt Vonnegut.* Jackson: U of Mississippi P, 1988.

Boon, Kevin A. "The Problem with Pilgrim in Kurt Vonnegut's *Slaughterhouse-Five.*" *Notes on Contemporary Literature* 26.2 (1996): 8–10.

Friedan, Betty. *The Feminine Mystique.* New York: Norton, 1963.

Hearell, Dale W. "Vonnegut's Changing Women." *Publications of the Arkansas Philological Association* 22.2 (1996): 27–35.

Hemingway, Ernest. "Soldier's Home." *In Our Time.* New York: Scribner's, 1925.

Merrill, Robert, and Peter A. Scholl. "Vonnegut's *Slaughterhouse-Five*: The Requirements of Chaos." *Studies in American Fiction* 6.1 (1978): 65–76.

Rampton, David. "Into the Secret Chamber: Art and the Artist in Kurt Vonnegut's *Bluebeard.*" *Critique* 35.1 (1993): 16–26.

Rooney, Andy, and Oram C. Hutton. *Air Gunner.* New York: Farrar, 1944.

Simpson, Josh. " 'This Promising of Great Secrets': Literature, Ideas, and the (Re)Invention of Reality in Kurt Vonnegut's *God Bless You, Mr. Rosewater, Slaughterhouse-Five,* and *Breakfast of Champions* or 'Fantasies of an Impossibly Hospitable World': Science Fiction and Madness in Vonnegut's Troutean Trilogy." *Critique* 45.3 (2004): 261–71.

Vees-Gulani, Susanne. "Diagnosing Billy Pilgrim: A Psychiatric Approach to Kurt Vonnegut's *Slaughterhouse-Five.*" *Critique* 44.2 (2003): 175–84.

Vonnegut, Kurt. *Bluebeard.* 1987. New York: Dell, 1998.

———. *Breakfast of Champions.* 1973. New York: Dell, 1999.

———. *Cat's Cradle.* 1963. New York: Dell, 1998.

———. "Custom-Made Bride." *Bagombo Snuff Box.* 1999. New York: Berkley, 2000.

———. *Galápagos.* 1985. New York: Dell, 1999.

———. *God Bless You, Mr. Rosewater.* 1965. New York: Dell, 1998.

———. "Lovers Anonymous." *Bagombo Snuff Box.* 1999. New York: Berkley, 2000.

———. *A Man without a Country.* New York: Seven Stories, 2005.

———. "Miss Temptation." *Welcome to the Monkey House.* 1968. New York: Dell, 1998.

———. "More Stately Mansions." *Welcome to the Monkey House.* 1968. New York: Dell, 1998.

———. *Palm Sunday.* 1981. New York: Dell, 1999.

———. *Player Piano.* 1952. New York: Dell, 1999.

———. *Slaughterhouse-Five.* 1969. New York: Dell, 1999.

———. *Timequake.* 1997. New York: Berkley, 1998.

CHAPTER 7

Apocalypse in the Optative Mood: *Galápagos*, or, Starting Over

Robert T. Tally, Jr.,

The epigraph to Vonnegut's *Galápagos* (1985) also reveals the novel's overall theme, and it marks a subtle shift in the career of one of America's greatest cynics. "In spite of everything, I still believe people are really good at heart." (That the line comes from Anne Frank's diary makes it all the more powerful, because we know exactly what the "everything" refers to.) *Galápagos* shares with Vonnegut's other works a poignant critique of the follies of man, a sense of the absurdity of life, but adds an element only hinted at before: hope. In earlier works, undoubtedly, Vonnegut had made gestures in this direction, such as Eliot Rosewater's volunteer firemen, but more often than not, his faith in humanity was overcome by a form of pessimism that might best be described as hopelessness.[1] *Galápagos*, however, embraces a process both random and superior to any human intelligence, the ultimate laissez-faire philosophy applied to the suprahuman process of natural selection itself.

In Vonnegut's postmodern iconography of American life, he frequently exhibits what I have elsewhere referred to as a "misanthropic humanism."[2] Vonnegut sees most people as fundamentally flawed, petty, avaricious, and prone to acts of almost incredible cruelty. Yet, for all that, Vonnegut also cannot abandon humanity; he marvels at man's folly, noting sadly or just curiously man's absurd perseverance, as in the bittersweet image of the triumphant Luddites who proudly put back together the very machines they had broken at the end of *Player Piano* (1952). In *Galápagos* Vonnegut takes further pity on people, arguing that it was never their fault that they were silly, arrogant, and cruel; it was all due to their grotesquely over-sized brains. A mental disease more powerful than Dwayne Hoover's schizophrenia in *Breakfast of Champions* (1973), the curse of the big brain doomed humans to a life of quiet, and sometimes noisy, desperation. In *Galápagos*, as in *Cat's Cradle* (1963), Vonnegut manages to wipe out most of humanity, but here it is not their fault; rather than the man-made *ice-nine*, an anonymous virus renders all but a small colony of the human race unable to reproduce. Reproduction, it turns out, is all that really matters, as the small colony on the northern tip of the Galápagos Islands evolves over millions of years into seal-like creatures, whose only troubles involve matters of fishing. The hope for humanity lies in that heroic perseverance witnessed in other novels, but here salvation comes from becoming animal, in losing the human, all-too-human characteristics that had defined human-ity. By my reading, Vonnegut overcomes his misanthropic humanism not by abandoning the *mis-* in misanthropy but by abandoning the *anthropos*. The result is a new humanism without the human. And, unlike Vonnegut's other apocalyptic novels, *Galápagos* embraces the posthuman world with a sense of hope and futurity that one normally associates with a utopian promise. With *Galápagos*, Vonnegut offers another apocalypse in his oeuvre; but here it is an apocalypse in the optative mood.

THE THING WAS . . .

In its opening lines, *Galápagos* establishes the bizarre premise that the story is being told in the year AD 1,001,986: "The thing was: One million years ago, in 1986 A.D., Guayaquil was the chief sea-port of the little South American democracy called Ecuador" (3). The mix of the utterly fantastic with the utterly commonplace is striking. There is a tremendous cognitive leap between the phrase "one million years ago" and "Guayaquil was the chief seaport." The reader is put on notice, right on the opening page, that the tale will involve an outrageous temporality: we must bear in mind that we are reading about things in the distant, perhaps prehistoric past while at the same time experiencing them almost as they are happening, in what is the reader's present, late–twentieth-century world. Hence, we have an almost God's-eye view of our present world, a view that comports well with Vonnegut's sense of the writer as "the Creator of the Universe" (as he suggests in *Breakfast of Champions* [205]). This is crucial for the novel's paradoxical apocalypse in the optative mood. Since we—through the narrator—know that everything works out for the best, we can watch sometimes horrific scenes of destruction without losing hope. Contrast this to the apocalypse presented in *Cat's Cradle*. There, although the narrator also recounted past events he had witnessed and participated in, the events were so new and so recent that one had little sense of how everything would turn out. Indeed, that novel ends with only the most minute glimmer of hope, as the ragtag band of survivors living on the fictional Caribbean island of San Lorenzo struggles to make sense of its postapocalyptic condition. The final scene of *Cat's Cradle*, when Bokonon himself at last appears, suggests that the final, meaningful act of one who truly understands the cosmos into which humanity has been thrown is an act of playful and defiant suicide: killing oneself while thumbing one's nose at the Creator.[3] In *Galápagos* the destruction of most of humanity is hailed as the great hope for a posthumanoid humanity on the remote island of Santa Rosalia. Thanks to the natural equivalent of *ice-nine*, the unassuming little germ that first appears at the 1986 Frankfurt Book Fair, the fur-covered humanity on that remote knoll of the Galápagos Archipelago flourishes. Rather than ossify in an attitude of playful defiance, humanity finally finds itself in vibrant harmony with the natural world.

The bulk of the narrative recounts events taking place in Guayaquil on November 28, 1986, although Vonnegut's style allows him to shift between flashbacks, flash-forwards, and lateral storytelling in order to create a nonlinear history. Readers would be familiar with such narrative techniques in, especially, *Slaughterhouse-Five* (1969), but Galápagos provides a different rationale. In *Slaughterhouse-Five* all of history could be viewed at once, as if time were really space, such that the various moments of history could be viewed just as one views a stretch of a mountain range.[4] Hence, time travel became as simple as space travel; so the narrative, like the protagonist Billy Pilgrim, could "become unstuck" in time, moving with ease among past, present, and future. Here, it is not that time is transformed into space but that the narrator is capable of witnessing a million years of history. To do this, Vonnegut created a new type of narrator, one especially apt for presenting an apocalypse in the optative mood.

Charles Berryman has noted that "Vonnegut's boldest experiments in fiction have always been with narrative strategy" (195), and Vonnegut employs a novel strategy here. *Galápagos* is narrated by the headless ghost of Leon Trout, the son of longtime Vonnegut-alter-ego Kilgore Trout, the science fiction writer who first appeared in *God Bless You, Mr. Rosewater* (1965) and played key roles in

Slaughterhouse-Five and *Breakfast of Champions* (he also makes an appearance in *Jailbird* [1979]). The father appears in this story as well, but in *Galápagos* Leon Trout gets to be the storyteller, and his own version of science fiction—specifically the science of Darwinian evolutionary biology—supplies the guiding thread of the novel's moral dimension. Vonnegut needed to create a narrator who could witness the events but also survive a million years of natural history. He could have created a god, an immortal alien, or the like; but with Leon Trout, he is able to combine the fantastic with the familiar in interesting ways. Obviously, a ghost-narrator is a far-fetched conceit, one that makes a mockery of the realism of the story taking place in Ecuador.[5] But likewise, this narrator makes possible the greater pathos and, in particular, empathy that illuminates the characters struggling with the horrors of the day. Leon Trout, by being a ghost, is thus able to become part of the story itself, a participant-narrator who is also a passive observer, one who sees into the minds of his characters and also reveals his own thoughts and feelings. And, as I will argue, Leon Trout—like his father, Kilgore—becomes a figure for the writer in general, and perhaps for Kurt Vonnegut himself. Leon Trout as narrator is thus a remarkable addition to the repertoire of storytelling styles employed by Vonnegut.

The cast of *Galápagos* is another colorful ensemble of oddballs, similar to those of his early novels; as in those earlier works, the characters are thoroughly flawed yet sympathetically presented. *Galápagos* is populated with the lovably motley assemblage that Vonnegut's fans have become accustomed to in other novels. Here we find Andrew MacIntosh, a captain of industry, with his blind daughter, Selena, and her seeing-eye dog, Kazakh;[6] Mary Hepburn, a recent widow from Ilium, New York, a town that regularly and generously provides Vonnegut with characters (literally and figuratively); James Wait, a sleazy confidence man looking to seduce, fleece, and abandon wealthy widows; Zengi Hiroguchi, a Japanese scientist and inventor hoping to become a businessman, and his depressed, pregnant wife, Hisako; Adolf von Kleist, a pompous, aging sea captain; and six illiterate girls from a lost tribe of rainforest dwellers, utterly bewildered and oblivious to most of the goings-on. Additionally, key roles are played by Jesus Ortiz, the good natured hotel employee who is pushed too far; Giraldo Delgado, a paranoid schizophrenic who is armed and extremely dangerous; Roy Hepburn, Mary's late and also schizophrenic husband; Guillermo Reyes, a sane fighter pilot; Hernando Cruz, a capable ship's mate; and Siegfried von Kleist, brother to an incompetent captain of a ship and the good-natured sufferer of the early stages of Huntington chorea. Leon Trout, the narrator and guardian angel or friendly ghost, rounds out this fine ensemble for an end-of-the-world farce.

The plot may be briefly summarized: Several of the aforementioned cast arrive in Guayaquil in order to participate in "The Nature Cruise of the Century," a globally marketed event that was supposed to feature celebrity guests such as Jacqueline Onassis, Mick Jagger, and Walter Cronkite. A severe financial crisis has put the cruise in jeopardy, as the celebrities have all dropped out, but the remaining guests, for reasons of their own, remain. Mary Hepburn had promised her late husband that she would attend, and she is suicidal with loneliness and despair when we first see her. James Wait, posing as a Canadian widower, had hoped to meet wealthy women to take advantage of. Andrew MacIntosh was planning to seal a lucrative business deal first with the government of Ecuador and then with Zengi Hiroguchi, the inventor of a new handheld device (the Mandarax) that, among its other useful features, operates as a nearly universal translator. MacIntosh is accompanied by his blind daughter, Selena, and Hiroguchi by his wife, Hisako, so the business arrangements may be discussed in the relatively informal surroundings of a family vacation. Later, in their postapocalyptic life on Santa Rosalia, Selena MacIntosh and Hisako Hiroguchi will live as spouses until they commit suicide together. Captain von Kleist, the captain of the cruise ship, *Bahia de Darwin* (or "Bay of Darwin"), and his brother Siegfried, the manager of the hotel, make possible the escape of the survivors from Guayaquil to the Galápagos island. Thanks to a series of accidents, this ensemble will also include six young girls from the lost tribe of Kanka-bono Indians. These girls will becomes the new Eves to all of humanity.

The worldwide economic crisis leads to the financial and social collapse of Ecuador, and poverty there is now compounded by starvation. Additionally, war between Ecuador and Peru is on the verge of breaking out. The new hotel has been cordoned off by the army, as mobs of hungry citizens become a growing danger. Giraldo Delgado, a paranoid schizophrenic soldier, will actually be responsible for breaking the cordon sanitaire, and he will also wind up killing Andrew MacIntosh and Zengi Hiroguchi as they are pacing the grounds. Realizing that the only hope for survival lies in escaping by sea, Siegfried von Kleist loads the survivors into a bus and drives them to the seaport, where he finds his brother thoroughly drunk and the ship completely stripped off all provisions and valuables. An explosion, which kills Siegfried von Kleist, unmoors the craft, and although the captain is not really qualified to operate the ship—his capable first mate having abandoned the vessel earlier—he sets sail to the West. A "Second Noah's Ark," as our narrator had called it, sets out for Mt. Ararat. James Wait, who has suffered a heart attack, dies shortly after "marrying" Mary Hepburn (the captain performed the ceremony), and Selena's seeing-eye dog goes missing (we soon learn that the Kanka-bonos have killed, cooked, and eaten it). Due to the captain's faulty and erratic navigating, the ship is far off course, and after five days, it eventually lands on the unpopulated northern Galápagos island of Santa Rosalia, best known for its indigenous species of vampire finches, as the former high school biology teacher Mary Hepburn recognizes. They stop there for provisions, but the *Bahia de Darwin*'s engines will not start again, so they are stranded. Thus, they are spared the ravages of a disease that first breaks out at the annual book fair in Frankfurt, Germany, a disease that destroys the reproductive capabilities of humans. What remains of human- ity, a million years later, descends from this initial colony of ten survivors—Captain von Kleist, Mary Hepburn, Selena MacIntosh, Hisako Hiroguchi, and the six Kanka-bono girls. Hisako soon gives birth to Akiko, who is covered in a light fur owning to a genetic defect in Hisako's family initially caused by exposure to radiation from the bombing of Hiroshima. Watching over all of this is Leon Trout, who worked and then died in the Swedish shipyard building the *Bahia de Darwin*, thus making both the craft and the story of the "Second Noah's Ark" possible.

APOCALYPSE REVISITED

In some ways, *Galápagos* is the apotheosis of Vonnegut's earlier work, an exemplary and perfected form of the narratives and argu- ments he had been laying out throughout his writing career, in what Peter Freese describes as "a baker's dozen of successful novels with apocalyptic themes and symbols" ("Natural Selection" 337). Certain themes audible in all of his writings reappear here as well. For example, the concern that human activities are increasingly performed by machines is the fundamental premise of Vonnegut's earliest novel, *Player Piano*, often thought to be a work of science fiction,[7] which depicts a dystopian near-future in the tradition of George Orwell's *Nineteen Eighty-Four* (1949). The apocalypse, a man-made end to the world, appears in *Cat's Cradle* as well as in more local versions in *Slapstick* (1976) and *Deadeye Dick* (1982). Schizophrenia and depression, key elements of *Slaughterhouse-Five* and *Breakfast of Champions*, make their timely reappearance here as well.

In *Galápagos*, the narrator notes, almost in passing, how humans with their big brains almost maniacally insisted on "having machines do everything that human beings did—and I mean *everything*" (70). The world presented in *Player Piano* is one in which computers and efficient machinery have eliminated the need for the vast majority of workers; with machines fulfilling all of society's material needs while denying the satisfaction of the less well-known "need" to perform meaningful work, the abject working class of the novel is forced to choose between absolutely menial nonwork or unemployment. A white-collar middle class, represented by the allegorically named Paul Proteus, is perhaps equally dejected, recognizing that the corporate identity and pseudofamily is destroying the individual and community identities so longed for. In what will serve as the climax of the novel, a band of neo-Luddites gleefully destroy the very machines that had taken not only their jobs but their meaning in life. Vonnegut, here, could have chosen to end the novel with the scenes of glorious destruction, depicting a victorious revolutionary working class rising up to demand a dignified life worth living. Vonnegut also could have chosen to show the brutal crackdown by a cold, heartless regime, thus turning the revolutionaries into martyrs. Both images are present in the book. But the lasting image, the one that haunts the reader and that provides the theme that is audible throughout Vonnegut's works, is slightly different. As the delirious rioters gloat over the smashed machines, several begin to take pleasure and, indeed, pride in repairing the recently broken devices. At first, fixing the machine is just a puzzle to be solved, but then the satisfaction of solving it leads to the desire of creating new, better machines. Vonnegut's message is clear: the dystopian world is entirely of human creation, and there is no human solution to the problem, since the ones who suffer from the life without meaning are the same ones who will create the conditions for that meaningless life.

I have referred to Vonnegut's attitude as a misanthropic humanism. Vonnegut's notion that the *human, all-too-human* (in Nietzsche's ironic but telling phrase) condition is absurd, that human behavior inevitably leads to ruin, is complemented by the thoroughly humanist belief that a striving, however meaningless in the end, has meaning in itself. The human spirit of perseverance is, for Vonnegut, the lovable quality that overcomes the absurdity of existence, if only for a while. *Cat's Cradle* is narrated by a wandering Ishmael—or worse, the bad luck Jonah—who sets out to write a book about the events that took place on August 6, 1945, the day that the atomic bomb was dropped on Hiroshima, Japan. He plans to call the book *The Day the World Ended*. The opening line of *Cat's Cradle*—"Call me Jonah"—invokes another great American novel, *Moby-Dick*, which also tells the tale of a fatal destruction of a figurative world. In each book, the seed of the world's destruction lies in human ingenuity coupled with the human, all-too-human desire for power, love, or understanding. Felix Hoenikker, the father of the atomic bomb and the inventor of *ice-nine* (the substance that will eventually bring about Armageddon in *Cat's Cradle*), is presented as an absentminded genius, someone who would not harm a fly but whose reckless and heedless knowledge-for-the-sake-of-knowledge actually is more destructive than the ill will of a thousand tyrants. Ahab, driven to distraction by "that inscrutable thing" of which the White Whale may be the agent or the principal, is willing to risk all to conquer it. In both cases, whether elicited by monomaniacal fury or innocent curiosity, the apocalyptic force is unleashed. The Faustian bargain is at the heart of Vonnegut's misanthropic humanism.

Leon Trout introduces and repeats a phrase, used to refer to the recently departed, throughout *Galápagos*: "Well, he wasn't going to write Beethoven's Ninth Symphony anyway." The line sums up what all of us, excluding Ludwig van Beethoven himself, amount to at death. A callous dismissal, perhaps. But Vonnegut also makes clear that the same brainpower that could write Beethoven's Ninth Symphony also made possible the bombing of Hiroshima, the famine spreading throughout Ecuador, and so on. The most ingenious device in *Galápagos* is surely the Mandarax, likened to the Apple of Knowledge in what will be humankind's New Eden on Santa Rosalia. When Hisako Hiroguchi lashes out at her inventor husband for creating the Mandarax, she discloses the frustration of someone whose life is measured by such outrageous standards as whether one might write Beethoven's Ninth Symphony. The Mandarax, a device initially designed to supplant the Gobuki (which could translate among ten different languages), could translate among a thousand languages, but it could also make medical diagnoses, provide thousands of quotations from world literature, and—apparently—teach ikebana, the Japanese art of flower arranging, also the area of Hisako's expertise. Although the Mandarax is clearly an extraordinarily useful thing, Hisako, in her anger and depression, recognizes a more baleful aspect of its creation:

> "You, *Doctor Hiroguchi," she went on, "think that everybody but yourself is just taking up space on this planet, and we make too much

noise and waste valuable natural resources and have too many children and leave garbage around. So it would be a much nicer place if the few stupid services we are able to perform for the likes of you were taken over by machinery. That wonderful Mandarax you're scratching your ear with now: what is that but an excuse for a mean-spirited egomaniac never to pay or even thank a human being with a knowledge of languages or mathematics or history or medicine or ikebana or anything?" (70)

(The asterisk, of course, is Vonnegut's way of letting the reader know that Zengi Hiroguchi will die quite soon, and certainly long before he will ever get the chance to write Beethoven's Ninth Symphony.) Even the Mandarax, imminently useful and ingeniously devised, can cause such anguish as the machines in *Player Piano*. The *ice-nine* that winds up destroying the world in *Cat's Cradle* is, like laborsaving machinery or nuclear weapons, another grand achievement in the human, all-too-human quest for knowledge. In his early writings, Vonnegut might have looked at such behavior with cynical detachment, but Vonnegut does not blame his characters personally for building or restoring the machines that had made them miserable, for creating and using weapons of almost unimaginable destructive power, or for using words and images to make each other unhappy. It is not their fault, and *Galápagos* reveals the actual source of human misery.

Big Brains

In *Galápagos* Vonnegut finally identifies the problem and proposes a solution. The problem with humans is that they have a terrible birth defect, passed down to their progeny throughout human existence. The defect is their big brains. Such big brains cause all the trouble, and if only humans could evolve to have smaller brains, they would be so much happier and more well-adjusted to the world in which they live. As the narrator puts it, looking back over a million years and with specific reference to the devious con man just introduced,

> It is hard to believe nowadays that people could ever have been as brilliantly duplicitous as James Wait—until I remind myself that just about every adult human being back then had a brain weighing about three kilograms! There was no end to the evil schemes that a thought machine that oversized couldn't imagine and execute.
>
> So I raise this question, although there is nobody around to answer it: Can it be doubted that three-kilogram brains were once nearly fatal defects in the evolution of the human race?

A second query: What source was there back then, save for our overelaborate nervous circuitry, for the evils we were seeing or hearing about simply everywhere?

My answer: There was no other source. This was a very innocent planet, except for those great big brains. (8–9)

Throughout the novel, Vonnegut blames those big brains for all of the problems facing humanity. Such enormous brains could not help but produce its own monsters, giving what the narrator describes as bad advice on crucial matters of survival. Thus, Mary Hepburn's brain tries to convince her that suicide is the right course of action; this is the same brain that will later have her perform experiments in artificial insemination with an unwilling sperm donor and with agreeable teenage virgins. Such big brains could create outlandish scenarios, as with the big brain of the trusting, hardworking hotel employee, Jesús Ortiz. "Ortiz's brain was so big that it could show movies in his head which starred him and his dependents as millionaires. And this man, little more than a boy, was so innocent that he believed his dream could come true" (75–76). Such big brains caused the Hiroguchis, and other married couples, to fluctuate between hating or resenting each other and wanting to do whatever possible to make each other happy, often changing whimsically from mere second to second. "Of what possible use was such emotional volatility, not to say craziness, in the heads of animals who were supposed to stay together long enough, at least, to raise a human child, which took about fourteen years or so?" (67). And, as Leon Trout himself confesses, "When I was alive, I often received advice from my own big brain which, in terms of my own survival, or the survival of the human race, for that matter, can be charitably described as questionable. Example: It had me join the United States Marines and go fight in Vietnam.

Thanks a lot, big brain" (29).

Another problem with these oversized brains, regardless of the naïveté or mendacity or goodwill of the person involved in the era of big brains, is that mere opinions themselves—notions formed in those brains with no real substance exterior to them—often had life-or-death consequences. Vonnegut uses the word *magical* to describe the process by which mere opinions, when agreed upon by a substantial number of people, could transform the value of things in human minds (18). The worldwide financial crisis that had disrupted the plans for the "Nature Cruise of the Century," which was causing famine in much of South America, and which would lead to war between Ecuador and Peru, was a simple result of the changing opinion of the value of paper representations of wealth exchanged in those places. "It was all in people's heads. People had simply changed their opinions of paper wealth, but, for all practical purposes, the planet may as well have been knocked out of orbit" (24).

Vonnegut also emphasizes that the problem with big brains is not that they are defective—the defect is that they exist at all. Leon Trout takes pains to explain this, especially since there are many dangerous characters in the story whose brains, in addition to being big, were actually malfunctioning. Not wanting to give the impression that "everybody a million years ago was insane," the narrator proclaims: "That was not the case. I repeat: that was not the case. Almost everybody was sane back then.... The big problem, again, wasn't insanity, but that people's brains were much too big and untruthful to be practical" (189). In the novel, we see Roy Hepburn's dementia, Giraldo Delgado's paranoia, and Siegfried von Kleist's nascent problems with Huntington's disease; but the real tragedy for mankind—Vonnegut insists—is not the brain that malfunctions, but the brain that functions properly and continues to cause misery in its owners and those surrounding them.

The solution, then, lies not in better mental health care or in learning to use our mental facilities more scrupulously or more effectively. The solution lies in ridding ourselves of those big brains. In *Galápagos* Vonnegut turns to real "science fiction," perhaps for the first time in his career. The science, of course, is evolutionary biology, specifically Darwin's theory of natural selection. Despite his aversion to being classified as a science fiction writer, Vonnegut has acknowledged his widespread use of "science fiction of an obvious kidding sort" (*Wampeters* 262). But *Galápagos* uses actual science to organize the fiction. As Peter Freese argues in "Natural Selection with a Vengeance: Kurt Vonnegut's *Galápagos*," Vonnegut uses "natural selection with a vengeance" to undermine the perceived superiority of human in the biosphere, and specifically to debunk the arrogant notion that the things that make humans superior are their big brains. Far from providing humankind with a superior weapon in the struggle for survival, the big brain is actually an evolutionary mistake, a congenital birth defect like Huntington's chorea. As Freese sums up Vonnegut's theory, "man is an evolutionary mistake, and the only chance to prevent the imminent destruction of the world is not to think ever better thoughts but to give up thinking all together" (339).

Vonnegut dramatizes a million-year experiment in creating a form of humankind best adapted to life on the planet. A million years ago, in 1986, there was a reasonable suspicion that the world was ending and that humankind and the world were not very good for each other. Leon Trout, from his God's-eye vantage over this span of a thousand millennia, can view everything and everyone as parts of an overall experiment, a research program conducted by Nature herself and using the law of natural selection as its method. Individual characters within the tale are themselves subjects in the experiment:

> If Selena was Nature's experiment with blindness, then her father was Nature's experiment with heartlessness, and Jesús Ortiz was Nature's experiment with admiration for the rich, and I was Nature's experiment with insatiable voyeurism, and my father was Nature's experiment with cynicism, and my mother was Nature's experiment with optimism, and the Captain of the Bahia de Darwin was Nature's experiment with ill-founded self-confidence, and James Wait was Nature's experiment with purposeless greed, and Hisako Hiroguchi was Nature's experiment with depression, and Akiko Nature's experiment with furriness, and so on. (82)

Whether any of these personality traits are beneficial for survival is unlikely to be seen during the lifetime of the persons who have them. That Nature has use for such things is doubtful, as the narrator concludes that "there are no such experiments, either with bodies or personalities, going on at the present time" (83).

At the end of history, or at least at the end of Leon Trout's story, the seal-like humans thrive in large part strictly because they have evolved in such a way as to lose the very capacity to have personalities. Nature, not some supernatural force, had "brought humanity into harmony with the rest of Nature" via the law of natural selection:

> It was the best fisherfolk who survived in the greatest numbers in the watery environment of the Galápagos Archipelago. Those with hands and feet most like flippers were the best swimmers. Prognathous jaws were better at catching and holding fish than hands could ever be. And any fisherperson, spending more and more time underwater, could surely catch more fish if he or she were more streamlined, more bulletlike—had a smaller head. (291)

Hence, no more big brains.

THE ERA OF HOPEFUL MONSTERS

Is it surprising that the virus that wipes out all of humanity—all, that is, except for the little colony on Santa Rosalia—first appears at the Frankfurt Book Fair? This annual event, though the largest of its kind, would not necessarily seem to be ground zero for the end of the world. But by using the world's largest book fair as the site where humanity ends, Vonnegut links the profession of writing to his apocalypse, an apocalypse written in the optative mood.

What is perhaps most striking about the apocalypse presented in *Galápagos* is its utterly quotidian nature. Contrary to the belief of some readers,[8] the destruction of the human race in *Galápagos* is not caused by World War III, by nuclear Armageddon, or by a substance like *ice-nine*; rather, what destroys all of humanity is a little virus or bacterium that destroys women's ova, thus making reproduction impossible. Those humans who initially survive, presumably, will lead long, healthy, and perhaps happy lives, only without having any more children. (Presumably, although the text does not specifically invite the inquiry, humans alive in 1986 could go on living for another 100 years or so; Vonnegut, or Leon Trout, does not tell what might have been happening outside of the isle of Santa Rosalia.) The absolute end of nearly all humankind is anything but spectacular. Far from the image of a meteor knocking the planet out of orbit, a nuclear holocaust, or a biblical Armageddon, Vonnegut buries the root of humanity's ultimate annihilation midway through the novel, mentioned as "another David-and-Goliath" story that is actually a simple, and natural, process.

As Mary Hepburn contemplates suicide in her hotel room in Guayaquil, she thinks of the lesson she taught her students about the great land tortoises. Once they could be found "lumbering over every temperate land mass of any size" (162), but then tiny rodents evolved to feed on tortoise eggs, and the great reptiles were wiped out everywhere but for those few remote places (like the Galápagos) that remained free of the rodents. This incidental piece of natural history provides a figure for the fall of man as well. As Vonnegut writes,

> It was prophetic that Mary should imagine herself to be a land tortoise as she suffocated, since something very much like what had happened to most of the land tortoises so long ago was then beginning to happen to most of humankind.
>
> Some new creature, invisible to the naked eye, was eating up all the eggs in human ovaries, starting at the annual Book Fair at Frankfurt, Germany. Woman at the fair were experiencing a slight fever, which came and went in a day or two, and sometimes blurry vision. After that, they would be just like Mary Hepburn. They couldn't have babies anymore. Nor would any way be discovered for stopping the disease. It would spread practically everywhere.

The near extinction of the mighty land tortoises by little rodents was certainly a David-and-Goliath story. Now here was another one. (162–63)

That this is the only mention of the cause of humanity's destruction in Galápagos is itself significant. Vonnegut, in passing, casually mentions the doom of man.

Of course, this germ that wipes out most of humanity winds up making possible the new, posthuman humanity that will evolve on the seemingly barren island of Santa Rosalia. This is, after all, the great hope for mankind. The pervasive optative mood of *Galápagos* is even given a label at one point. The title of a Kilgore Trout novel, *The Era of Hopeful Monsters*, about creatures hoping to succeed, biologically and otherwise, might be a good label for the novel as a whole. In that book, a humanoid race ignored the most serious problems with survival until, with forests dead, lakes poisoned with acid rain, and groundwater made unpotable, they began having children with monstrous birth defects. Some had "wings or antlers or fins, with a hundred eyes, with no eyes, with huge brains, with no brains, and on and on. These were Nature's experiments with creatures which might be better planetary citizens than the humanoids" (83). Most died or had to be shot, but a few survived, intermarried, and had young themselves. Such monsters had hopes for survival and, accordingly, embodied the hope for human (or humanoid) survival. Vonnegut, through the narrative voice of the disembodied Leon Trout, notes that his time—which is to say, our own time—might be dubbed "the Era of Hopeful Monsters." Specifically he refers to Nature's experiments with personalities, but Vonnegut's overall point is that we are the very monsters of the allegory. And hope is the intrinsic trait.

The persistence of hope in the face of a seeming hopeless situation is, perhaps, its own kind of madness. Leon Trout suggests as much in describing his mother's irrational belief that his father would become a great and popular writer, that the family would move into a nice house, and have friends, and dinner parties, and all that the American upper-middle-class can promise of the good life. Such a belief might be termed a "hopeless optimism." A paradox? Indeed, hopefulness is itself a hopelessly tragic condition, for those of us who ought to know better. But, in *Galápagos*, Vonnegut—for the first time in his long career—enables and even encourages us to embrace such an optative mood, to look upon the destruction of the human world we have known as part of the beautiful (and beautifully irrational) process of overcoming our human, all-too-human condition. There is an element of Nietzsche *fröhlich Wissenschaft* or "joyful wisdom" in Vonnegut's formulation.

Vonnegut even allows for the horrors of his own time to be incorporated into the more hopeful natural history he creates in *Galápagos*. The human race that thrives in the future descends from Akiko Hiroguchi, a child born with a beneficial mutation: she "was covered in a fine, silky pelt like a fur seal's" (58). Being exposed to the harsh equatorial sun on an island without trees or having to swim in the cold waters of the Pacific, the new kinds of humans to come could only benefit from such protective insulation. The narrator makes clear that this birth defect is an indirect result of the U.S. bombing of Hiroshima forty-one years earlier, as Akiko's grandmother had been exposed to nuclear radiation. Thus had the tragedy that sent Jonah, *Cat's Cradle's* narrator, off to write a book that led to his own apocalyptic tale become a source for the happily-ever-after postapocalypse of *Galápagos*. Thus had the Asian analogue of Vonnegut's own terrifying firestorm in Dresden in *Slaughterhouse-Five* made possible this tale written in the optative mood.

The epigraph to *Galápagos*, which Leon Trout asserts was his mother's favorite quote, expresses both the hope and the monstrosity well: "In spite of everything, I still believe people are really good at heart." At the beginning of the novel, the "everything" is on full display: greed, egoism, cruelty, and on. And, by the end of *Galápagos*, the goodness at heart is unquestioned. Vonnegut shows how humanity may be saved, and its salvation lies in shedding itself of the very human, all-too-human, qualities. The humans of AD 1,001,986 are happy and healthy planetary citizens. The broken machinery is repaired, not by some external force, but by Nature. As the narrator concludes,

> When my tale began, it appeared that the earthling part of the clockwork of the universe was in terrible danger, since many of its parts, which is to say people, no longer fit in anywhere, and were damaging all the parts around them as well as themselves. I would have said back then that the damage was beyond repair.
>
> Not so!
>
> Thanks to certain modifications in the design of human beings, I see no reason why the earthling part of the clockwork cannot go on ticking forever the way it is ticking now. (291)

The New Eden or the Second Noah's Ark experiment allows all of humanity, not least of which includes Vonnegut himself and his longtime readers, to start over.

Finally, *Galápagos* is Vonnegut's chance to make peace with the monster he is, the writer as monster. For Vonnegut, the role of the writer, perhaps best embodied by Kilgore Trout, is that of a social anomaly, an outsider who cannot help but fill the big brains of others with the distorted images of his own oversized thinking-machine. A writer is a monster, perhaps a hopeful monster, who does not fit in well with the world. Indeed, in *Galápagos*, we are given a suitably monstrous figure for the writer's horror-movie role in human affairs: a ghost. Leon Trout explains that the reason he chose to become a ghost, rather than stepping into the blue tunnel into the afterlife, was "because the job carried with it, as a fringe benefit, license to read minds, to learn the truth of people's pasts, to see through walls, to be many places at once, to learn in depth how this or that situation had come to be structured as it was, and to have access to all human knowledge" (253). Is it even necessary, to add in summation, *to become a writer*. Moreover, the ghost of Leon Trout does become a writer. In the final chapter, he famously explains that "I have written these words in air—with the tip of the index finger of my left hand, which is also air" (290). A million years in our future, where what remains of humankind is a race of seal-like fisherfolk, there are no more readers: "Nobody, surely, is going to write Beethoven's Ninth Symphony—or tell a lie, or start a Third World War. Mother was right: Even in the darkest times, there really was still hope for humankind" (259). The rendering of writers as spectral entities, floating above, within, or amid human society without being wholly of part of it, renders literature itself as a ghostly presence. But this is not viewed as a bad thing. Not at all. "Does it bother me to write so insubstantially, with air on air? Well—my words will be as enduring as anything my father wrote, or Shakespeare wrote, or Beethoven wrote, or Darwin wrote. It turns out that they all wrote with air on air" (290).

This is actually a very hopeful sentiment. Vonnegut's existential humanism had conceded that life was utterly meaningless, but here that sort of meaninglessness is embraced. What had caused so much pain and anxiety—for instance, Leon's dismay that his father had no readers—becomes a healthy acknowledgment of the transcendent power to make meaning in our own lives. In a famous interview in *Playboy Magazine*, Vonnegut had explicitly stated the role of the writer in the overall scheme of things, precisely in language resonant with the message of *Galápagos*: "Writers are specialized cells in the social organism. They are evolutionary cells. Mankind is trying to become something else; it's experimenting with new ideas all the time. And writers are a means of introducing new ideas into the society, and also a means of responding symbolically to life. I don't think we're in control of what we do" (qtd. in *Wampeters* 237).

In the end, *Galápagos* affirms our own era of hopeful monsters. It is the apocalypse in the optative mood that signals a new beginning, a starting over from scratch that cleanses the mind of the horrors instanced in *Player Piano*, *Cat's Cradle*, and *Slaughterhouse-Five*, among others. Vonnegut's *Galápagos* is thus a gift from the writer to his devoted fans. Its message, from Anne Frank, that "in spite of everything, I still believe people are really good at heart," also calls to mind that of another great writer from the middle of that troubled century, William Faulkner, who famously suggested in his Nobel Prize acceptance speech "that man will not merely endure, he will prevail." With *Galápagos*, Vonnegut imagines a potential end of man, but produces an apocalypse in the optative mood, a hopeful end-of-the-world romance that puts to rest the misanthropic humanism that typified Vonnegut's earlier works. Here, Vonnegut allows humanity to start over...happy, healthy, and covered in a light fur.

NOTES

1. In his autobiographic "collage," *Palm Sunday*, Vonnegut admits that after spending "two-thirds" of his life as a pessimist, "I am astonished to find myself an optimist now" (209). It seems to me that a sign of Vonnegut's newly acquired optimism is *Galapagos* itself.
2. See my "A Postmodern Iconography: Vonnegut and the Great American Novel."
3. The last lines of *Cat's Cradle* present the final paragraph of the Books of Bokonon: "If I were a younger man, I would write a history of human stupidity; and I would climb to the top of Mount McCabe and lie down on my back with my history for a pillow; and I would take from the ground some of the blue-white poison that makes statues of men; and I would make a statue of myself, lying on my back, grinning horribly, and thumbing my nose at You Know Who" (Vonnegut 191).
4. "All moments, past, present, and future, always have existed, always will exist. The Tralfamadorians can look at all the different moments just the way we can look at a stretch of the Rocky Mountains, for instance. They can see how permanent all the moments are, and they can look at any moment that interests them. It is just an illusion we have here on Earth that one moment follows another one, like beads on a string, and that once a moment is gone it is gone forever" (*Slaughterhouse-Five* 27).
5. Oliver W. Ferguson makes the even bolder argument that the "story" of Galapagos is really the hallucinatory fiction of a perhaps mad Leon Trout, who admittedly contracted syphilis and had psychological problems arising from his traumatic family life and military service. In

other words, the entire drama of the tourists on the "Nature Cruise of the Century" and the million years of evolution is just a fantasy, deliberately composed or otherwise, of a living Leon Trout.

6. Longtime Vonnegut fans will recognize the dog's name, which (with an additional "H") is the same as that of Winston Niles Rumfoord's beloved dog and fellow traveler on the chronosynclastic infundibulum in *The Sirens of Titan*, as well as the name of the vicious attack dog that frightens Vonnegut himself in *Breakfast of Champions*.

7. Vonnegut himself disagrees. See *Wampeters, Foma, and Granfalloons* 1–5.

8. See Klinkowitz.

Works Cited

Berryman, Charles. "Vonnegut and Evolution: *Galápagos*." *Critical Essays on Kurt Vonnegut*. Ed. Robert Merrill. Boston: G.K. Hall, 1990. 188–99.

Cowart, David. "Culture and Anarchy: Vonnegut's Later Career." *Critical Essays on Kurt Vonnegut*. Ed. Robert Merrill. Boston: G.K. Hall, 1990. 170–88.

Deleuze, Gilles, and Félix Guattari. *A Thousand Plateaus*. Trans. Brian Massumi. Minneapolis: U of Minnesota P, 1987.

Ferguson, Oliver W. "History and Story: Leon Trout's Double Narrative in *Galápagos*." *Critique* 40.3 (1999): 230–38.

Frank, Anne. *The Diary of a Young Girl: The Definitive Edition*. 1947. London/New York: Penguin, 2007.

Freese, Peter. "Natural Selection with a Vengeance: Kurt Vonnegut's *Galápagos*." *Amerikastudien/American Studies* 36.3 (1991): 337–60.

———. "Surviving the End: Apocalypse, Evolution, and Entropy in Bernard Malamud, Kurt Vonnegut, and Thomas Pynchon." *Critique* 36.3 (1995): 163–76.

Klinkowitz, Jerome. *The Vonnegut Effect*. Columbia: U of South Carolina P, 2004.

Melville, Herman. *Moby-Dick, or, The Whale*. 1851. New York: Norton, 1967.

Morse, Donald E. "Thinking Intelligently about Science and Art: Kurt Vonnegut's *Galápagos* and *Bluebeard*." *Extrapolation* 38.4 (1997): 292–303.

Orwell, George. *Nineteen Eighty-Four*. 1949. London/New York: Penguin, 2004.

Tally, Robert T., Jr. "A Postmodern Iconography: Vonnegut and the Great American Novel." *Reading America: New Perspectives on the American Novel*. Eds. Elizabeth Boyle and Anne-Marie Evans. Newcastle: Cambridge Scholars, 2008. 163–78.

Vonnegut, Jr., Kurt. *Bagombo Snuff Box*. New York: Putnam, 1999.

———. *Bluebeard*. New York: Dell, 1987.

———. *Breakfast of Champions*. New York: Delacorte, 1973.

———. *Cat's Cradle*. New York: Dell, 1963.

————. *Deadeye Dick.* New York: Dell, 1982.

————. *Galápagos.* New York: Dell, 1985.

————. *God Bless You, Mr. Rosewater.* New York: Dell, 1965.

————. *Hocus Pocus.* New York: Dell, 1990.

————. *Jailbird.* New York: Dell, 1979.

————. *A Man without a Country.* New York: Seven Stories, 2005.

————. *Mother Night.* New York: Dell, 1961.

————. *Palm Sunday.* New York: Delacorte, 1981.

————. *Player Piano.* New York: Dell, 1952.

————. *The Sirens of Titan.* New York: Dell, 1959.

————. *Slapstick.* New York: Dell, 1976.

————. *Slaughterhouse-Five.* New York: Dell, 1969.

————. *Timequake.* New York: Berkley, 1997.

————. *Wampeters, Foma, and Granfalloons.* New York: Delacorte, 1974.

————. *Welcome to the Monkey House.* New York: Dell, 1968.

CHAPTER 8

Folding Time:
History, Subjectivity, and
Intimacy in Vonnegut

Lorna Jowett

Science fiction can have immense temporal range, giving it epic scale. One novel can deal with the whole of time; a time travel story can shift between many different time periods. These perspectives inevitably alter the way we see time and how it functions in relation to individuals, to nations, and to humanity. Science fiction's epic temporal scale, like its potential spatial range (whole galaxies), means that it looks at things from a distance, an estranging distance. Estrangement is a key strategy of science fiction because, as any science fiction fan or scholar knows, it is not about aliens or other planets and not about the future. Putting distance (in time or space) between the reader and the events unfolded in its stories, science fiction comments on what is happening now, and how our past has brought us here. "Intelligent" science fiction can be deeply political, and it engages with history and the present in complex ways. Thus, Gene Rodenberry, creator of *Star Trek*, noted that during the 1960s, his show could "make statements about sex, religion, Vietnam, unions, politics and intercontinental missiles," and because it was science fiction, "they all got by the network" (Johnson-Smith 59). This is, perhaps, a problem inherent in using the fantastic to comment on the real: people are often distracted by the medium and do not perceive the message.

Another "problem" of science fiction, and something that causes it to be easily dismissed by those championing "real" literature, is that it may value the idea, the message, above the medium. Science fiction writing is not always great writing, and it usually avoids formal exper-imentation. This is not because science fiction writers cannot write, or are unwilling to experiment, but if science fiction is, as it is often described, a "literature of ideas" and uses the fantastic as a way to transmit those ideas, then its medium (writing in the case of novels or short stories) must be as transparent as possible. This is taken to an extreme in several Kurt Vonnegut novels that include, often as incidental throwaways, plots of stories by character Kilgore Trout, a science fiction hack. Vonnegut does not so much summarize the plot of these fictional fictions as he summarizes their ideas; in most cases the plot *is* the idea, and these roughed-out versions lay bare those ideas with great clarity.

Because of its foregrounding of (obviously fantastic) setting, some scholars have described science fiction as a "pseudo-realist" form:[1] the fantastic elements are grounded in a material reality. This applies equally to medium. The fantastic is, many believe, best served by a plain prose style that conveys that sense of grounded reality, "the reliance on a 'rhetoric of believability' that virtually defines it as a genre" (Ebert in Hollinger 204). The style and words are familiar (except those that function as signs of the genre, like technobabble); it is what they describe, the science fiction subject, that is unfamiliar and novel.

Vonnegut has certainly suffered from the first problem. Commentators have assumed that as science fiction is not "serious" writing, an author engaging with it has nothing serious to say. On a basic level, this is the fallacious argument that the fantastic is always escapist. Thus, it comes as a revelation to some that "in terms of sociohistorical background and theme, Vonnegut's novels are far more concerned with the very real here and now than he is often given credit for" (Mustazza 22). Other Vonnegut scholars suggest that he was dismissed by critics for so long, not just because he was labeled a science fiction writer, but also because his style was seen as too "simple" to convey anything complex.[2] Vonnegut uses time in his novels in similar ways to science fiction, and his style is as "simple," as serviceable, as most science fiction writing.

Decades of movies or television mean that audiences are accus-tomed to devices that render time, like flashback or even flash-forward, and are accustomed to seeing epic scale presented as a historical saga. Vonnegut's readers, therefore, are already familiar with some of the ways in which he manipulates time.[3] Other popular forms, like the comic, also deal with long-term narrative that may skip through time in a nonlinear fashion, and the constant reboots and ret-conning (retroactive continuity work) that go on in decades-old comic series provide a rather messier model for dealing with time. Common strategies to negotiate time are apparent in many types of popular fictions, then; yet, Vonnegut also consciously applies himself to developing narrative styles that use content to interrogate form or, perhaps, to developing a new form capable of fully exploring the content and of joining personal to public experience.

FUTURE/HISTORY

Vonnegut's novels engage with history by dealing with time in various science fictional ways. *Galápagos* gives us a huge sweep of evolutionary history, a story told from a million years in the future, while the near-future perspectives of *Cat's Cradle, Slapstick,* or *Hocus Pocus* offer another way to invent a future history, and to reinvent, or review U.S. history leading to this future. Far- and near-future settings allow Vonnegut to set in motion a basic science fiction operation. His "most crucial imaginative habit is to gaze down at humanity as if from another world," notes Martin Amis (Morse 28). Yet, instead of using alien creatures, Vonnegut uses time to offer this estranged perspective. At the end of *Player Piano*, Vonnegut's traditional science fiction dystopia, Paul Proteus and a group of rebels drink, not to success (the smashing of a machine-dominated society), nor even to failure (as the inhabitants start repairing the machines), but simply "to the record" (316), and the final words of the novel are "Forward march" (317). It is the apparent forward movement of time that creates the "record" of history, the record that will put our stories into perspective.

Cat's Cradle and Galápagos, while operating with rather different timescales, both make use of the notion of apocalypse as the end of time, or the end of history. The linear motion of history is seen to end (in *Cat's Cradle*) or continue in the evolutionary process (in *Galápagos*). Both novels foreground science as one discourse among others; but in *Cat's Cradle* science devastates the world and human life, whereas Darwin's theory of evolution is what explains the continuance of life in *Galápagos*, even though that life is no longer strictly human. The "big brain" of *Galápagos* is thus "the only real villain" (Vonnegut 216) of both stories, and many other Vonnegut novels. A religious discourse, as parodied in *Cats' Cradle*, might also suggest that apocalypse is part of a linear progression: "Traditionally, the Apocalypse represents a key moment in the linear movement of history from the Fall to ultimate redemption" (Schratt 67). However, in *Cat's Cradle* religion is visibly presented as "foma," that is, a set of "harmless untruths" (Vonnegut, epigraph), or comforting lies. Actually, both science and religion function as foma here: science is presented as creative progress, yet leads to complete destruction (a direct line is drawn from the first use of the atomic bomb to the apocalypse caused by *ice-nine*), while religion, even a deliberately manufactured one like Bokononism, cannot solve the problems of poor peoples' lives. The religious story of Noah's Ark is invoked in *Galápagos*, which also refers to Mother Nature, but these foma are subordinate to scientific explanation, which means that when some humans survive the apocalyptic plague, their big brain defect is happily corrected by centuries of evolution. In fact, several Vonnegut novels seem to suggest, as *Timequake* states, "For practically everybody, the end of the world can't come soon enough" (2). What constitutes the end of the world may be a point of debate, however, and the narrator of *Cat's Cradle* sets out to write a book called *The Day the World Ended*, intended as "an account of what important Americans had done on the day when the first atomic bomb was dropped on Hiroshima, Japan" (Vonnegut 1). In this sense, the world ends when it is fundamentally changed: time continues but the world we know does not, as demonstrated by the long view of *Galápagos*.

Thus, Vonnegut offers different scenarios that essentially prove Brian Attebery's point about the way science fiction works:

> the disorienting element that Darko Suvin calls a novum...corresponds to something already inherent in the characters: a buried fear, an unforeseen capability, a potential reshuffling of basic beliefs. *In confronting the novum, the characters are forced to rewrite their own stories, not only their individual life histories but also the historical, religious, and scientific trajectories—the masterplots—within which they make sense of their lives.* The SF writer, then, is not simply a popularizer of scientific ideas, but someone who links ideas to cultural narratives. (174, my emphasis)

In any apocalyptic scenario, the fact that characters are forced to "reshuffle...basic beliefs" is foregrounded by the narrative, as is the case in *Cat's Cradle* and *Galápagos*. History, religion, and science all offer competing discourses that explain our lives—Vonnegut's novels deal with all three, and he consistently links ideas (about the deadly potential of scientific thought, about the ongoing process of evolution) to cultural narratives about people and how they live their lives according to various foma, whether these are religious teachings or U.S. ideologies. He states, for instance, that he has "customarily written about powerless people who felt there wasn't much they could do about their situations," because such stories counter a body of U.S. fiction shaped by optimistic ideals.

> It goes against the American storytelling grain to have someone in a situation he can't get out of, but I think this is very usual in life. . . . There is that implication that if you have just a little more energy, a little more fight, the problem can always be solved. This is so untrue it makes me want to cry—or laugh. (Vonnegut in Irving 216)

Thus, some foma may not be as harmless as they appear.

On the one hand, then, such novels and their perspective on and in time mean that commonly held beliefs and assumptions about society are challenged by being made inappropriate and strange. On the other hand, the future viewpoint challenges the usual form of the novel itself: in any retrospective narrative the outcome is already determined. Vonnegut, therefore, is not "a trafficker in climaxes and thrills and characterization and wonderful dialogue and suspense and confrontations," as he describes writers in *Slaughterhouse-Five* (12). Characterization (as many commentators have pointed out) is often limited, subordinate to the demands of the idea or message,[4] but also subject to leveling (no villains, no heroes). Similarly, dialogue is often basic, since it simply demonstrates how characters' beliefs are challenged by their situation—they often respond in banal or clichéd fashion, saying "So it goes" at every death, for example (as in *Slaughterhouse-Five*). The confrontation of the character and the reader with our own society and our (mis)conceptions about it and our place within it is the main and only confrontation. Climaxes, thrills, and suspense are not much use to a story that is predetermined, and William Rodney Allen notes that Vonnegut "intentionally deflates suspense by mentioning in advance the outcome of any conflict he creates" (99). Similarly, Irving observes (of *Jailbird*, though it applies equally to other Vonnegut novels), "every character is introduced with a mini-history, and of many we are told, from the first meeting, what *would* become of them" (224). In *Galápagos* this is matched to the "survival of the fittest" theory, and characters soon to die have their names starred to forewarn readers that they "will shortly face the ultimate Darwinian test of strength and wiliness" (Vonnegut 24). A Vonnegut novel is not read to find out what will happen; we often are told that on the first page.

Early in *Slaughterhouse-Five* Vonnegut recounts how he mapped out its narrative many times, once with colored crayons on a roll of wallpaper. Lundquist develops this motif in an apt metaphor for Vonnegut's form: "It is as if he rolls the wallpaper into a tube so all of the characters and incidents are closely layered, so they are in effect one unit, and the reader must look at them from the side" (49). In other words, the story (in most Vonnegut novels, not just *Slaughterhouse-Five*) does not unfold as a linear chronology; instead, it is folded together so that different times and events meet. Such folded narratives do not reach neat conclusions. In *Breakfast of Champions* Vonnegut notes that he makes frequent use of phrases like "Etc.," "And," "So," "and so on" to denote the way life is continuous, resisting beginnings and endings (187). We might think that an apocalypse would offer an obvious conclusion, but *Cat's Cradle* ends with a *possible* final sentence for *The Books of Bokonon*. Bokonon tells the narrator, "The time for the final sentence has come" (Vonnegut 205), and the novel stops after it is quoted, sidestepping traditional closure.

Attebery points to connections between the development of narrative away from traditional form and the developments in science: "The shift to nonlinear mathematics or chaos theory...could not have taken place without a major reshuffling of basic concepts such as closure, predictability, and otherness" (161). Along the same lines, if from a slightly different angle, Lundquist suggests that Vonnegut's "method accords well with the major changes in the conception of reality that have come out of contemporary science" (45). It is certainly evident that Vonnegut wrote during decades when perceptions of time, history, and subjectivity changed. Science lost its innocence and objectivity, and so did history. Perhaps Vonnegut's persistent interest in writing about time and history stems from his own long career. He was born, as many commentators have and as his own writing often remind us, before the Great Depression and lived through the American Century, experiencing defining events such as World War II, the civil rights movement, the second wave of feminism, Vietnam, the development of capitalism, the onset of AIDS, environmental decline, mechanization, and the rise of new technologies. Such changes inevitably brought about the end of the world as we knew it, and the need to reexamine how history got us here. Vonnegut is able to challenge the ideologies and founding myths of U.S. society through rewriting U.S. history from a future perspective, drawing on how these myths have already been challenged in recent history.

Time and history are, thus, subject to change: they are also subjective. Evolutionary or national history are matched with individual, personal history. In his detailed exploration of how Vonnegut has spent his career "imagining being an American," Donald E. Morse argues that "Vonnegut has forged a moral identity composed of a mosaic of bits and pieces of experience and history, such as witnessing the Dresden massacre and taking seriously Eugene Debs's clarion call to end poverty" (3). Indeed, Vonnegut's novels suggest that history is changeable *because* it is subjective: both time and subjectivity (identity) are fluid and contingent. Kilgore Trout states in *Timequake* that to make sense of "the secrets of the Cosmos' time, matter, and energy need to be joined with another relative factor—human awareness or soul" (Vonnegut 213–14).

TIME TRAVEL/RELATIVITY

In writing about his real experience of the Dresden fire bombing in *Slaughterhouse-Five*, Jerome Klinkowitz observes that Vonnegut "knows he needs the arts of the defamiliarization" (*Kurt Vonnegut* 65), that the "recording of a personal and a historical horror in the world of fact calls for an act of style and fantasy" (63). Defamiliarization in this novel comes from the trope of time travel: *Slaughterhouse-Five* begins its second chapter with "Listen. Billy Pilgrim has come unstuck in time" (Vonnegut 25). Its first chapter describes Vonnegut's difficulty in approaching this personal history. The long perspective afforded by science fiction here folds into the "proper perspective" of a writer able to confront his experience for only the first time after quarter of a century has passed (Allen 106).

Bill Mistichelli notes that opposing notions of history present it as either subjective or impersonal; he judges that Vonnegut prefers the subjective (317). Others have attempted to convey the subjectivity of experience (history) and time through narrative point of view in popular forms like cinema, as films from Akira Kurosawa's *Rashômon* (1950) to Christopher Nolan's *Memento* (2000) demonstrate. But Vonnegut's subjective narratives of history do not just take a historiographic approach or an individual point of view; they also debate the ways we construct identity by re-viewing our lives. Vonnegut reiterates throughout his novels that life is not structured like a story, despite the ways various foma might persuade us that it can be. Thus, he writes the following in *Breakfast of Champions*:

> They were doing their best to live like people invented in story books. This was the reason Americans shot each other so often: It was a convenient literary device for ending short stories and books.... I resolved

to shun storytelling. I would write about life. Every person would be
exactly as important as any other. All facts would also be given equal
weightiness. Nothing would be left out. Let others bring order to
chaos. I would bring chaos to order, instead, which I think I have
done. (Vonnegut, 173)

(*Timequake* identifies two "subversive tales" that have never been
removed from reading lists, partly because they are simple stories often
told in simple forms to "children in intellectually humble American
homes": the story of Robin Hood and "the life of Jesus Christ as
described in the New Testament" (Vonnegut 36). Why don't more
people try to live like these stories?)

This sense of rendering life as chaotic rather than orderly is conveyed from early on, as in *The Sirens of Titan*. Often described as
space opera, this novel uses time travel to contrast two answers to
the question, why are we here? One argues that while we are shaped
by our life experiences, these experiences are simply "a series of accidents" (Vonnegut 161). The second suggests that we are manipulated
by beings more advanced than ourselves to accomplish some ineffable
purpose, and that even a human being caught in a "chronosynclastic
infundibulum" or timewarp cannot gain sufficient knowledge of the
future to prevent this. Since *Sirens* also presents time as relative, however, and its chronosynclastic infundibulum as a place where everybody is potentially right, both explanations may be true. As *A Child's
Cyclopedia of Wonders and Things to Do* tells us, "These places are
where all the different kinds of truths fit together as nicely as the
parts in your Daddy's solar watch" (Vonnegut 12).[5]

The relative nature of time disrupts the sense of linearity as
progression—Rumfoord knows exactly when Malachi Constant
will return to Earth in *Sirens*, for example, so suspense is not integral to narration—and subsequent novels dealing with time travel
address this. *Slaughterhouse-Five* is Vonnegut's most famous and
most discussed work, and critics often pick out the description of the
Tralfamadorian novel as key to his strategy here:

each clump of symbols is a brief, urgent message—describing a situation, a scene. We Tralfamadorians read them all at once, not one
after the other. There isn't any particular relationship between all the
messages, except that the author has chosen them carefully, so that,
when seen all at once, they produce an image of life that is beautiful
and surprising and deep. There is no beginning, no middle, no end, no
suspense, no moral, no causes, no effects. What we love in our books
are the depths of many marvellous moments seen all at one time. (71)

Certainly, the complex chronology of *Slaughterhouse-Five* undermines any sense of a linear narrative with beginning, middle, end, suspense, cause, and effect, though the constant shifting of time frames is not necessarily an impediment to understanding the story. Billy Pilgrim, the main character, is "unstuck in time" because he has been abducted by aliens, the Tralfamadorians. They explain their perception of time, and he adopts the notion that he can escape traumatic events in his life by shifting to another, more enjoyable, experience. He also adopts the philosophy that when anyone dies they continue to exist in other moments of their life, and, thus, "so it goes" is an appropriate response to death. Critics are divided on whether this means that Vonnegut also espouses these ideas, but since the book is about the process of looking back to the fire bombing of Dresden, it is clear that he does not. Both Vonnegut and many of his characters (who may appear in more than one novel) continue to timeshift, they "compulsively return, moving back and forth on their own lines," as Lundquist would have it, referring again to the wallpaper diagram (49). Just as people may fold back and forth in time, linking events with their lives, so the narrative also folds separate historical events together. The subtitle, "The Children's Crusade," links World War II to previous history, like Billy's story links it forward to contemporaneous wars, assassinations, and riots. The personal comments in the framing chapters (1 and 10) explain, not only the difficulty of looking back to such traumatic events, but also the necessity or "humanity" of doing so. Vonnegut uses the story of Lot's wife to make this point: "But she *did* look back, and I love her for that, because it was so human" (23).

In this sense, *Slaughterhouse-Five* develops a strategy used by subsequent novels that address America's brutal past. Both Octavia Butler's *Kindred* (1979) and Toni Morrison's *Beloved* (1987) seek to confront slavery as a history that has seriously scarred national ideals and, therefore, as a memory that must not be forgotten. Both, like *Slaughterhouse-Five*, use shifting time frames to tell their stories and, in doing so, examine how memories are repressed as well as how they continue to shape individuals and communities. Both also engage with fantastic elements: *Kindred* with time travel, *Beloved* with ghosts, proving that the "recording of a personal and a historical horror in the world of fact calls for an act of style and fantasy" (Klinkowitz, *Kurt Vonnegut* 63) indeed. That *Kindred* uses a more obviously science fictional trope, and that Butler is a science fiction writer, is certainly crucial to the two novels' respective reputations.

Vonnegut himself has suggested that his use of science fiction is both deliberate and to achieve a specific effect.

> The science fiction passages are just like the clowns in Shakespeare. When Shakespeare figured the audience has had enough of the heavy stuff, he'd let up a little, bring on a clown or foolish innkeeper or something like that, before he'd become serious again. And trips to other planets, science fiction of an obviously kidding sort, is equivalent to bringing on the clowns every so often to lighten things up. (qtd. in Rose 22)

That is, the science fiction elements allow readers to keep or recover their distance from the very real issues Vonnegut addresses. They are evidences of self-consciousness, from *Sirens* through to *Timequake*. Discussing a similar strategy in a different media, Steve Neale argues that science fiction or horror movies may "build in an element of camp, a tongue-in-cheek knowingness," especially if they are working with a small budget. "This element," he explains,

> is designed to protect the spectator (and hence the film) both from disappointment, should the effects fail to convince, or should their convincingness serve merely to highlight the improbable nature of that which they are used to represent; and also from genuine trauma, should the effects and what they represent be taken too seriously. (15)

Self-conscious use of the fantastic, then, can be a way out for the reader, and indeed many readers of Vonnegut managed to avoid his negotiation of "genuine trauma" for years, before *Slaughterhouse-Five* and its obviously historical referents forced them to take him seriously.

Self-consciousness extends beyond use of obviously science fictional tropes like time travel however. Since Vonnegut's treatment of time demonstrates that history is subjective, the subjective or personal approach becomes another self-conscious strategy. Stanley Schratt comments that "Just as Alfred Hitchcock makes an appearance in each of his movies, Vonnegut appears in each of his novels" (100), while Klinkowitz notes the "dominant personal presence" in *Slaughterhouse-Five* (*Kurt Vonnegut* 64). A version of Vonnegut does appear in several of his novels, which are also often infused with personal presence. This is where he diverges most from science fiction and, despite Schratt's Hitchcock comparison, from popular fictions too. Hitchcock appears in his films, yet does not comment on them when he does so: his appearance shakes but does not break the narrative frame.[6] The epic scale of science fiction, the defamiliarized viewpoint, tends to work against intimacy or the personal, yet, nevertheless, "Intimacy noticeably characterizes Vonnegut's fiction" (Morse 5). The personal is integral to Vonnegut's subjective view of time and narrative, and he frequently uses the notion of nonlinear and relative time to interrogate the form of the novel to the point that it becomes intertwined with autobiography, most notably in *Slaughterhouse-Five* and *Timequake*, both of which involve time travel.

Using a scientific metaphor, Lundquist describes the timeshifting Billy Pilgrim as "becoming his history, existing all at once, as if he is an electron" (46), later developing this into a slightly different description of Billy as "many personalities, many selves existing together at once. He is a living Tralfamadorian 'clump'" (50). Just as time is folded together like a roll of wallpaper, versions of Vonnegut's characters, like versions of himself as author, are folded together in his oeuvre. Kilgore Trout is often taken as another version of Vonnegut—he admits Trout "has been my alter ego in several of my other novels" in *Timequake* (xiii). These recurring characters may shift and change from novel to novel, suggesting that identity, subjectivity, is as fluid and contingent as time is relative.

Klinkowitz argues that the structure of *Slaughterhouse-Five* "creates a radical reconnection of the historical and the imaginary, the realistic and the fantastic, the sequential and the simultaneous, the author and the text" (*Kurt Vonnegut* 69). *Timequake* takes this even further, to the point that we might hesitate to describe it as a novel. Vonnegut consistently "violates the convention that the author must keep a certain distance from his or her work," but as Klinkowitz concludes, "It is this personal relationship that makes the novel interesting" ("Emerging from Anonymity" 109). Certainly, *Slaughterhouse-Five*, *Breakfast of Champions*, and *Timequake* are some of Vonnegut's most powerful works. Science fiction's long perspective affords distance, but Vonnegut's voice creates intimacy. "His is a human voice, not just that of an omniscient narrator" (Lundquist 53) and in many novels distance is simultaneously created and collapsed. Where Vonnegut himself does not appear, the story is often narrated by a character with a uniquely subjective view. In each case "simple" prose denotes a "simple" narrator who mediates complex events in ways we can understand. The narrative voice connects wider, universal issues to us as individuals (by giving us an individual perspective) while at the same time "this naïve style...actually helps defamiliarize what we have come to accept as ordinary everyday truth" (Morse 102), as with Leon Trout, the ghostly narrator of *Galápagos*.

AND SO ON

Other contemporary fictions have engaged with experiments in time, history, and chronology or with subjectivity. Novelists like Bret Easton Ellis or Chuck Palahniuk present twisted versions of U.S. society that draw on the Gothic rather than science fiction (as *Beloved* does), but nevertheless manipulate their fantastic elements to provide a critique of U.S. society, just like Vonnegut. Other works, then, have come to some of the same conclusions and have used similar tools to develop their ideas. Comics, in particular, have been creating "chaos from order" in terms of time and subjectivity for at least as long as Vonnegut, though they have waited even longer to receive serious attention as narrative forms. Other media are now also adopting Vonnegut's mixture of social comment and intimacy of address. Michael Moore's documentaries, for example, have an equally demotic style and feature the "author" in the work itself. "These two poles of autobiography and creative self-reflection are extremes that conventionally realistic fiction avoids" (Klinkowitz, *Kurt Vonnegut* 74), and in a nonfiction form like the documentary it has been, if anything, even more controversial than in Vonnegut's novels. Yet, like Vonnegut, Moore attracts a wide audience, and both offer challenges to U.S. history and ideology in ways acceptable to audiences, partly, perhaps, because they do it with humor. Since Moore is working in documentary, he does not use fantastic elements like science fiction to distance his subject matter. He does, however, adopt other distancing techniques, including montage (a different mediation of time; a typical strategy of documentary) or animation (a different mediation of "reality"; a more atypical strategy) to allow audiences to safely confront his often powerful material.

It may be more forgivable in a fiction writer to manipulate the personal and even the "facts" for effect; "But never is mere confession or simple autobiography [Vonnegut's] method," observes Klinkowitz, "rather his way is to engage this personal self in larger issues" ("Emerging from Anonymity" 124). Vonnegut uses future history and time travel to bring us to the present, as science fiction often does, and his personal approach encourages us to confront that present in the same way his fiction allows us to confront the traumatic and brutal past of the United States and nations like it. *Timequake* tells us that Kilgore Trout accepts the timequake of 2001 and the consequent rerun of the preceding decade because "It was just more foolishness in the world outside his own, and no more worthy of his respect than wars or economic collapses or plagues, or tidal waves, or TV stars, or what you will" (Vonnegut 92), neatly encapsulating the detached perspective of science fiction in the character of a science fiction writer. However, Trout's message to others affected by the timequake, later adopted far and wide as a philosophy to live by, is somewhat antithetical to this apparently detached view: "You've been sick but now you're well again, and there's work to do" (167). We cannot sit back, as if devoid of free will, while history marches on. Vonnegut was well aware that if the United States wants to live up to its ideals of freedom and democracy, there is certainly work to do based on the lessons of history. He'd been telling us this all along, just, perhaps, never so clearly, because never so directly and personally.

NOTES

1. For example, see Roberts 18.
2. See, for instance, Irving 213.
3. Lundquist even admits that the film of *Slaughterhouse-Five* makes its timeshifts unremarkable, because they are "merely cinematically familiar on the screen" (53).
4. This is often the case in science fiction, and Kilgore Trout argues the same in *Timequake* (Vonnegut 63).
5. Here, a rare use of science fiction technobabble is gently undermined by the childish language of the explanation.
6. One example that does, like Vonnegut, rupture the frame is when the artist of a cartoon or comic strip interrupts the action, usually to debate issues of authorial control with the character being drawn, exactly the issue raised by Vonnegut in *Breakfast of Champions*.

WORKS CITED

Allen, William Rodney. "Slaughterhouse-Five." *Kurt Vonnegut's* Slaughterhouse-Five: *Modern Critical Interpretations*. Ed. Harold Bloom. Broomall: Chelsea, 2001. 95–106.

Attebery, Brian. *Decoding Science Fiction*. London: Routledge, 2002.

Hollinger, Veronica. "Cybernetic Deconstructions: Cyberpunk and Postmodernism." *Storming the Reality Studio*. Ed. Larry McCaffery. Durham and London: Duke UP, 1991. 213–25.

Irving, John. "Kurt Vonnegut and His Critics: The Aesthetics of Accessibility." *The Critical Response to Kurt Vonnegut*. Ed. Leonard Mustazza. Westport: Greenwood, 1994. 213–25.

Johnson-Smith, Jan. *Science Fiction Television: Star Trek, Stargate and Beyond*. London: I. B. Tauris, 2004.

Klinkowitz, Jerome. *Kurt Vonnegut.* London: Methuen, 1982.

———. "Emerging from Anonymity." *Kurt Vonnegut's* Slaughterhouse-Five: *Modern Critical Interpretations.* Ed. Harold Bloom. Broomall: Chelsea, 2001. 107–25.

Lundquist, James. "The 'New Reality' of *Slaughterhouse-Five.*" *Kurt Vonnegut's* Slaughterhouse-Five: *Modern Critical Interpretations.* Ed. Harold Bloom. Broomall: Chelsea, 2001. 43–54.

Mistichelli, Bill. "History and Fabrication in Kurt Vonnegut's *Hocus Pocus.*" *The Critical Response to Kurt Vonnegut.* Ed. Leonard Mustazza. Westport: Greenwood, 1994. 313–25.

Morrison, Toni. *Beloved.* New York: Knopf, 1987.

———. *Kindred.* Boston: Beacon, 1988.

Morse, Donald E. *The Novels of Kurt Vonnegut: Imagining Being an American.* Westport: Greenwood, 2003.

Mustazza, Leonard. *Forever Pursuing Genesis: The Myth of Eden in the Novels of Kurt Vonnegut.* Lewisburg: Bucknell UP, 1990.

Neale, Steve. "'You've Got to Be Fucking Kidding!': Knowledge, Belief and Judgement in Science Fiction." *Liquid Metal: The Science Fiction Film Reader.* Ed. Sean Redmond. London: Wallflower, 2004. 12–16.

Roberts, Adam. *Science Fiction (New Critical Idiom).* London: Routledge, 2000.

Rose, Ellen Cronan. "It's All a Joke: Science Fiction in Kurt Vonnegut's *The Sirens of Titan.*" *The Critical Response to Kurt Vonnegut.* Ed. Leonard Mustazza. Westport: Greenwood, 1994. 15–23.

Schratt, Stanley. *Kurt Vonnegut Jr.* Boston: Twayne, 1976.

Vonnegut, Kurt. *Breakfast of Champions.* London: Paladin, 1990.

———. *Cat's Cradle.* London: Penguin, 2008.

———. *Galápagos.* London: Flamingo, 1994.

———. *Hocus Pocus.* London: Vintage, 2000.

———. *Player Piano.* London: Paladin, 1986.

———. *The Sirens of Titan.* London: Hodder, 1967.

———. *Slapstick.* New York: Dell, 1976.

———. *Slaughterhouse-Five.* London: Paladin, 1989.

———. *Timequake.* London: Vintage, 1998.

CHAPTER 9

Resilience, Time, and the Ability of Humor to Salvage Any Situation

Jessica Lingel

By Kurt Vonnegut's own admission, the stories in *Bagombo Snuff Box* would most likely never have "seen the light of day again" had it not been for the renown and success of his later books, such as *Cat's Cradle* (1963), *Slaughterhouse-Five* (1969), and *Timequake* (1997). *Bagombo Snuff Box* is comprised of fiction previously published in magazines and journals in the 1950s and 1960s, with short stories that range from science fiction to depictions of daily domesticity to quirky vignettes of office life. Against the formidable reputations of his more critically acclaimed texts, several of the narratives included in this anthology can seem somewhat outdated (particularly those with leading female characters[1]), or even stiflingly flat when removed from the contours of the publications in which they were first printed. Readers conditioned by the concise abruptness and dry, acerbic wit characterizing Vonnegut's more well-known work may be startled by stories that sometimes read as somewhat unfinished and a little bare, rather than purposefully terse. Refuting (or at least confronting) these claims of miffed criticism are the bookend chapters by Vonnegut, explaining, in part, the resilience of his work. If there are stories in *Bagombo Snuff Box* that strike readers as problematically simplistic, Vonnegut's insights on his work, in particular, and the process of writing, in general, offer an intricate framework through which to process the collection's patterns of characterization, symbolic sequences, and narrative motifs, literary devices that can be traced along themes of coping, survival, and resilience. Within the cast of characters assembled here, some of the most compelling are those that embody Vonnegut's interpretation of storytelling as a redemptive, reclaiming act meant to defy trauma, survive loss, and (re)connect one human being to another. Stories come to comprise their own kind of resilience, where the connection between author and text is made definitive and concrete through the text as an apparatus exchanged between people separated by some kind of injurious distance. The book has become both the telephone and the phone call to a (lost, loved) reader. Through close readings of republished, recontextualized stories and consideration of Vonnegut's thoughts on his own work over the course of his career, resilience takes on an undertone of authored empowerment, an established role of literary creation that just might have the ability to bring back (or at the very least beckon to) the dead.

Vonnegut on Writing as It Was and Is

Beyond obvious structural divergences, there are conceptual differences between the republication of a novel and the gathering of previously published short stories, disparate and lacking chronology, into an allegedly cohesive collection. In the latter instance short story sequences lend themselves to analysis of the themes that consistently and insistently haunt an author. As settings and characters shift, disappear, and form a diverse strain of human behavior, tracking symbols from story to story allows for the grounded crafting of a narrative framework from which to develop and interpret an author's central thematic concerns, preoccupations, and obsessions. According to Vonnegut,

> the short story, because of its physiological and psychological effects on a human being, is more closely related to Buddhist styles of meditation than it is to any other form of narrative entertainment. What you have in this volume, then, and every other collection of short stories, is a bunch of Buddhist catnaps. (6)

In *Bagombo Snuff Box* the themes of these Buddhist catnap meditations include how resilience functions in the face of personal trauma, the emotional complexities of the most basic human relationships, and the simple process of surviving (and perhaps even succeeding throughout) the progression of time, where resilience is a function of storytelling that calls for interpretation of both the changing situations of characters and Kurt Vonnegut as an author.

Vonnegut's reputation as a writer should not be the fundamental lure for readers of *Bagombo Snuff Box*; what is offered in the collection is the transportative ability of narrative to place the reader in an earlier historical, social, and cultural context, to grasp the components of fiction that survive from one decade to the next and manage to remain significant, even imperative. This is not to imply that Vonnegut's earlier efforts were somehow lacking in essential proficiency. In the midst of any overt criticisms of the merit of these short stories (and critical attention to *Bagombo Snuff Box* was in many instances lukewarm[2]), it is worth remembering that these fictions were decidedly successful at the time of their original publication and achieved a degree of popularity. The success of Vonnegut's short stories indicates that he had "found a winning formula, a structure appealing to and reflective of America's popular image of itself" (Klinkowitz 48). The notion of popularity is critical to Vonnegut's ability both to tap into a collective sense of humor and to accurately reflect certain characteristics, flaws, and attributes common to the "average" reader. As Klinkowitz notes, through the author's fiction, it is possible to

> see how Vonnegut gauged culture and more significantly, the direction in which it was heading. At their simplest, his stories reaffirm certain satisfying notions middle-class Americans might have about themselves: that simple virtue outweighs and outlasts more sophisticated pretensions, that there can be such a thing as too high a price for success, that the poor can often be happier than the rich. (48)

Plotlines coalesce around questions of commodities, communities, and the human condition in general, where interaction requires the recognizing (or reclaiming) of what is shared culturally, socially, and politically.

In the introduction to *Bagombo Snuff Box*, Vonnegut is interested in the passage of time and the sociological impact stories from forty and fifty years ago might still generate. His ostensible aim is that the collection "may be interesting, nonetheless, as relics from a time, before there was television, when an author might support a family by writing stories that satisfied uncritical readers of magazines, and earning thereby enough free time in which to write serious novels" (3). Vonnegut's historical context is not limited to general historical or political circumstances—it also includes unromantic, unsentimental statements of the pressures of economic viability and the ever-present ideological strains behind the means of production surrounding his written work. To be able to fulfill this professed hope for the collection's publication requires more than the quaintness of hearkening back to an earlier time when writers and writing were somehow different. If the premise of *Bagombo Snuff Box* is that some of Vonnegut's "earliest tales, for all their mildness and innocence and clumsiness, may, in these coarse times, still entertain" (2), this entertainment will be achieved not simply through an anachronistic quirkiness but rather through both literary resonance and humor. To entertain, to be an unexpected source of play, is a pivotal tenet of Vonnegut's gospel for writing. Humor is a critical component in Vonnegut's work, alternately evidenced through facets of absurdity, cynicism, sarcasm, slapstick, and morbidity. In an interview with *The Paris Review* from 1977, Vonnegut argues that writing should be an act of "learning to play practical jokes" in that "if you make people laugh or cry about little black marks on sheets of white paper, what is that but a practical joke? All the great story lines are great practical jokes that people fall for over and over again" (Hayman). By no means would Vonnegut place the work in *Bagombo Snuff Box* in a category of greatness; indeed, Vonnegut is quite upfront in his assertion that "there is no greatness in this or [his] other collection, nor were there meant to be" (3). The collection's very existence defies the author's initial expectations for these stories, which at the time of their initial publication he "expected to be among the living about as long as individual lightning bugs" (2). It is undoubtedly humor and unexpected instances of prescience that defy chronological lapses in publication that salvage this collection from obscurity, but the process of salvation via comedy and wit in these particular fictions becomes delightfully complicated with Vonnegut's discussion of writing as it pertains to his sister, Allie.

Amusement, alternately goofy and subversive, is more than a mechanism for engaging a reader regardless of the passage of time; it is, in fact, a conduit for remembrance that enables Vonnegut to maintain a vital relationship with his sister. For Vonnegut, paying homage to Allie, whom he defines as his ideal reader in perpetuity, is inextricably linked with making her laugh: Vonnegut writes that his editorial process regarding the publication of these stories was to eliminate everything Allie wouldn't like and leave everything that she would "get a kick out of" (13). Comedy is the connective tissue between brother and sister, author and reader, living and dead. That his stories are shaped as constructs of his sister's sense of humor can be seen as an offering of hope for Vonnegut, indicating a willful agency in carrying on in spite of his loss, but carrying on specifically through the implementation of inside jokes, long lost comedy routines, and a shared sense of irony. Allie is consequently both the end and the means of *Bagombo Snuff Box* in that "the boundaries to the playing fields of [these] short stories...were once the boundaries of the soul of [Allie]. She lives on that way" (14). Remembrance and recapturing drive this text, where forms of textual restoration operate along three paths. First, a text can reanimate its author—Vonnegut refers to this kind of restoration in largely pragmatic terms of financial sustainability, but also refers to the success of his early work as "cardiopulmonary resuscitation of this author who was all but dead" (2). Second, an engaging text stimulates its readers, forming a symbiosis of interaction; a reader must, after all "pick [a text] up, or it will go on lying there, dead as a doornail" (Vonnegut 4). Finally, texts can serve as a homage to or a revoicing of the stories from the dead, a claim that Vonnegut makes specifically regarding his sister Allie.

Of the twenty-three stories in *Bagombo Snuff Box*, three stand out as particularly evidential of characters in crisis, in need of a story to tell. In "Thanasphere" Vonnegut demonstrates some of his humanist concerns through the lens of civilization's view of progress; "The Cruise of the *Jolly Roger*" describes the transition from war to peace as a harrowing psychological challenge requiring redefinition at some of the simplest levels of human identity; and in "This Son of Mine" Vonnegut works through questions of obligations, expectations, and dreamy ambition in both domestic and work environments, where politics work equally in families and factories. Throughout these fictions, Vonnegut's characters crave a sustained and sustainable narrative, and it's precisely in that crisis of needing a story to survive (or to be the thing that survives instead) that they illustrate the possibility of a resilient text.

Lost in Space:
Commodification versus the Soul

A frequent narrative tension in *Bagombo Snuff Box* is the navigation of financial, work-oriented obligations with the intimate, philosophical demands of one's private life. A second, related motif prevalent in this selection is the steady encroachment of technology as a pervasive, problematic force, threatening to overwhelm and override simple but essential human instincts. Both are endemic to the central conflict of "Thanasphere." In the collection's opening short story, Major Allen Rice makes a doomed, solitary pilgrimage into the earth's outer atmosphere as part of an air force intelligence-gathering mission. Rice is characterized as a calculating, rational, analytical man, "as much like a machine as possible . . . quick, strong, unemotional," who is further-more attractive as a candidate for this military mission as a "childless widower, melancholy and solitary, a career soldier, a demon for work" (Vonnegut 17–18). With even his surname evoking an image of prag-matic, predictable, unassuming sustenance, Rice is (at least initially) a figure of mechanical reliability. This image of objectified machin-ery is reinforced by the ordered, methodical military context of his work, the technological components of Rice's immediate spacecraft surroundings, and the transmitters, radios, and technological devices in the background of the corresponding ground crew, whose major characters are General Dane and Dr. Groszinger. Instead of obedi-ently relaying required information by reporting on weather patterns and detailing the contours of the enemy's geography, Rice finds him-self trespassing through a world of ghosts, all impatient to make con-tact with loved ones and relations below. The dichotomy between the mechanical and the ethereal manifests itself in the apparitions, ghosts, and voices occupying outer space, where Vonnegut positions the latter as being potentially disruptive to the former. In his hypoth-esizing about the effects of the news of the Thanasphere reaching the public, Groszinger is "baffled, miserable" as he wonders "would Death unmasked drive men to suicide, or bring new hope? . . . Would the living desert their leaders and turn to the dead for guidance?" (Vonnegut 30). His preoccupation settles on the consequences of the dissolution between the living and the dead, the grounded and the ghostly, where Rice's discovery effectively threatens not just the immediate military operation but the underpinnings of empowered authority structures.

Vonnegut spends very little time on reactions of surprise or alarm in response to this diaphanous world of the dead, focusing instead on alternate attempts at coping with their existence. Confronted with this spiritual barrage that is insistent upon various forms of agitated communication, Rice succumbs fairly quickly, substituting their messages of supernatural intervention for military insight. Within moments of his second transmission to his superiors, Rice transi-tions from remarking on "clear patches over Zones Eleven, Fifteen, and Sixteen" to "there's an old woman calling out something in a German accent" (Vonnegut 24), who turns out to be Groszinger's mother, advising him not to work so hard. In place of statistics, ana-lytics, and military stratagems, Rice's transmissions are the lingering missives of the dead, consisting of pleas for vengeance, for placation, offerings of advice, and solace. Irrespective of the messages' specific content is the fact of their claim on some sort of vibrant reanimation, where the successful communication of their personal history constitutes a possible redemption, restoration, or pacification, any one of which contradicts (and leaves nonplussed) the ostensible aim of Rice and Dane. The poles of transmitted narrative are, thus, established as Dane's insistent demands for technology-oriented data and Rice's disturbing offerings of otherworldly revelations. The climax of "Thanasphere" becomes the reconciliation between Rice and his late wife, Margaret, in the midst of his commitments to Dane's military objectives and Groszinger's scientific pursuits. Unlike Rice's early radio conversations with Dane, which included increasingly brief bits of mission-related data, by this point all pretenses of fulfilling obligations to Dane have been supplanted by the jubilant relaying of his ghostly companions: "thousands of them, thousands of them, all around... standing on nothing, shimmering like northern lights— beautiful, curving off in space, all around the earth like a glowing fog" (Vonnegut 31). If Dane and Groszinger had expected an ecstatic coup from the undertaking of this mission, it was to be from a technological triumph of sending a man into orbit, the ultimate execution of infallible engineering. They are less bewildered by the obstacle of the undead than how to proceed with circumstances in which their supposedly stable soldier relapses into a state of vulnerability. In this manner, the story suggests that susceptibility to the spiritual trumps the presumed superiority of ever-advancing technology.

Although Rice chooses to surrender to the realm of ghosts over compliance with the demands of the living, there is no clear victor in the conflict between institutional, militarial ideology and the emotive, cathartic presence of the human spirit. Dane's response receives the most negative characterization, where his determination to pursue this operation of military stealth epitomizes a hollow callousness to the extraordinary with a narrow directive of garnering information of solely procedural import, in line with Jerome Klinkowitz's analysis that "automation's threat to human values was another important critique" (48) of Vonnegut's short stories. Even when confronted with the inexplicably incredible, Dane's only use for communication is to gain tactical advantages; the only data of interest to him is that which contributes directly to his strategic causes. Dane insists that communicative spirits in outer space hold no interest for him, that his lone interest is for "a man out there to tell [him] that [he's] hitting what [he's] shooting at," and that beyond that, he doesn't "give a damn what's going on in outer space" (Vonnegut 25). This relationship to information is completely subverted by the impalpable feedback obtained by Rice, who quickly casts off an obligatory stance to communication as strategic information, becoming absorbed in the emotional, confessional dialogue of the Thanasphere. In addition to channeling his wife and Grozinger's mother, Rice is deluged by pleas from Mrs. Pamela Ritter, who "wants her husband to marry again, for the sake of the children" (Vonnegut 21); Andrew Tobin, who "claims his brother murdered him" (Vonnegut 21); and Grantland Whitman, "the Hollywood actor, [who] is yelling that his will was tampered with by his nephew Carl" (Vonnegut 27). Where Dane's motives lie in an almost grimly comical obstinacy for tactical facts, Rice's communication derives from moments of purely human emotions, ranging across comfort, anger, revenge, and compassion. These forces effectively upend Dane's churlish demand that communication consist solely of facts, numbers, and military stratagems.

Effectively straddling this spectrum of relationships to information is Dr. Groszinger, whose initial interest in the project seems to be limited to the technical efficiency and scientific advances promised by the experiment rather than the political parameters surrounding it. With Rice's breakdown, however, Groszinger shifts from a figure of rational pragmatism to one of melancholic, philosophical musings as he attempts to work through the implications of a vociferously active realm of ghosts hovering just above the realm of the living. By the conclusion of "Thanasphere," Dane has disappeared into the machinery of his military endeavors, and Rice has given himself up to the occupants of the Thanasphere entirely, leaving Groszinger as the inheritor of the stories of the dead. For Groszinger, technology seems largely indicative of a juggernautlike progression toward war, in that

> science had given humanity forces enough to destroy the earth, and politics had given humanity a fair assurance that the forces would be used. There could be no cause for awe to top *that* one. But proof of a spirit world might at least equal it. Maybe that was the shock the world needed, maybe word from the spirits could change the suicidal course of history. (Vonnegut 29)

The cynical tone indicates more than a post–World War II suspicion of (and exhaustion with) international war;[3] it further forms part of an ethical inquiry into the struggle to maintain a coherent form of accountable integrity in the midst of human ambition that has given rise to technological machinations bent on his pursuing a path of perceived scientific, political, or cultural progress (or prowess).

The supposed inevitability of maturation, advancement, and betterment through technology is a tenuous claim for Vonnegut, who sees progress as "an illusion of motion going somewhere...a delusion of society advancing...or a series of chimerical detours through life" (Morse 102). Less a triumphant pursuit of perfection and more a masked circumnavigation miscategorized as improvement, projects like Dane's will always find themselves subordinate to instances of intimate human exchanges. Momentarily setting aside his experiments and scientific ambitions, Groszinger speculates on the powerfully disruptive influence of transmissions from the dead, and the subsequent meaning of an awareness of "a world in constant touch with the spirits, the living inseparable from the dead...would it make life heaven or hell? Every bum and genius, criminal and hero, average man and madman, now and forever a part of humanity—advising, squabbling, conniving, placating" (Vonnegut 30). The ambiguity of Groszinger's character is solidified in the story's concluding sequence, in which he is called upon by the press to explain the crash of Rice's satellite, which he dutifully positions as a falling meteorite. When asked by an eager and "imaginative" group of journalists about the possibility of sending a ship into space, Groszinger replies that perhaps in twenty years he'll "have a story" for them (Vonnegut 33). This glaring falsification (and quasi-betrayal) can be read cynically as evidence that there can be no recognized triumph over ever-advancing technology, even from the persistent demands of the supernatural. In "Thanasphere" specifically, there is also a subtler perspective that perhaps Groszinger found himself psychologically incapable of taking up the task of serving as storyteller for the dead. The willingness to bear witness and testify on behalf of ghosts, to bear the burden of cathartic storytelling may be rooted in inability rather than reluctance or (more cynically still) resignation.

In addition to its inclusion of survival, technology, and the intricate fallacies of human arrogance as thematic concerns, "Thanasphere" also offers one of the clearest examples of Vonnegut's humanist leanings in *Bagombo Snuff Box*. Characteristic of institutional insistence of the significance of technology are assumptions that place

> human beings at the pinnacle of evolution as they once placed themselves at the pinnacle of creation. But substituting evolution for creation still leaves unresolved the problem of the absence of evidence for assuming that humans are indeed the goal of evolution rather than adaptation to local conditions. (Morse 93)

Vonnegut never takes the assumption of human primacy for granted, recognizing all too well the absurdity and baseness of humanity without forgetting what it means to be (or how to describe) the human. The dark theme of "Thanasphere" is the difficulty of traversing multiple strata of the human experience, a difficulty that is made ironic in comparison with avowals of technological superciliousness. Groszinger's initial prediction for Rice's mission borders on smugness as he reasons "there were no unknowns...the man in the spaceship two thousand miles from earth had no unknowns to fear...he could only confirm what reason had already revealed" (Vonnegut 17). Vonnegut offers a grim humor here of expectations and redefinitions of tendentious attempts toward progress, even when progress comes to require critical reinterpretations of growth, evolution, and accommodation of a place for the human spirit. He also makes clear an argument for the importance of fidelity to the departed and of deliberate acts of commemoration. Storytelling in "Thanasphere" takes places through haunting, where the experience of intercepting messages from the dead is stubbornly ignored, ruefully puzzled over, or happily allowed to consume.

Narrative, Trauma, and the *Jolly Roger*

The protagonist of "The Cruise of the *Jolly Roger*" is Nathan Durant, a lonely, migratory figure who works on piecing together civilian life after seventeen years in the army. His departure from the military at the age of thirty-six was forced on him by wounds sustained in combat, leaving Durant with "a deep scar across his cheek, with the lobe of his right ear gone, with a stiff leg" (Vonnegut 122). Progress in and obstacles to recuperation are central to this short story, where recovery is a process of learning how to narrate an individual history. For somewhat obtuse reasons, Durant takes up life on a cabin cruiser he christens *The Jolly Roger*, but his restless travels result in a melancholic dissatisfaction, in which he is "depressed by the tranquility and permanence, by the feeling of deep, still lakes of time, by men and women so at one with the peace of the place as to have nothing to exchange with an old soldier but a few words about the weather" (Vonnegut 122). Durant's inability to connect through speech seems tied to his perceived lack of a cogent, cataloged identity. His mariner's life reiterates the malleability of his surroundings and the subsequent search for indentifying structure. When Durant eventually ventures into sustained contact with others, he feels out of place, fundamentally inadequate, and subsequently becomes aware of a desire to show that "while he couldn't speak [their] language, he could speak one of his own that had life to it" (Vonnegut 125). Ultimately, however,

Durant finds himself rendered incapable of relating his own history; when asked to describe his wartime experiences specifically, a request that should be a welcome invitation to reinscribe himself in a recognizable context of his military past, Durant is, instead, unable to locate sufficient narrative terms to make his story relatable.

The paradox of storytelling in "The Cruise of the *Jolly Roger*" involves the simultaneous desperation to voice one's story with a muting incapacity to make trauma comprehensible. In this way

> Vonnegut's fiction questions the possibility of developing discourses of morality and identity in the face of contingency: How is it possible to speak of morality or identity once one accepts that there is no Truth or meta-discourses to access outside of human-made languages or contacts? (Gholson 135)

This general impossibility of the human condition is perhaps made more familiar in the figure of a shell-shocked veteran attempting acclimation to a "peaceful" life. Durant's experiences as a civilian leave him helplessly exhausted as a result of his struggle to communicate effectively. His one attempt at divulging the most difficult of narratives results in a "formless, unwieldy description of war as it had really seemed: a senseless, complicated mess that in the telling was first-rate realism but miserable entertainment" (Vonnegut 125). Durant's frustration stems from an unmanageable expectation to deliver a narrative that will captivate, disabuse, and perhaps even restore, but instead proves to be trapped in the "glib and urbane" (Vonnegut 125), where it languishes rather than compels. This dilemma of communication is a familiar tenet of trauma theory, in which "unable to assimilate such disturbing events, the survivor visits the traumatic memories again and again, tends to his or her wounds, in an involuntary effort to attach meaning to the horrors" (Dodman 259). For Durant, this struggle is, ultimately, articulated largely through his eventual pilgrimage to the hometown of a fellow veteran, George Pefko.

The emotional landscape of Durant's decision to visit the nameless town that Pefko claimed as home takes shape only as he is attempting to converse with local townspeople while he's in search of information. Upon being informed by Annie, a secretary at a law firm who happens upon Durant while he's making inquiries at the post office, that the Pefko family were "drifters" with minimal local connections, Durant protests his friend's apparent anonymity, feeling that it was "unbearable that every vestige of George had disappeared, unmissed" (Vonnegut 129). Where an inured resignation surfaced from his earlier frustrations to express accurately his wartime experiences, the possibility of a similarly untellable narrative displacing the memory of Pefko elicits a starker, more desperate response. Vonnegut refuses to allow a direct narrative of war into the text, but the image of roaming wanderlust at the crux of this short story indicates a canvassing for a cogent grounding of traumatic experiences in narrative. This unsettled (and unsettling), seemingly circular procedure "reveals a desire for a whole and perfect retelling of the past; his narration functions as a prosthesis meant to stave off a sense of the self as a disarticulated scar. His embodied subjectivity, like the wounds he suffers to represent, call out for prosthetic completion" (Dodman 250). Contemporary perspectives on war narrative would likely label Durant as a victim of posttraumatic stress disorder, terminology that would not have been available to Vonnegut and his readers,[4] however recognizable the figure of a veteran struggling to reengage in civilian life may have been.

Resolution in "The Cruise of the *Jolly Roger*" can read as objectionably facile. Overcoming Durant's dissatisfied embitterment is the patriotic performance of a young boy participating in a memorial parade. A brief dialogue between Annie and the boy yields simple but heartfelt responses of honoring military sacrifice, which prove capable not only of penetrating Durant's cynicism but of restoring his ability to identify himself in legible terms. This transformation is immediate and empowering, allowing Durant to invite Annie back to his boat, a bold gesture that would have been impossible when he felt critically deficient in decipherability. The implied ease with which Durant embarks on his recovery[5] perhaps borders on maudlin insufficiency, but however swift the transformation, the basic function of agency as redemptive is maintained. In this story, as elsewhere in Vonnegut's work, "narrative is the fundamental means by which we encounter the world, understand the self and inquire about moral questions" (Gholson 14). This (re)constitution via retextualization of personal trauma demonstrates Vonnegut's pathology of recovery, which argues for a kind of psychological irredentism requiring a careful reacquaintance with language, humor, courage, and storytelling.

FATHERS, SONS, AND THE FAMILY BUSINESS

Having set narrative friction against backdrops of technological infringement and institutional recovery, in "This Son of Mine," Vonnegut places emotional conflict in both domestic and work spheres. This refiguring of the psychological struggle to come to terms with identity and obligation is evident in the relationships between the fathers and sons of two families: Merle and Franklin Waggoner and Rudy and Karl Linberg. The dialogue between Merle and Franklin is a familiar one. With a financially successful business—Waggoner Pump—to manifest his personal ambitions as well as financial security, Merle turns to Franklin, home on vacation from college, as the presumed heir to his accumulated efforts. Completely, unavoidably aware of these responsibilities, Franklin's response is one of bewilderment and resignation, in which he "felt like crying, because he didn't care, couldn't care—and would have given his right arm to care. The factory whanged and banged and screeched in monstrous irrelevance—Franklin's, all Franklin's, if he just said the word" (Vonnegut 253). Rather than don the corporate mantle prepared so fastidiously by his father, Franklin intends to use his trip home from college as the occasion to announce his intention to pursue a career in acting. Vonnegut avoids expected tropes of an overly restive romantic eager for the glamor of the stage by encapsulating the specific intent to act within the more general follies of the young, in which Franklin's declaration represents the "bittersweet, almost formless longings of youth. Saying he wanted to be an actor gave the longings a semblance of more fun than they really had. Saying it was poetry more than anything else" (Vonnegut 254). It is the formlessness of Franklin's aspirations that make him further vulnerable to lingering hesitations of disappointing Merle. Pressed by his father to specifically articulate his plans for financial viability, Franklin's stuttering response is critically insufficient because "he was being asked to match his father's passion for the factory with an equal passion for something else. And Franklin had no such passion—for the theater or anything else" (Vonnegut 254). In contrast to his diffused visions of the future, Franklin, named after Benjamin Franklin, a further indication of the pressure to fulfill impossible expectations of someone else's success, is surrounded by characters besieged by intensely purposeful (as well as interrelated and intergenerational) ambitions revolving around the economic success of Waggoner Pump.

Characters in "This Son of Mine" have firmly established roles of interaction, derived from years of latent expectations and occasionally brazen manipulations. Merle remains devoted solely to the direct inheritance of his life's work where specific appreciation for related craftsmanship or quotidian processes (or indeed even a genuine interest in pumps) can happily be overlooked in favor of the basic agreement to keep the company a family business. Rudy, Merle's first employee who turned down the chance of becoming a partner in the company's earliest years, seems intent on substituting Karl as an investment in the company. For his part, Karl, seems fundamentally exhausted from an entire childhood of anticipatory comparisons with Franklin,[6] but his upbringing makes it impossible to avoid either a hyperawareness of his relationship to the company or even to undermine any part of those long-crafted obligations. The slightest deviations from these weighty, obligatory machinations, so entrenched in a generation's worth of oft-thwarted expectations, give rise to revelatory discord.

Unable to combat Merle's visions with a sufficiently vibrant ambition of his own and recognizing that he "could never dream two million dollars' worth, could never dream anything worth the death of his father's dreams" (Vonnegut 256), Franklin's resolve collapses, and he wearily succumbs to Merle's vision of the future. In addition to forestalling the sellout of Waggoner Pump to corporate entities characterized as greedy and gargantuan, Merle sees Franklin's shift as a singular bulwark of fidelity that stands in stark contrast to the blithe decisions of Franklin's peers to abandon filial contracts in favor of an easier, jauntier approach to wealth. Even Franklin comes to think of his fellow youths in positions similar to his own as

> the killers of their fathers' dreams. Their young faces were the faces of old men hanging upside down, their expressions grotesque and unintelligible. Hanging upside down, they swung from bar to ballroom to crap game, and back to bar. No one pitied them in that great human belfry, because they were going to be rich, if they weren't already. They didn't have to dream, or even lift a finger. (Vonnegut 259)

On one level, Franklin's dilemma echoes Vonnegut's thematic concern regarding the primacy of corporate interests and their unyielding invasion into intrinsically human and domestic arenas. Franklin identifies his dreams as part of his youthfulness, whereas Merle identifies with the company that he has build over the course of a lifetime. Both view the possibility of a buyout as a looming, perilous threat that would render inconsequential some indispensable part of their lives. Beyond the corporate peril, within this dynamic of Waggoner Pump versus heartless business conglomerates, the defensive devotion to the factory on behalf of Merle and Franklin is experienced quite differently by father and son; where Merle feels a dread of losing the physical manifestation of his work, Franklin is only aware that he lacks such a manifestation, although his love and respect for his father's pride in workmanship is sufficient to create a willingness to make certain sacrifices.

The intertwining of machinery, humans, and existentialism is a familiar tangle for Vonnegut. Discussing *Cat's Cradle*, David Morse writes that "Vonnegut cannot reflect upon the role of technology in the twentieth century without also reflecting on human metaphysical anguish" ("We are Marching to Utopia" 24). Vonnegut's characters are often asked to make incredible adaptations to hardship, but their successful evolution depends on the ability to derive survivability from a purposeful clarity, from a vivid confirmation of intent based on their individual narratives. Lacking any sort of compelling inner directive, at least at this point in his life, Franklin's aimlessness signals an important counterpoint in Vonnegut's focus on the obligations, decisions, and relationships that come to define a life. The desperation of characters in "This Son of Mine" to make good on various promises and come to terms with shortcomings, impossibilities, and missed opportunities is all the more heart-wrenching due to the lack of any clear resolution. Despite the ardency of convictions held by characters in "This Son of Mine," at the conclusion of this short story, no one's destiny is certain. A visit by both families to a local shooting range pits generation against generation and eventually Franklin against Karl. Although their contest provides a rare (if brief) moment for open communication between the two boys in which Karl encourages Franklin to strike out on his own, citing his inability to define himself outside of Rudy's (and vicariously Merle's) expectations. The relationships realign family to family as the Linbergs play a duet, and the Waggoners are left to witness a speechless conversation that was "saying what they had all been saying haltingly, sometimes with pain and sometimes with anger and sometimes with cruelty and sometimes with love: that fathers and sons were one" (Vonnegut 264). Complex webs of alternately hopeful and hateful interactions have been reduced to a redefinition of family. Whatever Merle may lack in sympathetic understanding of his son and despite Franklin's unformed vision of the future, they can at least identify along the binding lines of family, opening up a moment of congruity owing to the brief but significant space of sharing the same story.

Given Vonnegut's admission of the importance of family in his process of crafting a text, the domestic dynamics in "This Son of Mine" are perhaps particularly indicative of the importance of returning to the most primal relationships humans share, relationships of family, with the pursuant demands of sacrifice and hope. There is no confirmation of financial security or corporate success in this story, but there is an affirmation of the imperviousness of family bonds, a survivability that can defy the artifice of economics, politics, and machinery.

CODA, CONCLUSION, CREATION

Closing a chapter of his writing career as well as concluding a collection of his work, in "Coda to My Career as a Writer for Periodicals" Vonnegut offers additional criteria (outside of the earlier framework outlined in the introduction) for the hermeneutics of his work, fixating on consequential conditions of regionalism and endemicity. Despite his travels abroad and stints on the East Coast, it's the Midwest that seems to have made the most critical claim on Vonnegut's attention. Although still engaged in questions of writing, Vonnegut has refigured his inquiry to accommodate matters of origination, place, and geographical belonging. These musing queries reorient themes of resilience, grounding the faltering gestures of coping in the solidity of a region, lending them the credence of being part of a larger, physical entity. This quasi-spiritual relationship to place stems from the fact that "what geography can give all the Middle Westerners, along with the fresh water and topsoil, if they let it, is awe for a fertile continent stretching forever in all directions. Makes you religious. Takes your breath away" (Vonnegut 357). One possible sublimation of this awe, religion, and breathlessness is art. Although the formation of one's personal history into a coherent, creative assemblage is no longer possible as a career enabled by publication in periodicals, as it was for Vonnegut, he nevertheless claims that

> participation in an art is not simply one of many possible ways to make a living, an obsolescent trade as we approach the year 2000. Participation in an art, at bottom, has nothing to do with earning money. Participation in an art, although unrewarded by wealth or fame, and as the Middle West has encouraged so many of its young to discover for themselves so far, is a way to make one's soul grow. (355)

An insistent yet good-natured call to arms for writers, artists, inventors, and humorists, the coda is also a swan song for the institutions, people, and places that fostered and enabled Vonnegut's work.

Given Rice's propulsion to and revelations in outer space, Durant's migratory wandering of the seas and psychoanalytical well-being, and Franklin's unresolved generational oscillation, the applicability of Vonnegut's interest in place becomes part of the search for identity. The conflict in these fictions revolves around a need, not only to develop the ability to tell one's own story, but also to map that story concretely to surroundings. Vonnegut's self-awareness of his writing (from where he hails, to whom he writes) grafts his narratives securely to the parameters of his personal history. In some sense, generalized interpretation is necessary to encompass stories published in a variety of forums over a space of two decades, when the author fully admits to being in a period of developing his craft. And yet there are identifiable, powerful strands of narrative to be traced throughout this collection. Vonnegut observes that his work is written for his sister and is deeply indebted to his roots in the Midwest. These are two of the conceptual fixtures that provide a framework for thinking about, not only how Vonnegut's characters survive, but why he writes about survivability. Even as he's constructing the tones and tools that will come to define him as an author, Vonnegut remains firmly in the grip of his obligations to family and his home, which can be posited as entrenching, guiding figures throughout his artistic growth. That same need to revert to the most intrinsic parts of the human experience, to the most basic things that resonate, are critical narrative aspects in *Bagombo Snuff Box*. They are the components of literary endurance, the literary devices that enable resilience.

NOTES

1. Vonnegut directly addresses the issue of his works' portrayal of women in an interview with the *Paris Review*, stating that "there aren't any women" in his books because of a "mechanical problem. So much of what happens in storytelling is mechanical, has to do with the technical problems of how to make a story work....I try to keep deep love out of my stories because, one that particular subject comes up, it is almost impossible to talk about anything else. Readers don't want to hear about anything else. They go gaga about love. If a lover in a story wins his true love, that's the end of the tale, even if World War III is about to begin, and the sky is black with flying saucers." Although several short stories in *Bagombo Snuff Box* include descriptions of and conflicts within marriage, as a whole the collection complies with Vonnegut's stated embargo against the inclusion of "deep love" in his texts, typically opting instead to focus on characterizations through navigation of conflicts of class, economics, and culture.

2. *People* magazine effectively summarizes narrative flaws with the assessment that "there are some clunkers in the collection, lines that sound painfully naïve" (Novak 56). A common refrain of *Bagombo Snuff Box* reviews is to comment on the text as a worthwhile read by virtue of being a Vonnegut publication, as evidenced in the *Entertainment Weekly* review stating that "mild as most of [the short stories] are, these tales are worth reading...they provide fans the complete test tube Vonnegut" (Klepp 70).

3. Given the success of Vonnegut's account of his experiences in World War II, it may be tempting to hypothesize a significant connection

between Vonnegut the veteran and Rice, where both are serving as hapless interlocutors of the dead. I have opted not to pursue this course of biographical analyses in favor of limiting the scope of interpretive reference to Vonnegut's personal life to those factors that he mentions directly either in the introduction or coda.

4. PTSD was first recognized and named as a disorder in 1980 by the Diagnostic and Statistical Manual of Mental Disorders, although the symptoms had been recognized at least since World War I (Felt).

5. Vonnegut describes this incident of induced resilience by writing that "the old spark was back. Major Durant, home from the wars, was somebody" (Vonnegut 132).

6. Karl is described as an identical copy of his father in that he "seemed sobered by fifty-one years of life, though he'd lived only twenty" (Vonnegut 249).

Works Cited

Dodman, Tervor. "'Going All to Pieces': *A Farewell to Arms* as Trauma Narrative." *Twentieth Century Literature* 52.3 (2006): 249–74.

Felt, Gary. "The Relationship of Posttraumatic Stress Disorder to Law Enforcement." *aaets.org*. The American Academy of Experts in Traumatic Stress. 12 Dec. 2007 <http://www.aaets.org/article92.htm>.

Gholson, Bill. "Narrative, Self and Morality in the Writing of Kurt Vonnegut." *At Millennium's End: New Essays on the Work of Kurt Vonnegut*. Ed. Kevin Alexander Boon. Albany: State U of New York P, 2001. 135–47.

Hayman, David, David Michaelis, George Plimpton, and Richard Rhodes. "The Art of Fiction No. 64: Kurt Vonnegut." *The Paris Review* Spring 1977. 10 Dec. 2007 <http://www.theparisreview.org/viewinterview.php/prmMID/3605>.

Klepp, L. S. "*Bagombo Snuff Box*: Uncollected Short Fiction." *Entertainment Weekly* 1 Oct. 1999: 70.

Klinkowitz, Jerome. *The American 1960s: Imaginative Acts in a Decade of Change*. Ames: Iowa State U, 1980.

Morse, David E. "You Cannot Win, You Cannot Break Even, You Cannot Get out of the Game: Kurt Vonnegut and the Notion of Progress." *At Millennium's End: New Essays on the Work of Kurt Vonnegut*. Ed. Kevin Alexander Boon. Albany: State U of New York P, 2001. 91–104.

———. "We Are Marching to Utopia: Kurt Vonnegut's Player Piano." *The Utopian Fantastic: Selected Essays from the Twentieth International Conference on the Fantastic in the Arts*. Ed. Martha Bartter. Westport: Greenwood, 2004. 23–32.

Novak, Ralph. "*Bagombo Snuff Box*." *People Weekly* 6 Sept. 1999: 56.

Vonnegut, Kurt. *Bagombo Snuff Box*. New York: Berkeley, 1999.

PART III

Vonnegut and Other Writers

CHAPTER 10

Duty Dance with Death:
A Farewell to Arms and
Slaughterhouse-Five

Lawrence R. Broer

When Kurt Vonnegut describes "the soul's condition in a man at war" as hideously deformed (*Mother Night* 117), he indicates the plight of his and Ernest Hemingway's protagonists, alike. The horrors of war, the idiocies of battle permeate the works of both writers. However, while Frank McConnel accurately views Vonnegut as the most recognizably Hemingwayesque of the new generation of writers to emerge after World War II (163), it is usually to separate himself from Hemingway, to damn not praise, that Vonnnegut speaks of his fellow artist-warrior. While admiring Hemingway's best stories, Vonnegut scorns the Hemingway mystique, his idealization of valor and physical prowess. If Hemingway's soul is large, it is also in Vonnegut's critique a soul corrupted by a primitive delight in the killing of animals and by the so-called arts of war (Broer, *Vonnegut's Goodbye* 66). Indeed, Vonnegut's satire of Hemingway in *Happy Birthday Wanda June* (1970)—self described as "a simple minded play about men who enjoy killing and those who don't"—can be read as a critique of Hemingway's work as a whole. More specifically, Vonnegut might well have had the protagonist of *A Farewell to Arms*, (1929), Frederic Henry, in mind as a likely candidate for what the Vonnegut persona, Norbert Woodley, derides in Harold Ryan as macho posturing, "heroic balderdash." Finding it disgusting and frightening that a killer should still be a respected member of society, Woodley articulates Vonnegut's moral outcry from *Player Piano* (1959) to

Timequake (1997)—"Gentleness must replace violence everywhere, or we are doomed" (2). As opposed to Harold Ryan's association of manhood with toughness and physical challenge, Woodley says he wants to cry whenever he comes into a room containing animal heads, a "monument to a man who thinks that what the world needs most is rhinoceros meat." "Any one of these poor dead animals," Norbert tells Harold, "was a thousand times the athlete you could ever hope to be" (7). Woodley plays violin in a doctor's quartet, was a stretcher bearer in the Korean War, doesn't play sports, always takes the path of least resistance, uses his brains instead of his brawn, and attempts to change people with the weapons of compassion, unselfishness, and maudlin concern (7).

In *Timequake* Vonnegut continues to challenge what he sees as Hemingway's relatively romantic treatment of war and death, his hard-boiled pose that mixes heroism with physical valor and killing with honor. Contrasting his own Purple Heart for frostbite, this country's second lowest decoration, with Hemingway's War Cross and Silver Medal of Honor for being shot, Vonnegut accuses Frederick Henry of *A Farewell to Arms* of getting Catherine Barkley pregnant to prove his manhood, declaring that the novel really proclaims Hemingway's detestation of civilian life, of marriage (81). The tears Henry sheds are those of relief for having been saved from an unglamorous life of civilian responsibilities—getting a regular job, a house, life insurance. Despite Hemingway's vivid depiction of the horror of war, Vonnegut suggests that Frederic and Catherine have too many wonderful experiences, thus representing the most popular story a writer can tell about a good-looking couple having a really good time copulating outside wedlock and having to quit for one reason or another in the full blush of romantic feeling (80–81).

Vonnegut portrays his own, more sardonic version of war in *Slaughterhouse-Five* (1969) and in *Timequake* through several stories by Kilgore Trout, a soldier-artist who shares both Vonnegut and Hemingway's military background. In Trout's account of Albert Hardy, Vonnegut's World War I soldier not only has his penis shot off like Jake Barnes in *The Sun Also Rises*, his body is atomized and his penis, his "ding-dong," is blown into oblivion (*Timequake* 79). In a Trout story that appears to parody the ending of *A Farewell to Arms*, reflecting what McConnel calls the "stylized brutality" (84) of Hemingway's depiction of war and bullfighting, the Knights of the Round Table are equipped with Thompson submachine guns. Probably with Frederick Henry in mind as Lancelot and Guinevere as Catherine, Lancelot, the "purest in heart and mind," puts a slug through the Holy Grail and makes "a Swiss cheese of Queen Guinevere" (*Timequake* xiii). Vonnegut shares with Trout a real-life, similarly antiheroic tale about his friend, David Craig. Craig shoots a German tank with a bazooka, but no Germans pop out of the turret, no one celebrates. As if again parodying Frederick Henry's convenient exit from humdrum domesticity, Kilgore Trout concludes that at least the tank's occupants died in glory, that David Craig's true heroism was in sparing his victims years of disappointment and tedium in civilian life (*Timequake* 80).

We might explain Vonnegut's hostility by supposing he draws apart from Hemingway just as Hemingway had done from his immediate mentor, Sherwood Anderson, to better define his own stylistic identity. Or we might wax Freudian, citing the fact that, as McConnel explains, every artist must kill or castrate his artistic father before he can function on his own, especially the symbolic father who liked to be called "Papa" (163). Vonnegut, himself, suggests in *Fates Worse than Death* that differences in their respective cultures and war experiences made Hemingway his natural adversary. Explaining that they were divided by booms and busts and wars radically different in mood and purpose and technology, which separated not only himself from Hemingway but the first half from the last half of the twentieth century (*Fates* 6), Vonnegut declares that while only twenty-three years apart in age, the difference might have been a thousand years (*Fates* 60). In particular, Vonnegut attributes their differences in temper to the differences between World War I and World War II, and between both of these wars to the war in Vietnam. The nature of true battle stories by Americans was utterly debased by World War II, he explains, "when millions of us fought overseas and came home no longer needing a Hemingway to say what war was like" (*Fates* 62). Vonnegut declares that while neither he nor Hemingway ever killed anyone, he himself "almost killed his first German" when he got home, and his Uncle Dan clapped him on the back and bellowed, "You're a man now" (*Timequake* 70).

Vonnegut suggests that the nightmare of hydrogen bombs and the atrocities of the Nazi death camps necessarily created a new historicist sensibility, one that no longer believed that "Death before dishonor" was a fate worse than death, since the military death of one man might easily mean the death of everything (*Fates* 144). What made the Vietnam soldier particularly "spooky," Vonnegut explains, is that he never had illusions about war, never had Hemingway's need to return from war with the shocking news that war was repulsive, stupid, and dehumanized (*Fates* 146). Rather, the Vietnam veteran was the first American soldier to know from childhood that war was a meaningless butchery of ordinary people like himself and that death was plain old death, the absence of life. This is precisely what Harold Ryan's wife, Penelope, reminds Harold of in *Wanda June* when she accuses him of confusing heroism and honor with killing and death. "It is not an honor to be killed," she chides, "It is still just death, the absence of life—no honor at all" (174).

The irony of Vonnegut's description of their differences—the thousand years Vonnegut says divides him from Hemingway—is that it obscures more than it illuminates about their significant artistic affinities. Vonnegut acknowledges that, though not a soldier,[1] Hemingway was one of the best war reporters. Vonnegut and Hemmingway's war experience and resultant wounds were remarkably similar,[2] as was their literary response in *A Farewell to Arms* and *Slaughterhouse-Five*. At the age of eighteen, Hemingway was literally blown up by an Austrian trench mortar while serving as a civilian ambulance driver on the Italian front. As a lowly twenty-year old PFC, albeit an intelligence and reconnaissance scout, Vonnegut first was captured "in tact" during the Battle of the Bulge while looking for enemies and was then forced to witness the hideous firebombing of Dresden.

In spite of the fact that Vonnegut is witness to horrors in different wars from Hemingway, or that his wounding was less visible, probably no two works more aptly demonstrate the common art and vision of these literary figures than *A Farewell* to *Arms* and *Slaughterhouse-Five*. The fact that both writers are engaged in a struggle with guilt and pessimism, that both write from a seemingly numbed and detached point of view, suggests their common purpose: to portray the wound, the psychic fragmentation, and the quest of the wounded soldier for positive values and for ways of ordering his life in a hostile, naturalistic world. It is clear their war experiences were equally complex and traumatic, requiring a purging of fear and bitterness Vonnegut calls his "duty dance with death" (*Slaughterhouse-Five* 21). In the autobiographical preface to *Slaughterhouse-Five*, Vonnegut cites the example of the French soldier/novelist, Ferdinand Celine, who said that only by writing about his war wounds could he cure them. With reference to his own designs as a healer-writer, Vonnegut explains that "Celine was a brave French soldier in the First World War—until his skull was cracked. After that he couldn't sleep, and there were noises in his head. He became a doctor, and he treated poor people in the daytime, and he wrote grotesque novels all night" (21). Celine explains that he had fought "nicely" against the ravages of death as long as he could, "danced with it, festooned it, waltzed it around...decorated it with streamers, titillated it..." (21). Identifying metaphorically with Celine's head wound, Vonnegut agrees that "No art is possible without a dance with death" (21). As with Celine, Vonnegut also knows that it is an obligation he has too long deferred. It would, in fact, take years and successive attempts before either Vonnegut or Hemingway could face their war experience directly. Though Vonnegut, like Hemingway, plays down the long-term trauma of his war experience, J.G. Keogh and Ed Kislatis contend that for Vonnegut, the shock of personally witnessing the war's greatest massacre, nearly two hundred thousand civilians incinerated, had to be exorcised over a long period of writing. *Slaughterhouse-Five*, where Vonnegut tackles the experience head on, releases his Dresden tensions spread out over a lifetime, intensifying from novel to novel. Similarly, it took Hemingway over a decade to deal directly with Fossalta, though his wound, too, reproduced in *A Farewell to Arms* exactly as it happened, recurs throughout his work as Dresden does for Vonnegut. A case can be made that for both writers, what was at stake in turning to art as therapy was nothing less than their preservation of sanity, let alone the efforts to find an orderly way to live in the world that crippled them. Putting their nightmare to paper—survival through the healing powers of imagination—was as necessary to one writer as the other.

The wounded soldier unable to sleep is, of course, one of the central themes of Hemingway's work, merely one of the proofs that violence and the meaningless butchery of war have traumatized and demoralized Hemingway's Frederic Henry and Vonnegut's Billy Pilgrim.

In the authors' mutually powerful portrayal of the slaughterhouse of war—the brutality of battle, the impermanence of love, and the impossibility of any metaphysical solution for Frederic Henry or Billy Pilgrim—it would at first seem to be feelings of futility and helplessness war creates in both writers, rather than solutions to the violence of war, that occupy them from beginning to end. Frederic Henry is psychically as well as physically shot to pieces by the end of his story, and Billy Pilgrim emerges from his underground bomb shelter a broken kite on a stick, headed for a mental hospital. The panorama of death and violence that defines Billy Pilgrim's world prompts Vonnegut to say that, "even if wars didn't keep coming like glaciers, there would still be plain old death" (4). "War time is all time," Arthur Waldhorn explains about Hemingway's world, a metaphor for the "hostile implacability" of the universe toward living and loving (22). In such a savage world, Waldhorn says, "when men occasionally fail to destroy one another, nature leaps into the breach" (22).

Reminiscent of the scene in which Frederic Henry likens human beings to ants burned alive in a camp fire, the slaughterhouse where Billy is kept as a prisoner in Dresden becomes a grotesque image of human beings dehumanized by war, hanging like butchered animals on hooks. Billy also sees himself as a "bug trapped in amber" (Vonnegut, *Slaughterhouse-Five* 77). Such images portray a world where suffering and death are commonplace. In his famous denunciation of the phony ideals for which the war has been fought, Frederic Henry decides that war so dehumanizes individuals they become no different than butchered cattle. "I had seen nothing sacred," he says, "and the sacrifices were like the stockyards at Chicago if nothing was done with the meat except to bury it" (Hemingway, *Farewell* 191). In "A Natural History of the Dead" Hemingway sees no more spiritual significance to these inglorious deaths than to the deaths of horses and mules. After the explosion of a munitions factory, Hemingway comments upon the ghoulish carcasses of mules and horses as well as men, women, and children. He identifies the dead, their different conditions, by sex or race; by the division of their bodies along anatomical lines; the difference in color change; the effect of heat on their decaying flesh; their smell; the "maggots working where their mouths had been." "The first thing that you found about the dead," Hemingway reports, "was that, hit badly enough, they died like animals" (*Short Stories* 440). Sandra Spanier Whipple summarizes Hemingway's world at war as "one in which things do not bear fruit, but explode, break, decompose, or are eaten away" (14).

For both protagonists, everything eventually dies or goes to pieces. Frederic Henry declares late in *A Farewell to Arms* that there is simply no defense against the ravages of death, that the world has to kill people to break them. "They killed you gratuitously like Aymo. Or gave you syphilis like Rinaldi. But they killed you in the end. You could count on that" (Hemingway 350). Billy Pilgrim would certainly concur: "So it goes," Billy wearily laments about the endless death and violence around him, now, as always, without cessation or sense. The shell that wounds Frederic Henry is "flung blindly" (88) just as the plane crash that kills everybody but Billy happens randomly and senselessly. Catherine's death—a freak biological accident that defies a sense of meaning or justice in the world—is as arbitrary as the death of Edgar Derby, who enters the war out of pure motives, and whose efforts to provide helpful leadership to Billy and his fellow prisoners proves futile in protecting Derby from the stupidity and absurdity of war.[3] While Dresden goes up in flames, Derby is arrested for taking a teapot and shot by a firing squad.

For both men, there comes a moment when the madness of war overwhelms them, and only personal survival matters. For Henry, after the desperate retreat at Caporetto, any remaining notions of patriotism or devotion to duty are nullified by countless instances of cruelty, betrayal, and incompetence by his own fellow soldiers, climaxing in needless executions where Henry is mistaken as a German imposter and is nearly executed himself. Overwhelmed by similar displays of human madness and injustice, Billy Pilgrim experiences a final unbalancing he likens to being stretched on the rack (Vonnegut, *Slaughterhouse-Five* 172–73) when he remembers the night Dresden was destroyed—the firestorm that "ate everything...that would burn, that turned the city into a desert and people into little petrified human beings" (178). Billy's experience consists of the same maddening contrasts between human ideals and the grotesque realities of war that force Henry to seek a separate peace: "bucolic interludes sandwiched between bouts of violence...and sanctioned public murder" (Spanier 91–92). The horrors of war become so unbearable that each man renounces not only the war but the forces that make it. Because both have seen death en masse, Pilgrim shares Henry's embarrassment over such hollow abstractions as "sacred, glorious and sacrifice, and the expression in vain" (Vonnegut, *Slaughterhouse-Five* 191). Thus, both men, as Penn Warren says of Henry, "cut themselves off from the herd" (xxxii).

Threatened with annihilation and potentially disabled by fear and cynicism, the dilemma of the Hemingway/Vonnegut hero is precisely the same: how to manage existential despair so great that insanity or suicide pose real threats. As men who hunger for the sense of order and assurance that most find in religious belief, but who cannot find grounds for such belief, how do Billy and Frederic avoid the "complete dispiritedness" (Tetlow 15) for which they appear headed, retaining faith in the value of human effort that nevertheless dooms noble human beings like Catherine Barkley and Edgar Derby? More than mere personal survival, however, Penn Warren and Loree Rackstraw agree that for Frederic and Billy, successfully confronting the existential void means more than personal survival. It means staying alive with "decency" in the world that has crippled them (Rackstraw 54): the world of Hemingway's "nada" and Vonnegut's "chaos." From Penn Warren's perspective, Frederic and Billy must adopt an ideal of behavior that gives meaning and moral significance to the confusions of living (xii).

It is the critical difference between each author's definitions of "moral significance" that best explains the worldview that divides them. Hemingway acquires ideas about how to live humanly, with courage and stoical bearing, from the world of the bullfight, whereas Vonnegut formulates ideas of conduct from Christ's "Sermon on the Mount," adopting kindness and restraint as moral imperatives. The contrast seems striking in light of Hemingway's story, "Today is Friday," about Christ's crucifixion. While the story says nothing about ideals of charity or compassion, it conspicuously praises Christ's manly bearing—his courage and ability to endure suffering. Tetlow offers us a useful way to distinguish the two modes of conduct. In Hemingway's case, the world as essentially cruel and predatory is "accepted and assimilated" (Tetlow 70). Even violence is justified, because that is what it takes to prevail in a violent world, the willingness to prove that you are tougher and more courageous. Vonnegut chooses to repudiate animal instinct, encouraging a loving rather than adversarial relationship with nature. As I noted in *Sanity Plea: Schizophrenia in the Novels of Kurt Vonnegut* (1989) as an ardent primitivist, Hemingway joins Faulkner, Steinbeck, Lawrence, and Norman Mailer in believing that the solution to a dehumanized world lies in throwing off the trappings of civilization and retreating to a golden age in the past; in contrast, Vonnegut believes that our only hope for salvation is intelligently and humanely directing our course into the future. He would have us move up the evolutionary ladder, not down.

Throughout *A Farewell to Arms* and *Slaughterhouse-Five*, however, the only way Billy Pilgrim and Frederic Henry find to deflect pain is to continue the dangerous evasive strategies of their younger selves. Frederic masks feelings of vulnerability behind a tough-guy stoicism that borders on cruelty, and Billy, his emotional fuses completely blown, practices a numbness of response that leaves him robotically dazed and compliant. The authors' ironic, understated styles convey the protagonists' escape into what Millicent Bell calls "the dreamless sleep of apathy" (121)—a screen of simple words and short, declarative sentences meant to numb emotional pain and protect the hero from further potential horrors. But as Wendolyn Tetlow explains, the reader hears the silent screams just beneath the iceberg's surface (Vonnegut, *Slaughterhouse-Five* 102).

In their mutual strategies of disengagement from the war, the adoption of false selves and dangerously escapist fantasy worlds is foreshadowed by the presence of playacting, numerous instances of masquerading, and game playing. Frederic, an American in an Italian uniform, wants to pretend to be Catherine's dead fiancé (Hemingway, *Farewell* 39). Love is compared to a game of chess and to cards.

Henry sees his conquest of Barkley "all ahead like the moves in a chess game" (Hemingway, *Farewell* 26). The couple attends a fixed horse race. After deserting from the army, Henry disguises himself as a woodcutter (Hemingway, *Farewell* 323) and a "fake doctor" (340). Life is theater for Frederic as much as for Billy Pilgrim. Thomas Strychacz notes that "Real helmets, pistols, and salutes become stage props" (92). Similarly, Billy can relate only to imaginary scenes and people. "Theatrical grief" (Vonnegut, *Slaughterhouse-Five* 125) becomes more real to him than anything in the outside world. In the prison camp performance of Cinderella, Cinderella's boots fit him perfectly—"Billy Pilgrim was Cinderella, and Cinderella was Billy Pilgrim" (Vonnegut, *Slaughterhouse-Five* 145).

No wonder that Billy and Frederic's self-protective masks lead them to disengage from war completely. Henry seeks refuge through flight to Switzerland with Catherine in what he calls their "separate peace," a womblike condition in which the lovers determine to survive by being loyal to a world composed only of themselves. In turn, Billy Pilgrim hallucinates the "morphine paradise" (Vonnegut, *Slaughterhouse-Five* 49) of Tralfamadore, an equally dubious utopia in which he secludes himself with the movie star Montana Wildhack, who, like Catherine, becomes pregnant, but whose promises of sanctuary and new life prove as abortive as the flight to Switzerland by Hemingway's doomed lovers. Not only do the Tralfamadorians, with their "earthly combination of ferocity and spectacular weaponry and talent for horror" (Vonnegut, *Slaughterhouse-Five* 115), not improve Billy's visions but Billy's flight from the responsibilities of "wakeful humanity" (17) leads directly into what John Tilton calls "a spiritual oubliette" (46). Billy trades his dignity and self-integrity for an illusion of comfort and security, becoming himself a machine like his Tralfamadorian captors.

Just as delusively, Frederic and Catherine's flight from outer reality results in what Millicent Bell calls "an almost animal-like isolation and state of numbness and ennui" (216), a loss of selfhood exactly like Billy's abdication of humanity, canceling any hope of new life. Many readers view the "separate peace" the escaped lovers make in Switzerland as an opportunity for Frederic to practice what Catherine has taught him about the value of selfless love. Catherine's remark, "you're my religion" (Hemingway, *Farewell* 116), suggests the spiritual intensity of the connection she feels or desires to feel for Frederic, establishing her as his moral guide. Without question, Catherine displays the wisdom, courage, and honesty appropriate to her role as Frederic's tutor. It is Catherine, Sandra Spanier explains, who gives

Frederic ample lessons in the tragic heroic declaration that "a man can be destroyed but not defeated" (100). Frederic is supposedly "tenderized" by love and made to care like the caring Catherine, in whom his selfhood is invested (Spilka 212). For a while, at least, Frederic abandons hunting, sports, and war for a world circumscribed by the lovers' bed.

Yet, under the "impress of war," Strychacz argues, Frederic's "caring" about Catherine develops too rapidly to be anything more than "self conscious role playing" (98), more "sexual excitement" than love, as the priest has defined that more transcendent experience: "When you love you wish to do things for" (Hemingway, *Farewell* 55). "If I ever get it," meaning true love, Frederic tells the priest, "I will tell you" (Hemingway, *Farewell* 75). We wonder if that moment ever comes. As Strychacz asks, "Can we really tell when Henry first loves, or if he ever does love Catherine Barkley?" (101). In its place, Frederic daydreams of being with Catherine in a hotel room, where he conceives of her as a magnificent whore, evoking the image of Billy Pilgrim with Montana Wildhack, Billy's face pressed to Montana's swelling bosom in a similar masquerade. "I was not made to think," Frederic acknowledges, "I was made to eat. My God, yes. Eat and drink and sleep with Catherine" (Hemingway, *Farewell* 242). When Catherine agrees to flee with him to Switzerland, Henry says, "You're a fine girl. Let's get back into bed" (Hemingway, *Farewell* 82). Whereas Henry's animal appetite never lags, his capacity for caring is suspect.

Linda Wagner Martin argues that love for the Hemingway hero generally means "erotic desire," blended with the concept of courtly love (55). Catherine, she says, exists as lady to Henry's knight errant (61). Bolstering Vonnegut's point that Frederic and Catherine represent "a good looking couple" having too much fun outside wedlock, Wagner-Martin sees "blocked desire" as the "energizing element" of Hemingway's romantic treatment of sexual love: "The intensity of the lover's passion is directly related to the extent to which their love is doomed" (56). A genius at replicating the conventions of popular romance, Hemingway creates the moral fantasy that love is all-sufficient, and even if the story ends in death of one or both lovers rather than a permanently happy marriage, it ends in such a way as to suggest that the love relationship has been of lasting and permanent import (56).

While Billy Pilgrim's disguises leave him dazed and identity-less, his passivity seems, in Vonnegut's view, less morally objectionable than Frederic Henry's mask of stoical toughness, misogyny, and occasional cruelty. Apropos of Vonnegut's moral to *Mother Night*, "We are what we pretend to be, so we must be careful about what we pretend to be" (v), Frederic's soldierly masquerade becomes unnervingly real. What Strychacz calls Henry's "shifting articulations of identity" (98) returns us to Vonnegut's essential critique of *A Farewell to Arms*, and the authors' contrary views of what it means to fill the existential void "decently" or "humanly." We have noted that Vonnegut accuses Hemingway of glorifying war—of heroic posing and the idealization of manly toughness—and of associating honor with death and killing. How fair are these criticisms, and what do they portend in understanding differences in each writer's vision of life and war?

Certainly, Hemingway's numerous descriptions of war wounds in *A Farewell to Arms* portray war as anything but "romantic" or "glorious." His scenes showing the random horrors of death and suffering on the battlefield not only rival but exceed Vonnegut's in realistic detail. Linda Wagner Martin points out that Hemingway's readers cannot escape the recognition of "relentless blood and dreadful death" and the frustration of medical knowledge that fails to save lives (62). At the moment of Henry's own terrible wound, when he learns it was a "mistake to think you just died" (Hemingway, *Farewell* 57), he describes the suffering of a particularly brave Italian soldier named Passini, hit by the same trench-mortar shell: "His legs were toward me and I saw in the dark and the light that they were both smashed above the knee. One leg was gone and the other was held by tendons and part of the trouser and the stump twitched and jerked as though it were not connected." Passini screams in pain until Henry reports, "Then he was quiet, biting his arm, the stump of his leg twitching" (Hemingway, *Farewell* 57). Henry tries in vain to make a tourniquet but notices that Passini was "dead already. I made sure he was dead" (Hemingway, *Farewell* 58). At the dressing station, Frederic sees doctors working "red as butchers" (Hemingway, *Farewell* 59). After a doctor, indifferent to Henry's pain, finishes probing and bandaging his wounded knee, "doing things that hurt sharply and severing tissue" (Hemingway, *Farewell* 62), Henry finds himself in an ambulance, placed beneath a hemorrhaging soldier in the cot above him. Henry tries to move out of the way but can't avoid the steady stream of blood from above, turning him "warm and sticky," dripping as if "from an icicle after the sun has gone" (Hemingway, *Farewell* 64). One would be hard-pressed to view Frederic Henry's famous denunciation of the usual base motivations for war (Hemingway, *Farewell* 191), his contempt for the patriotic platitudes that send young men off to die, as something other than a protest against war. When we hear the battle police during the retreat from Caporetto speaking of "the sacred soil of the fatherland" and the "fruits of victory" as they execute their own soldiers (Hemingway, *Farewell* 232), we understand Henry's disgust.

Yet, Thomas Strychacz's argument that Hemingway's episodes of war function "as an alibi for the violence that is being celebrated" (108), if valid, suggests that Vonnegut's concerns are not misplaced. In Strychacz's view, Hemingway's descriptions perform the "double task of exploring the guilty pleasures of militarism" (108), decrying, for instance, the pain of brave soldiers, whose suffering and death nevertheless bring them glory. The merciless killings during the retreat are terrifying, certainly not an endorsement of the glory of battle or the nobility of death. Reynolds argues, in fact, that Henry is a decidedly "non-heroic figure," someone "never quite brave" (*Hemingway's First War* 259); yet, Henry's confrontations during the retreat inspire in Henry exactly the self-conscious machismo Vonnegut disparages in Harold Ryan, codelike exhibitions of toughness, bravery, and stoical fortitude, a markedly different response to war than Billy Pilgrim's.

It is not difficult to view Frederic Henry's capacity for violence in light of Harold Ryan's assertion in *Happy Birthday Wanda June* that "You've got to fight from time to time or get eaten alive" (Vonnegut 176). According to Robert Penn Warren and John Killinger, Henry's violence simply represents an appropriate response to "the great nada" (Penn Warren 44). Yet, naturally combative, Frederic fights not only to survive but because he likes it, taking pride in himself as a tough guy who enjoys intimidating other men and even inflicting pain. When he bloodies the face of an Italian officer with a single blow (Hemingway, *Farewell* 230), takes pleasure in "scaring" the professor he boxes with in Lausanne, noting "he went all to pieces if you started after him" (Hemingway, *Farewell* 321), or relishes seeing the Italian artillery captain cower when they want the same seat on a train (165–66), Henry takes the same pride in his masculinity as he does watching himself shadow box. There is little difference between this Frederic Henry and the Harold Ryan who thrives on physical threats and enjoys "twitting weaklings" (Vonnegut, *Happy Birthday* 110) or who proclaims that the "core of his life" was the pleasure of watching someone make the choice between fleeing and fighting, or making the choice himself (Vonnegut, *Happy Birthday* 72). "This is a moment of truth," Harold Ryan tells his buddy Shuttle contemptuously, when Shuttle won't fight him, "and you're almost crying" (Vonnegut, *Happy Birthday* 164–65).

We know that when Frederic dispatches the suffering Passini—"I made sure he was dead" (58)—he acts from pity. But a far darker emotion surfaces—a seeming enjoyment of killing—when he shoots fleeing Italian officers who resist Henry's orders to help dig a car out of the mud. He describes the killing as coolly and indifferently as if he were shooting pheasant or quail, consistent with violence that he perversely enjoys and that increasingly desensitizes him. "I shot three times," he says, "and dropped one. The other went through the hedge and was out of sight." "Did I hit the other one at all?" he asks someone (Hemingway, *Farewell* 211). When Bonello puts his pistol against the head of one of the fallen soldiers, Henry responds coldly, "You have to cock it" (Hemingway, *Farewell* 211).

If Vonnegut's portrait of the bellicose Harold Ryan indicts Hemingway for the kind of aggression that shows up in Frederic Henry, aggression Vonnegut believes would eventually destroy the world, Ryan and Henry also share an unnerving propensity for heroic braggadocio. There are several episodes where Hemingway appears, disingenuously I think, to undercut the kind of heroic posing Vonnegut detests. When Frederic says, "Nothing ever happens to the brave," Catherine smartly answers, "the brave die of course" (46). Yet, her view that the truly brave are quiet about it evokes a concept of heroic fortitude that seems staged and even pretentious. Frederic seems to congratulate himself for the very heroism he pretends to deny, likening himself to a "ball-player that bats two hundred and thirty and knows he's no better" (Hemingway, *Farewell* 146). His modesty accentuates unspoken assumptions of moral superiority. We see that Frederic suffers, but his valor requires he denies its seriousness. When he describes his swollen and bleeding forehead—his personal red badge of courage—as "nothing" (Hemingway, *Farewell* 239), waits to have his knee wound dressed because "there are much worse wounded than me" (61–62), and understates the ordeal of the retreat on foot, then swimming the Tagliamento with "this knee," there is an unmistakable element of self-congratulation reminiscent of the bravado of the British prisoners of war in *Slaughterhouse-Five*. Though Henry ostensibly resists being viewed as a hero, Penn Warren appears on track by asserting that both Hemingway and Frederic celebrate their wounds to "Certify their manliness and provide a source of masculine authority" (212). While Rinaldi tells Frederic, "You are so brave and quiet I forget you are suffering" (*Farewell* 67), Hemingway makes certain we do not.

While Vonnegut's criticisms simplify the complexities of text and characterization in *A Farewell to Arms*, they nevertheless illuminate essential differences in each writer's management of war wounds at almost identical phases of their careers. Vonnegut's portrait of his own suffering war hero, Billy Pilgrim, constitutes the very antithesis of Hemingway's tough, violent, and sometimes brutal Frederic Henry. Like Norbert Woodley, Harold Ryan's peacenik counterpart in *Happy Birthday Wanda June*, Pilgrim epitomizes Vonnegut's dictum that "There's no time for battle, no point to battle any more" (176). Woodley, Penelope says, represents the new heroes who refuse to fight: "They're trying to save the planet" (Vonnegut, *Happy Birthday* 176). Billy's gentleness and subsequent refusal to participate in the world's destructiveness contrasts conspicuously with what we see of Henry's truculence and enjoyment of physical confrontation. Richard Erlich notes that even Billy's virtue as a "fool among knaves" [from Swift's *Tale of a Tub*] is a laudable ideal (qtd. in *Sanity Plea* 87–88). We see Billy as a latter day Christ who spends three days entombed in a slaughterhouse shelter. On the way to his Dresden prison camp, Billy suffers a sleepless agony, clinging to a "cross-brace" (Vonnegut, *Slaughterhouse-Five* 78) he is found "lying at an angle on the corner-brace, self crucified" (80). He cries at the sight of a suffering German horse, a moment that begs comparison with the narrator's impersonal response to the crippled baggage animals thrown to drown in the water in Hemingway's "On the Quai at Smyrna."

Billy's natural gentleness and innocence, appropriate to his role as chaplain's assistant, hardly prepares him for the idiocy of battle, anymore than Frederic Henry's boyish exuberance prepares him for the war's destruction. Yet, if anything, Billy grows more docile, while Frederic becomes increasingly militant. In contrast to Frederic's self-conscious virility, Billy is loath to discover that his wife associates sex and glamor with war (Vonnegut, *Slaughterhouse-Five* 121). Rather than show off his personal sexual prowess, Vonnegut in the opening chapter jokes that the war has made his own phallus inoperable—a "tool" that "won't pee anymore" (*Slaughterhouse-Five* 23). All in all, Billy experiences war as an interminable nightmare of victimization and madness, an "acrimonious madrigal" (Vonnegut, *Slaughterhouse-Five* 79) in which everyone around him exhibits some form of insane, mechanically conditioned behavior, that which is overtly aggressive or which allows aggression to happen. Hemingway's denunciations of war are more problematic, war viewed as a process of tempering the writer's craft and sensibility,[4] a stage upon which to enact what Penn Warren calls "the lessons of lonely fortitude" (xxxii), shows of courage and strength necessary to endure in a world that kills and maims with impunity.

Whereas Frederic Henry thinks to himself, "One had so many friends in a war" (Hemingway, *Farewell* 163), we are hard pressed to think of Billy as similarly blessed. Instead, we encounter the mindless-hating-and-killing, super-patriot machines of Howard Campbell, Colonel Wild Bob, and Bertram Copeland Rumfoord, whose glorifications of war and exhortations to battle appear ludicrous alongside the pitiful suffering of Billy and his comrades (Vonnegut, *Slaughterhouse-Five* 67). In addition to the death of Edgar Derby and the execution of Private Eddie Slovik, shot for challenging authority, Billy represents Vonnegut's view that despite all the popular movies that glorify war and soldiering, and star manly figures like John Wayne or Frank Sinatra, it is usually the nation's young and innocent who are first sent to be slaughtered. One cannot escape the contrast to war movies made of *A Farewell to Arms, For Whom the Bell Tolls,* and *Islands in the Stream,* starring exceedingly masculine figures like Tyrone Power, Humphrey Bogart, Gary Cooper, and George C. Scott or the more pointed irony that, whereas Billy is appalled at the execution of Derby, Frederic Henry, sans pity or remorse, performs just such an execution of a fleeing Italian officer.

In an episode reminiscent of the chaotic retreat at Caparetto in *Farewell,* but conspicuously devoid of Frederic's bravado, Vonnegut's portrait of the demented Colonel Wild Bob exhorting his beaten soldiers to battle epitomizes Vonnegut's refusal to glamorize war in any form. As Billy joins the "river of humiliation" of marching prisoners, being spat upon by their German captors, violent, "bristly men" with "teeth like piano keys" (Vonnegut, *Slaughterhouse-Five* 65), he hears "Wild Bob," who has lost an entire regiment, about forty-five hundred men—"a lot of them children"—speaking patriotic nonsense to Billy through lungs that "rattled like greasy paper bags" (66). He tells Billy and the agonized, uncomprehending soldiers around him that there were dead Germans all over the battlefield who "wished to God" they had never heard of Billy's outfit, "the Four-fifty-first." He says that after the war he was going to have a regimental reunion in his home town of Cody, Wyoming, and "barbecue whole steers" (Vonnegut, *Slaughterhouse-Five* 67). Other than the fatherly ministrations of Edgar Derby, the only other representation of heroism in the novel occurs when Billy encounters the British prisoners of war, described in hilariously parodic terms. The Brits have put up a sign reading, "Please leave this latrine as tidy as you found it" (Vonnegut, *Slaughterhouse-Five* 125), signaling an obsessive pretense of order and cleanliness nearly as mad as the war itself. While Vonnegut comments about the ineffectiveness of war protests, the antiwar element in this novel is direct and powerful. Vonnegut tells his sons to not work for companies that make war machinery (Vonnegut, *Slaughterhouse-Five* 19) and to express contempt for people who think we need machinery like that. True to his promise to O'Hare's wife, Vonnegut demonstrates that wars are fought by children, subtitling his novel "The Children's Crusade." Ironically, Frederic and Catherine hope their son will be a lieutenant commander or, better yet, a general (Hemingway. *Farewell* 147). Billy's son, on the other hand, a decorated Green Beret, achieves the military distinction Frederic and Catherine have in mind, but as a mindless, former high school dropout and alcoholic, hardly qualifies as a poster child for war. In one telling image, a war movie run in reverse, Vonnegut demonstrates the power of art to subvert the destructive process of war. Fires go out; dead or wounded soldiers are made whole; bombs fly back in to planes which fly backwards to friendly cities; the bombers are dismantled, and minerals used for bombs are returned to the earth (Vonnegut, *Slaughterhouse-Five* 73–75).

Just as neither Frederic's aggression nor Billy's passivity offers a meaningful adjustment to the trauma of war, so their adoption of what Earl Rovit calls "studied forgetfulness" (15) prevents them from understanding the submerged fears Spilka sees as the Hemingway hero's deeper wound, "a secret and ambivalent language about repression and infantile longings, mother love, and a desire for mergence with the feminine" (216). This deeper, more personal wound evokes the loveless marriages, nonnurturing mothers, and defeated, will-less fathers of Hemingway's Nick Adams stories and the painful adolescent experience of Vonnegut's Rudy Waltz and Wilbur Swain. Until Billy and Frederic Henry face taboo fears and desires that link the traumas of childhood with the wounds of war, accessing the buried or denied feminine, they invite the fate of Nick and Rudy, and that of their immediate predecessors, Jake Barnes of *The Sun Also Rises* (1926) and Howard Campbell of *Mother Night* (1961), the former impotent, the latter a suicide. By continuing to associate women with death and suffering, cursing life, itself, Henry and Pilgrim move further away than ever from a cure to what ails them.

Yet while *Slaughterhouse-Five* and *A Farewell to Arms* both end on a note of despair, the fact is that it is Vonnegut's greater willingness to explore buried or denied fears and desires that explains the relative affirmation of Vonnegut's text, and which highlights Vonnegut's critique of *A Farewell to Arms* as a novel that retreats from consciousness and authorial responsibility. We must first of all understand that the heroes' deeper wounds—feelings of ambivalence toward, if not a

fear and hatred of, the feminine—result from their authors' own profoundly conflicted feelings of loss and betrayal, the personal reason
for writing that underlies all their work.[5]

For both writers, war becomes an objective correlative for successive personal tragedies, confirming their feeling that death, as readily
as life, was the consequence of sexuality, stirring feelings of hostility
and guilt toward their parents whom they felt powerless to restrain
but compelled to write out. For Hemingway, the loss of Agnes Von
Kurowsky's love, the ensuing loss of Grace Hemingway's regard and
approval, the frustrations with Duff Twysden, the loss of Hadley's
love through separation and divorce, and his father's suicide all combine to intensify his most buried anxieties about death and sex. As
Spilka explains, Hemingway despairingly concludes that either one
will somehow kill marriage, as the author had done with his own first
marriage, or it will kill you, or at least emasculate you, as his mother
had emasculated his father. In either case, "death and destruction
arrive in the end" (221–22).

Similarly, numerous personal blows surrounding the writing of
Slaughterhouse-Five activate in Vonnegut what Eliot Rosewater's doctor in *God Bless You Mr. Rosewater* calls "the most massively defended
neurosis I've ever seen" (17). Billy Pilgrim and Eliot Rosewater share a
mental ward partly because of what they have seen in war (Vonnegut,
Slaughterhouse-Five 101), but also because of unresolved hostilities
toward their parents, feelings of fear and guilt associated with the
financial failures and emotional collapse of Vonnegut's father, the suicide of Vonnegut's mother, the allied firebombing of Dresden, the
death of Vonnegut's sister, Alice, from cancer within hours of her
husband's death in a train crash, and a sense of futility about the
Vietnam War that significantly deepens Vonnegut's pessimism. These
are the real-life events that produce what Spilka calls the "hidden
agenda" of these novels, taboo desires and fears submerged or denied
because, in Ann Putnam's words, they are too "dangerous...forbid-
den, and fraught with sorrow" (126).

It is this conflicted state of mind that causes Billy and Frederic
Henry to reject women who represent female parts of themselves,
particularly the mother figure who in real life has forsaken them, yet
for whom they feel repressed infantile longings. Spilka explains that
even though Hemingway expressed the belief his mother destroyed
his father, he must have longed for her approval, feeling a need both
to reject and to be wanted (125). While Hemingway's mother in
Farewell is conspicuous by her absence, we know Hemingway has
her in mind from the angry sentiments Hemingway removed from

the final text: "But what if you were born loving nothing and the warm milk of your mother's breast was never heaven" (qtd. in Spilka 129). Spilka observes that Hemingway's wounded feelings toward his mother began in "passive resentment," then hardened into permanent adolescent hatred (123).

By contrast, Vonnegut's mother, whom Vonnegut chides numerous times for her coldness and insensitivity,[6] appears prominently in *Slaughterhouse-Five* in scenes that represent severely repressed Oedipal desires. Just as Billy is being undressed and deloused as a prisoner of war, feeling his penis shriveled and his testicles retracting, he thinks of his mother.

> And Billy zoomed back in time to his infancy. He was a baby who had just been bathed by his mother. Now his mother wrapped him in a towel, carried him into a rosy room that was filled with sunshine. She wrapped him, laid him on the tickling towel, powdered him between the legs, joked with him, patted his little jelly belly. Her palm on his little jelly belly made potching sounds. Billy gurgled and cooed. (84–85)

Billy's long suppressed desire for his mother emerges in guilty reactions to her presence at his hospital bedside after he commits himself to a mental hospital during his senior year at the Illium School of Optometry. He feels himself getting "much sicker" at her approach and pulls the covers over his head until she goes away. He becomes disoriented at the sight of her lipstick-smeared cigarettes on the bedside table.

Billy recoils from his mother because, like the mother figure in Hemingway's fiction, she is insipid, materialistic, and morally obtuse, but he is mystified that his aversion, his embarrassment and weakness in her presence, should be so strong simply because she gave him life (102). We are reminded of Paul Proteus' Oedipal breast and womb fixations in *Player Piano*, which cause him to confuse his wife's bosom with his mother's,[7] and cause him to see his vision of an angry, punishing father as he dreams of awakening in the night alongside his mother-wife (246). Billy fails to associate fears of his father's aggression (throwing him into the deep end of the YMCA swimming pool, then taking him to the rim of the Grand Canyon) with Oedipal desire for his mother conveyed by the womb/vortex imagery of rims and dark, foreboding holes. It is notably at his mother's touch that Billy wets himself. Montana Wildhack, a surrogate mother in Billy's Tralfamadorian fantasy, later causes Billy to have wet dreams (Vonnegut, *Slaughterhouse-Five* 134).

In Montana Wildhack, Billy produces an imaginary woman, an onanistic dream who can do him no harm. Catherine Barkley, however, is a very real part of Frederic Henry, partly the mother-goddess carrying associations of maternal solicitude and sympathy, but also the terribly real mother he is bound to fear and reject.[8] Confined to his hospital bed, Frederic lives out Billy Pilgrim's fantasy of being tended to like a baby in its bassinet, comforted by female caretakers, particularly the caring, maternal Catherine. For a while his wounds allow Frederic to enjoy his childlike vulnerability, free of associations of weakness, fragility, or, more troublesome yet, feelings of being female. Even the lovemaking that takes place in his hospital room at night is pleasantly passive, where he assumes the conventional female position as Catherine lies on top. Catherine's tender ministrations return us to her role as someone who nurtures and guides, with whom fused identities represent the Jungian quest for union that balances male and female aspects of soul.[9] Spilka explains that Catherine's efforts to teach Frederic the value of womanly caring manifests the very trait Grace Hemingway expected of Ernest and taught him to show his sisters. It was an ideal formed also by Clarence Hemingway's medical world, where male and female caring intermix, and by his own experience as a caring Red Cross corpsman who recovered from war wounds in a Milan hospital (Hemingway, *Farewell* 212). From Millicent Bell's perspective, Frederic's efforts to access the feminine through Catherine—to become the more womanly man we now know Hemingway secretly desired to be[10]—is as inauthentic as Pilgrim's fantasized relationship with Montana Wildhack. Frederic, Bell explains, only delusively attaches himself to an "otherness" (121), what Ann Putnam calls "the bountiful mother" (114) the hero must harmonize with rather than attempt to master or destroy.

Yet while Henry and Pilgrim fail at this point in their struggle with the suppressed feminine, it is the subtle difference in narrative frames that most importantly distinguishes Vonnegut's more positive vision from Hemingway's—his greater success at exorcising his demons and healing his complex wounds—and that crystallizes Vonnegut's essential critique of Hemingway's novel. While both retrospective narratives distance the teller of the story from the protagonist, the Frederic Henry who narrates *A Farewell to Arms,* presumably after the same ten-year interval that defines Hemingway's writing of the novel, bears significantly closer resemblance to his author than does Billy Pilgrim to Vonnegut. As we have seen, Vonnegut enacts his duty dance with death by repudiating the conscienceless apathy of his hero, opening himself to the female within. Hemingway, on the other hand, resists humanizing awareness that might mend his wounded psyche, retreating from the feminine while sanctioning aggression as a way to live "humanly" in the world.

When Frederic declares that even after Catherine's death, there are still things he cannot tell (Hemingway, *Farewell* 14), we may surmise this includes a deeper analysis of the forces underlying masculine pretense. Continuing to equate the female mother with suffering and death, the protagonist retreats into further pessimism and an increasing propensity for violence, failing what Bell calls "the responsibilities of response" (qtd. in Spilka 221). Spilka observes that for the next ten years, Hemingway will turn to the problem of "shoring up his own male identity" (215). Conversely, whereas Hemingway kills off the extremely female Catherine so that he may save his male identity, Vonnegut eliminates Billy Pilgrim as a symbolic repudiation of male aggression, more specifically, the passivity that allows aggression to happen. Vonnegut is careful to dissociate himself from Billy as from no character before, signaled by the fact that the author speaks to us directly about the impact of the war on him in the important first chapter and the fact that with references such as "I was there" and "that was me," he personally turns up in the narrative four times. Billy, like Frederic, may choose to close his eyes to unpleasantness, but Billy's regress is Vonnegut's progress. The true hero of *Slaughterhouse-Five* is the author himself, the revelation of which Vonnegut remarks in *Breakfast of Champions*: "I see a man who is terribly wounded, because he has dared to pass through the fires of truth to the other side, which we have never seen. And then he has come back again to tell us about the other side" (180). If Hemingway dodges the responsibilities of thoughtful response, Vonnegut embraces what Doris Lessing calls "the ambiguities of complicity" (351), causing the reader to think carefully about degrees of responsibility for violence and injustice (qtd. in *Sanity Plea* 212).

With the help of Phoebe Hurty in *Breakfast of Champions*, that mother surrogate who at the spiritual crossroads of his life helped him develop the necessary moral sense and faith in human development to survive the Great Depression, Vonnegut no longer identifies women with death and destruction. Rather, Phoebe Hurty represents the feminine will to love and serve, the projection of anima we see in Catherine Barkley, but is here embraced rather than dismissed. Whereas Hemingway's rejection of Catherine precludes the possibility of inner wholeness, Kathyrn Hume argues that Vonnegut's exorcism of the mother that once so contaminated his picture of women allows him to accept the creative female principle in himself and espouse "a more active response to the hurts of the world" (qtd. in *Sanity Plea* 199). It is perhaps the great personal depression Vonnegut has survived that *Slaughterhouse-Five* (and *Breakfast of Champions* [1973]) are most about, and that best explains Hemingway as Vonnegut's bête noire, the troubled and troubling Secret Sharer of Vonnegut's literary imagination. Vonnegut purposefully targets Hemingway as he does Billy Pilgrim, Kilgore Trout, and Kurt Vonnegut Senior, as the embattled author's chief scapegoats, carrying his heaviest burden of trauma and despair. Hemingway is the Jungian "shadow," the dark side of himself he knows he must not become, symbolic of flight from the primal mother, and the unconscious aggression and cruelty Vonnegut believes will eventually destroy the world. Vonnegut's willingness to look deeply into his own *Mother Night* shows him that Billy Pilgrim's passivity, Hemingway's fatalism, Frederic Henry's violence all represent the same universal will to destruction. With the specter of Hemingway's suicide never far from mind, Vonnegut believes that resisting the pull of his defeatist self was necessary, not only to fulfilling his role as canary bird in the coalmine, but to life itself.

In Volume IV of Michael Reynolds' authoritative biography of Hemingway's life, *Hemingway: The 1930s*, Reynolds confirms judgments I had made twenty some years earlier in *Hemingway's Spanish Tragedy* (1973) that the author's assumption of an increasingly belligerent, tough-guy public persona threatened to harden permanently into the caricature of Hemingway later portrayed as Harold Ryan in *Happy Birthday Wanda June*, obscuring the more complex human being beneath. In the wake of *Wanda June* (1971), Vonnegut's fiction from *Breakfast of Champions* to *Timequake* becomes not only a critical rejoinder to a world of violence and death but a rebuttal of Hemingway's response, the Hemingway who equates manhood with heroic comportment, and who associates emotional and artistic integrity with the killing of animals. As if to bear out Vonnegut's indictment, not only does Hemingway not say "farewell" to violence and aggression with the death of Catherine Barkley, in the immediate works to follow, *Death in the Afternoon* (1932) and *Green Hills of Africa* (1935), he defines himself and his literary aspirations in markedly masculine terms.[11] In *Green Hills of Africa*, as if to revenge himself upon that cruel mother for birthing him into the Garden he would only lose, Hemingway not only takes delight in killing big animals for pleasure but determines to become an even better killer than the beasts of the jungle. In Spilka's views, these texts become a veritable handbook for manly violence and heroic behavior, the crux of Vonnegut's critique of Hemingway as a hunter and a lover of blood sports. In *The Young Hemingway* Reynolds suggests that the author, invents the man he wished to be or have people believe he was from his earliest days in Oak Park: a warrior; an outlaw; a rough character, capable of extreme violence; a man always in control, always all-knowing, competent; a man who is never weak, uncertain, self-doubting, insecure, or afraid of anything. It was a mask, Reynolds suggests, and Vonnegut believes, that was no longer removable. Vonnegut, we recall, sees Hemingway trapped in a "forest" of machismo, an aggressively male persona that undermines Hemingway's personal and artistic growth and contributes to his tragic death (*The Young Hemingway*).

If Vonnegut were right that Hemingway was written out after *The Old Man and the Sea*, there might be little more to say of Hemingway as a brutalized and artistically diminished writer who could go only so far in examining his deepest needs and anxieties. Yet if Vonnegut had read Hemingway's posthumous works—*Islands in the Stream* (1970), The *Garden of Eden* (1986), and *Under Kilimanjaro* (1999)— he would have found Hemingway engaged in an increasingly open conversation with the suppressed "other" dramatically like his own. In fact, Hemingway's work from *For Whom the Bell Tolls* to *Under Kilimanjaro*, like Vonnegut's from *Slapstick* to *Hocus Pocus*, is similarly about confession, redemption, and rebirth, distinguished by the hero's willingness to access what Jung calls "dangerous knowledge" about himself, knowing "what I myself desire" (85). I believe that Hemingway's self-critical introspection in these works, especially his struggle to understand the richly ambiguous gender potentialities or contraries within himself,[12] suggests creative as well as moral advance, greater risk than all the bullfights Hemingway ever saw. The grand irony of Vonnegut's critique, then, is that Hemingway himself produces the reborn and reformed author Vonnegut imagines as the end of *Wanda June*. He creates an androgynous hero who not only does not celebrate *cajones* power but interrogates and distances himself from the hunter, the matador, the predator in himself, and whose moments of truth have less to do with physical confrontation than with facing the stresses in his own divided nature. Jung explains that recognizing and accepting the feminine aspects of the split persona requires a moral effort beyond ordinary, painstaking, psychotherapeutic work, extending over a long period of time (165). It requires the courage of the tragic hero, in this case, the willingness to not only acknowledge the destructive consequences of the masked anima but to recognize that the tragedy originates in himself. Such self-understanding may have come to Hemingway at a slower, more gradual rate, but raising the Jungian "shadow" of self-doubt and feminine denial to consciousness is exactly the achievement of Kurt Vonnegut and his Secret Sharer, Ernest Hemingway.

NOTES

1. James Jones, author of *From Here to Eternity*, told Vonnegut that he did not consider Hemingway a fellow soldier since Hemingway had never submitted to training and discipline either in World War II or in the Spanish civil war (*Fates* 61). Vonnegut quips in *Palm Sunday* that Irwin Shaw's *The Young Lions* was such a good book that it made Hemingway mad: "He thought he had copyrighted war" (138).

2. Hemingway sustained a physical injury at Fossalta, Italy in World War I, while Vonnegut suffered psychological trauma as a result of his experiences in Dresden, Germany during World War II.

3. John Killinger explains how violence reveals the absurd for characters like Henry and Pilgrim. The individual's awareness of the contrast between reality and ideal expectation produces Sartre's "nausea," a palpable spiritual disgust the hero experiences as early as the Indian camp episode of Nick Adams and the accidental murder of a pregnant housewife by Rudy Waltz.

4. In *Green Hills of Africa*, Hemingway argues that war was a vital part of his education as man and artist, and that no writer should be without it. He cites Tolstoi as someone war benefited inestimably and Thomas Wolfe as a writer who missed something irreplaceable (50).

5. Philip Young, Robert Penn Warren, and Millicent Bell concur that Hemingway's main text was always profoundly personal, a projection of problems in Hemingway's secret inner life he was deeply concerned to write about, and write out.

6. Though Vonnegut eventually reconciles with the mother figure in his work, in a way that eludes Hemingway, both mothers represent what I call the Black Widow, someone painfully insensitive to the adolescent protagonist's emotional needs.

7. See *Sanity Plea* 24.

8. Jung explains that the loving or terrible mother of mythology, saint or whore, associated with both light and darkness, draws the male protagonist into life's "frightful paradoxes" (170).

9. Jung stresses the artist's need to embrace the feminine to forge a more hopeful and integrated disposition. He contends that, "Just as a man brings forth his work as a complete creation out of his feminine inner nature, so the inner masculine side of a woman brings forth creative seeds which have the power to fertilize the feminine side of the man" (98).

10. In *Strange Tribe*, John Hemingway argues persuasively that Hemingway's work was always about trying to get in touch with his feminine side—in Jungian terms, to achieve a balance between the masculine animus and female anima. He praises the recent work of scholars like Carl Eby, Nancy Comley, Rose Marie Burwell, and Debra Moddelmog for bringing to light what the author had been hinting about for years, the strongly resisted desire to be a woman.

11. Thomas Strychacz discusses Hemingway's richly complex management of "competing possibilities" of a masculine/feminine split in his main characters. He sees the attraction to violence and power in protagonists like Frederic Henry undercut by what he calls a feminine "counter-masculinity" (122), a process that functions in *Death in the Afternoon* in subtle, surprising ways.

12. Scholars like Rose Marie Burwell and Robert Fleming agree with Vonnegut that Hemingway's later work, particularly his posthumous novels and stories, represent artistic decline, arguing that the defensive mask of machismo prevented the ailing writer from pushing far enough into the process of vigorous self-examination of conflicts that might have added even more to the stature of his life's work. I suggest we evaluate the posthumous works not for what Hemingway didn't do, but in light of his continuing efforts to understand and resolve the painful divisions within himself.

Works Cited

Bell, Millicent. "Pseudoautobiography and Personal Metaphor." *Ernest Hemingway's* A Farewell to Arms. Modern Critical Interpretations. Ed. Harold Bloom. New York: Chelsea, 1987. 113–29.

Benson, Jackson, ed. *The Short Stories of Ernest Hemingway*. Durham: Duke UP, 1975.

Broer, Lawrence. *Hemingway's Spanish Tragedy*. Tuscaloosa: U of Alabama P, 1973.

———. *Sanity Plea: Schizophrenia in the Novels of Kurt Vonnegut*. Tuscaloosa: U of Alabama P, 1994.

———. "Vonnegut's Goodbye: Kurt Senior, Hemingway, and Kilgore Trout." *At Millennium's End: New Essays on the Work of Kurt Vonnegut*. Ed. Kevin Boon. Albany: State U of New York P, 2001. 65–90.

Erlich, Richard. "Unpublished Teaching Notes to *Slaughterhouse-Five*." Teaching notes. Dept. of English, Miami (of Ohio) University.

Hemingway, Ernest. *Death in the Afternoon*. New York: Scribner's, 1932.

———. *A Farewell to Arms*. New York: Scribner's, 1929.

———. *For Whom the Bell Tolls*. New York: Scribner's, 1940.

———. *From Here to Eternity*. New York: Scribner's, 1976.

———. *Garden of Eden*. New York: Scribner's, 1986.

———. *Green Hills of Africa*. New York: Doubleday, 1954.

———. *Islands in the Stream*. New York: Scribner's, 1970.

————. "A Natural History of the Dead." *The Complete Short Stories of Ernest Hemingway.* New York: Scribner's, 1987. 335–41.

————. *The Old Man and the Sea.* New York: Scribner's, 1987.

————. "On the Quai at Smyrna." *The Complete Short Stories of Ernest Hemingway.* New York: Scribner's, 1987. 63–64.

————. *The Short Stories of Ernest Hemingway.* New York: Scribner's, 1927.

————. *The Sun Also Rises.* New York: Scribner's, 1926.

————. "Today is Friday." *The Complete Short Stories of Ernest Hemingway.* New York: Scribner's, 1987. 271–73.

————. *Under Kilimanjaro.* Kent: Kent State UP, 1995.

Hemingway, John. *Strange Tribe: A Family Memoir.* Connecticut: Lyons, 2007.

Hume, Kathryn. "Vonnegut's Self-projections: Symbolic Characters and Symbolic Fiction." *The Journal of Narrative Technique* 12.3 (1982): 177–90.

Jung, C.G. *Aspects of the Feminine.* Trans. R.F.C. Hull. Princeton: Princeton UP, 1982.

Keogh, J.G., and Edmund Kislaitis. "*Slaughterhouse-Five* and the Future of Science Fiction." *Media and Methods* Jan.1971: 38–40.

Killinger, John. *Hemingway and the Dead Gods: A Study in Existentialism.* Lexington: U of Kentucky P, 1960.

Lessing, Doris. "Vonnegut's Responsibility." *The New York Times Book Review* 4 Feb. 1973: 35.

Martin, Linda Wagner. "The Romance of Desire in Hemingway's Fiction." *Hemingway and Women: Female Critics and the Female Voice.* Ed. Lawrence Broer and Gloria Holland. Tuscaloosa: U of Alabama P, 2002. 54–69.

McConnel, Frank. "Stalking Papa's Ghost: Hemingway's Presence in Contemporary American Writing." *Wilson Quarterly* 10.1 (1986): 160–73.

Putnam, Ann. "On Defiling Eden: The Search for Eve in the Garden of Sorrows." *Hemingway and Women: Female Critics and The Female Voice.* Ed. Gloria Holland and Lawrence Broer. Tuscaloosa: U of Alabama P, 2002. 109–30.

Rackstraw, Loree. "Dancing with the Muse in Vonnegut's Later Novels." *The Vonnegut Chronicles: Interviews and Essays.* Ed. Peter J. Reed and Marc Leeds. Wesport: Greenwood, 1996. 123–45.

Reynolds, Michael S. *Hemingway: The 1930s.* New York: Norton, 1997.

————. *Hemingway: The Final Years.* New York: Norton, 1999.

————. *Hemingway's First War: The Making of* A Farewell to Arms. Princeton: Princeton UP, 1976.

Rovit, Earl, and Gerry Brenner. *Ernest Hemingway.* Rev. ed. TUSAS 41. Boston: Twayne, 1986.

Shaw, Irwin. *The Young Lions.* London: Hodder, 2008.

Spanier, Sandra Whipple. "Hemingway's Unknown Soldier: Catherine Barkley, the Critics, and the Great War." *New Essays on* A Farewell to Arms. Ed. Scott Donaldson. New York: Cambridge UP, 1990. 75–108.

Spilka, Mark. *Hemingway's Quarrel with Androgyny*. Lincoln: U of Nebraska P, 1990.

Strychacz, Thomas. *Hemingway's Theaters of Masculinity*. Baton Rouge: Louisiana State UP, 2003.

Swift, Jonathan. *A Tale of a Tub and Other Works*. New York: Oxford UP, 2008.

Tetlow, Wendolyn E. *Hemingway's In Our Time: Lyrical Dimensions*. Lewisburg: Buckness UP, 1992.

Tilton, John. *Cosmic Satire in the Contemporary Novel*. Lewisburg: Bucknell UP, 1977.

Vonnegut, Kurt. *Breakfast of Champions*. New York: Dell, 1975.

———. *Deadeye Dick*. New York: Delacorte-Seymour Lawrence, 1982.

———. *Fates Worse than Death: An Autobiographical Collage*. New York: Berkley, 1992.

———. *Happy Birthday, Wanda June*. New York: Delacorte-Seymour Lawrence, 1971.

———. *Jailbird*. New York: Delacorte, 1979.

———. *Mother Night*. 1961. New York: Dell, 1974.

———. *Palm Sunday*. New York: Delacorte, 1981.

———. *Slapstick*. New York: Dell, 1976.

———. *Slaughterhouse-Five*. 1969. New York: Dell, 1972.

———. *Timequake*. London: Vintage, 1998.

Waldhorn, Arthur. *A Reader's Guide to Ernest Hemingway*. New York: Octabon, 1981.

Warren, Robert Penn. Introduction. *A Farewell to Arms*. New York: Scribner's, 1929.

Young, Philip. *Ernest Hemingway*. Minneapolis: Minnesota UP, 1965.

CHAPTER 11

"Somewhere in There Was Springtime": Kurt Vonnegut, His Apocalypses, and His Post-9/11 Heirs

Chris Glover

INTRODUCTION

In 1970 Kurt Vonnegut spoke at the graduation ceremony at Bennington College in Vermont.[1] As was typical of Vonnegut, he drew heavily on his life experience in his remarks, talking about the events surrounding the destruction of Dresden; yet on this particular occasion, the author also spoke about the atomic bombs in Japan, the fall of Biafra (which he had narrowly escaped), and the events in Vietnam (at that time beginning to demand worldwide attention). Not surprisingly, he chastised Americans and their government for allowing such historical mistakes to repeat themselves. Curiously, though, he also hid this comment amidst the rant:

> I know that millions of dollars have been spent to produce this splendid graduating class, and that the main hope of your teachers was, once they got through with you, that you would no longer be superstitious. I'm sorry—I have to undo that now. I beg you to believe in the most ridiculous superstition of all: that humanity is at the center of the universe, the fulfiller or the frustrator of the grandest dreams of God Almighty.
>
> If you can believe that, and make others believe it, then there might be hope for us. Human beings might stop treating each other like garbage, might begin to treasure and protect each other instead. Then it might be all right to have babies again. (qtd. in *Wampeters, Foma, and Granfalloons* 163–64)

In the same speech, Vonnegut goes on to explain that while science may have damaged the credibility of some of the supposedly literal stories of the Bible (Adam and Eve, Jonah), most of the overall principles have the potential to still ring true, "particularly the lessons about fairness and gentleness" (166). True, a hefty number of self-proclaimed religious believers have betrayed the very values they have professed over the millennia (the crusades seem like a more-than-adequate example of this; Vonnegut himself wrote that "Earthlings who have felt that the Creator clearly wanted this or that have almost always been pigheaded and cruel"[2]), but this should not be taken as a knock against the values themselves. The values, claimed Vonnegut, hold up nicely; rather, it is those who claim to value those values who are often problematic.

Kurt Vonnegut was no Christian. He has been described by critics as a nihilist and by himself as an atheist, a humanist, and an incorrigible pessimist. But he was not admonishing these recent graduates to convert; rather, he saw a common set of religious beliefs or values as a means to an end. He said numerous times that what drove many of his novels was his desire to give a voice to the notion that humanity's—in particular, America's—love affair with technological (read: superficial) improvement is a poor substitute for interpersonal relationships.[3] What humans call progress has come at the expense of its soul; technological development occurs in inverse proportion to human connectedness. He wrote elsewhere that if Americans were indiscriminately given new middle names, people assigned to these new "families" would, regardless of how artificial those families may be, come together and embrace their new brothers and sisters. A common religion, be it Christianity, Islam, Voodoo, or even some bizarre, otherworldly mythology, would perform the same unifying act as astrological signs or bogus middle names, and even provide a set of guiding principles in the process. Over and over in his novels, Vonnegut maintains that what will bring humanity together is an acceptance of its role vis-à-vis the universe and the importance of its bond to itself: the sagacious beings from Trafalmadore appear in *Slaughterhouse-Five* (1969) and *The Sirens of Titan* (1959) and teach a few of us about our insignificance in the galactic scheme; chemical imbalances plague the citizens of Midland City in *Breakfast of Champions* (1973), evidence of our vulnerability to things outside of our control (or even knowledge); our common destiny as the playthings of fate and the creations of our own stupidity figures heavily in such novels as *Galapagos* (1985), *Deadeye Dick* (1982), and *Timequake* (1997). Finding religion, then, is not the desired goal, although it certainly would help.

Readers and critics of Kurt Vonnegut have long found it difficult to discern "the real Vonnegut" amidst the serious polemics and the famously dark humor, and between the science fiction stories and the opinion pieces. Yet, central to much of Vonnegut's output is the notion of hope. In a piece that appears in Vonnegut's final work, the nonfictional *A Man without a Country* (2005), Vonnegut notes that in his octogenarian years, as he observes the "guessers" (as opposed to the educated and informed) calling the political shots in the nascent years of the twenty-first century, he has experienced a rebirth of pessimism: "What can be said," he asks, "to our young people, now that psychopathic personalities, which is to say persons without consciences, without senses of pity or shame, have taken all the money in the treasuries of our government and corporations, and made it all their own?" (88–89). But he does not end this essay with a rhetorical question as he does in many of his novels; instead, he attempts an answer, even as he undercuts his commentary's power to operate as one, by making an example of Ignaz Semmelweis. Semmelweis, a surgeon who pioneered the practice of washing his hands between surgeries to dramatically reduce the chance of spreading disease, insisted on this practice in the face of severe consequences. Vonnegut knows, as do we of course, that germs are taken seriously by every medical professional in the world now; so by invoking Semmelweis, he challenges us to be pioneers for truth as well, even if, as in Semmelweis' case, it drives us to grief, expatriation, shame, and suicide. In the Bennington address, when he insists that the naïve optimism of his youth has been replaced by the pessimism that accompanies life experience (William Blake would be proud), he shows us that there just might be a way out of the darkness, this pessimism. In one breath he tells his young audience that although they should not concern themselves with saving the world from itself, it is their obligation, and it is within their ability, to help plan for a better future.[4]

In his role as canary in the mine,[5] it was Vonnegut's job to warn us about the future, the vehicle for these warnings being science fiction stories. Often heartbreaking and humorous at the same time, these stories were also incisive, cutting to the very heart of human nature. However, since these stories featured the characteristic elements of science fiction, elements on par with those of pulp fiction, these stories were not viewed with the serious critical treatment reserved for more "legitimate" literature. Shortly after the release of *Slaughterhouse-Five*, Robert Scholes claimed that "serious critics have shown some reluctance to acknowledge that Vonnegut is among the best writers of his generation. He is, I suspect, too funny and too intelligent for many" (Merrill 38). Scholes might well have included "and because he is thought of as a science fiction writer" as a reason too, since his books often included such hallmarks of that niche like space aliens, other planets, time travel, extrasensory perception, and, what will be the focus of this chapter, apocalypse. By the time Vonnegut began to employ these subjects and tropes, they had been somewhat discredited due to their association with B-movies, comic books, and other genres that were perceived as subpar. The Trafalmadorians might as well have been the stock space aliens of the 1950s, come to Earth in flying saucers from a distant world to challenge our nationalism, conquer our planet, and frighten our women.[6] But Vonnegut infamously recoiled from the "science fiction" label—"I have been a sore-headed occupant of a file drawer labeled 'science fiction,'" he wrote in an essay called simply "Science Fiction" that appears in *Wampeters, Foma, and Granfalloons,* "and I would like out, particularly since so many serious critics regularly mistake the drawer for a urinal" (1)—because to him, it connoted a lack of seriousness, and he felt he could be frightfully serious if the subject matter warranted it. And of course, as any serious student of Vonnegut knows, his novels are less about the fantastic than about the human.

Part One: Vonnegut the Apocalptycist

In 1985 Charles Berryman, referring to Vonnegut, asked, "Is there another contemporary novelist more concerned with visions of destruction and mortality?" (99). As support for this rhetorical question, Berryman cites destructive evidence from several of Vonnegut's novels, some of which I will examine here. Apocalyptic events of one sort frequently serve either as backdrops for the worlds he creates or as key moments the plots lead to. Given his personal history and the world scene at the time Vonnegut did most of his writing—major and minor wars in far-off places, certainly, but also the cold war at home; Vonnegut lived the bulk of his adult life under the threat of possible nuclear annihilation—little wonder that his characters frequently find themselves facing extinction in some manner.

Before proceeding, it is important to note the inherently misleading nature of the term "apocalypse." While it suggests the end of the world as we know it, it is true to say that no apocalyptic tale would be complete without survivors, their stories, and sometimes, in the more overtly didactic ones, the conveyance of moral lessons. Peter Freese notes that apocalypticists are less interested in the specifics of humanity's ultimate end and more interested in who can survive it and how a "new beginning can be wrested from an all-embracing apocalypse, in the redirection of evolutionary processes" (163). An apocalypse like Vonnegut's is less The End than "a story that begins with the very end and sounds out possibilities of a new beginning" (Freese 164). Indeed, the sounding out of those possibilities is for our benefit, positioning us, as interpreters of the text, as arbiters of humanity's future. Commenting from a religious standpoint, John R. May writes that "apocalyptic literature, moreover, uses the mythic framework of the regeneration of the world as a macrocosmic idiom for another important Christian concern, the *metanoia* [fundamental transformative change] of the individual" (23). Furthermore, Douglas Robinson notes that "one of the most revealing cultural facts to be noted about the American preoccupation with the apocalypse is that it has always been forcefully contested" (3). From Michael Wigglesworth's 1662 poem *The Day of Doom* to F. Scott Fitzgerald's 1920 novel *This Side of Paradise* (and well beyond), the literal End of the World has always been a useful metaphor, used to offer didactic lessons about the importance of living a proper life.

Vonnegut, in his fiction as in his nonfiction, often found a way to undercut his vision of The End by allowing for the possibility of hope. In this way he helped to pave the way for contemporary writers to present an apocalypse that includes a degree of positivity. In the years following the events of 9/11, a new subgenre has begun to emerge on the literary landscape, one driven by a need to explicate the horror of the terrorist attacks and the subsequent violence, both physical and psychological, we continue to suffer. While novels like Ian McEwen's *Saturday* (2005) and John Updike's *Terrorist* (2006) use 9/11 as plot devices to various degrees in order to serve as reminders of the world we inhabit now, other novels like Ken Kalfus's *A Disorder Peculiar to the Country* (2006) and Don DeLillo's *Falling Man* (2007) detail the relationship fallout of 9/11 survivors and empower their protagonists by giving them choices about what forms their reconstructed lives might take rather than forcing them to make the best of an authorially created situation. In this way "post-9/11 fiction" represents a rebirth of the American obsession with apocalyptic fiction, or, put differently, a refocusing of apocalyptic fiction in the light of a world-altering event that allows for—even demands—such focus. Interestingly, modern writers have taken up Vonnegut's banner of hope in seemingly hopeless times.

What makes this development in the novel so attractive to modern writers may be that it enables invention—or, perhaps more accurately, rearrangement. The postapocalyptic novel in which humanity has been reduced to its barest elements gives writers the freedom to mold society in their image. Leonard Mustazza divides Western culture's shared creation myth, presented in the early chapters of Genesis, into three parts: Creation, Innocence, and the Fall. So many modern writers, Vonnegut among them, pick up at the point in the narrative that exists at the precipice of Innocence. This is the moment of fascination, the moment in which human potential experiences its fullest spectrum of possibility. Mustazza, writing about the characters in Vonnegut's *Cat's Cradle* (1963) who, having survived the world-altering effects of the introduction of the destructive element *ice-nine* into the ecosystem by hiding among the ruins of a destroyed castle, emerge from the remains to discover that they are among a very few left alive on a new and frightening planet, says that

> Like other characters in Vonnegut's fiction, they are constantly pursuing geneses, beginnings, new ways of looking at life, and like the God of Genesis, they are constantly engaged in coaxing some kind of form and order out of the chaos around them. Unlike God, however, they seem often to have little or no control over the outcomes of their inventions, nor do they seem to take much responsibility for those inventions. (76)

Mustazza's first point, that characters in Vonnegut novels are often put in situations that force them to adapt to and, in a sense, create the specifics of their reality, is well-taken and can be applied not only to the work of Vonnegut but also to other, more contemporary works. His second point, however, is not so broadly applied; characters may not have divine control over the events they initiate, but they often do dictate the initial terms of those events' outcomes, as I hope to show a little later.

In "Why They Read Hesse"[7] Vonnegut closes by talking about Hitler's Germany, suggesting that "The next holocaust will leave the planet uninhabitable....Not only would *Steppenwolf* be homesick on some other planet. He would die" (*Wampeters, Foma, and Granfalloons* 115). However, not all holocausts or apocalypses are global; oftentimes, they are limited to one person. In Nicole Krauss' recent novel, *Man Walks into a Room* (2002), for example, Greene's apocalypse is the test atomic blast; it kills no one but changes his entire world dramatically. In Vonnegut the personal apocalypse figures heavily in *Breakfast of Champions*. As early as the first chapter, he sets his audience up to believe that something on a far grander scale is going to happen. The novel principally concerns Dwayne Hoover, owner of a Pontiac dealership in Midland City and a man who we know from page one is on the verge of insanity (Vonnegut is never one to keep his plot points a secret); but a character who at first appears to play a minor role, the author Kilgore Trout, is only a few pages later seen musing, " 'Any time now.... And high time, too.' It was Trout's theory that the atmosphere would become unbreathable soon" (18). This is not an objective analysis by Trout, either: Vonnegut tells us explicitly that Trout believed "that humanity deserved to die horribly, since it had behaved so cruelly and wastefully on a planet so sweet" (18). Those unfamiliar with the world and style of Kurt Vonnegut may be led to believe that the novel is in danger of unfolding in a painfully predictable manner: the audience knows who the protagonist is and what will happen to him, who the most pivotal minor character is, and what type of event just might be foreshadowed by Trout's end-of-the-world talk. Later in the novel, Trout describes coming to the realization "that God wasn't any conservationist," citing volcanoes, tornadoes, and "the Ice Ages he arranges for every half-million years" as proof that the natural progression of things is on a declining arc toward destruction (85).

But the world does not end in *Breakfast of Champions*; Kilgore Trout is wrong, at least for now. The only thing that explodes is Dwayne Hoover, just as we were told he would, but nothing else. (Vonnegut has said in interviews that his study of body chemistry coincided with his writing of *Breakfast*.) After reading one of Trout's books, Dwayne is convinced that his life is the only one with meaning and that he is the only creature on earth with free will, and once this last bit of information clicks into place, his sudden spree of madness and violence begins. After it is over, Dwayne's formerly successful life is destroyed, and Dwayne himself is consigned to the local mental ward. By Vonnegut's own admission, *Breakfast* is not one of his better books; in *Palm Sunday*, his 1981 collection of previously unpublished material, he gave it a grade of "C." Indeed, toward the end of the novel, the thrust of the book shifts radically away from Dwayne Hoover's solipsistic crisis, and the last few chapters focus instead on Vonnegut's authorial intrusion into his own fictional world and his creator/creation relationship with Kilgore Trout. *Breakfast of Champions* may not be one of Vonnegut's finest, but it does exemplify the hopeless personal apocalypse: Dwayne Hoover's previous life is over, ruined by one book (written by a hack) in one night.

The personal apocalypse of *Mother Night* (1961) is a more explicitly gradual one. One of the themes running throughout *Mother Night* is that responsibility is not easily shirked. Vonnegut plays the role of editor for the fictional Howard W. Campbell, Jr., in this novel, providing the framework for (and, therefore, the lens through which to view) Campbell's jail cell biography/confession/suicide note. The moral of the story, says the "Vonnegut" of the introduction, is that "we are what we pretend to be, so we must be careful what we pretend to be" (v). In the case of "Vonnegut"'s subject, Campbell pretends to be, and so is, an accomplice to world war. That Campbell is unknowingly and constantly manipulated by forces greater than he—the Nazi regime, the American government, George Kraft, Resi Noth—bespeaks a more significant comment, offered up by authorial intent (rather than editorial commentary), which is that these two behavioral traits, stupidity and manipulation, work in destructive tandem.

Howard W. Campbell is a nobody. Jerome Klinkowitz says that he "acts out an Ionesco drama"; he and real-life Nazis Rudolph Hoess, Heinrich Himmler, and Adolf Eichmann are presented in their "utter banality," ironically underscoring their claims as regular people, nothing special (83). As two horrible truths begin to dawn on Campbell, that as a man without convictions, he was duped and that as an American agent, he was actually more of a Nazi puppet since he did his job a little *too* convincingly, his conscience catches up with him. Finally, he finds himself a captured prisoner of war in an Israeli prison cell. He has been a coconspirator in death on a massive scale, and he is about to play a part in one last death, his own. Campbell's closing words are of his resolution to hang himself in his cell rather than face a trial, and he closes by writing, "I *know* that tonight is the night.... Goodbye, cruel world! *Auf Wiedersehen?*" (Vonnegut, *Mother Night* 268). The fictional Vonnegut does not comment on Campbell's word choice; but the real Vonnegut may have intended some ambiguity here. The second of the two goodbyes, appropriate because of Campbell's (and Vonnegut's) ties to Germany, carries with it the connotation of "until we meet/speak/see each other again." Since the audience can safely trust that Campbell's corpse will not literally rise from the grave, we are left with a figurative interpretation of this phrase; and that it is put across as a question only raises the stakes. Will he see us again? If he is a type of all humanity, will we live to be seen again? And if we do, will we be recognizable? The apocalyptic event, in this case World War II, has come and gone. Both Vonneguts, the author and the proxy editor, leave us with the opportunity to write our own conclusion. The question mark signifies the possibility of hope for humanity.

This glimmer of hope is slightly more pronounced in *The Sirens of Titan*. According to Joseph Sigman ("Science and Parody in Kurt

Vonnegut's *The Sirens of Titan*"), Vonnegut takes out science and faith in one fell swoop. The chronosynclastic infundibula are the agents of discord here; only a universe ungoverned by the comfortable and generally agreed-upon rules of physics could allow for the presence of so strange an anomaly, and only Vonnegut's sense of irony would place them so close to Earth. From a religious standpoint, the discovery of the infundibula is a paradoxical one indeed: although "it was a situation made to order for American fundamentalist preachers" who are "quicker than philosophers or historians or anybody to talk about the truncated Age of Space" (Vonnegut, *Sirens* 26) and how people, in a tradition as old as the Tower of Babel, are guilty of reaching beyond their station. The discovery also leads, at least for Winston Niles Rumfoord, to the truth of humanity's and Earth's astounding—even insulting—unimportance in the cosmic order as a spare-part delivery system for the stuck Trafalmadorian Salo. God figures—Rumfoord himself, whose omniscience turns out to be limited, and the Trafalmadorians, whose creation and manipulation of Earth are often ineffective to say the least—are poor substitutes for an actual deity, and Sigman writes that the end result of all this theological destruction is a "totally relativistic cosmos" (33). However, by the novel's end, Titan becomes a new Eden. The first having been rendered illegitimate, even dishonest, in light of our new knowledge of the Trafalmadorian master plan, humanity's second "first family" lives in isolation on Titan. While their living conditions are far from ideal or biblical, hope lies in Chrono, the boy. Free from Trafalmadorian manipulation and the visitations by Rumfoord, Chrono is no longer influenced by outside forces and instead, following the death of his mother, chooses his own life, living among the mysterious Titanic bluebirds. "Malachi Constant[8] said good-by to her when the sky was filled with Titanic bluebirds.... And in that night in the midst of day, Chrono, the son of Beatrice and Malachi, appeared on a knoll overlooking the new grave. He wore a feather cape which he flapped like wings. He was gorgeous and strong" (Vonnegut, *Sirens* 318). Humanity's path promises to be totally different on Titan.

Like *Breakfast of Champions* and *Mother Night*, *The Sirens of Titan* is another of Vonnegut's novels that features the elimination of one man's good fortune; it also features the darkly humorous recruitment, training, and utter annihilation of the Martian invasion fleet. But the real apocalypse in *Sirens* may be of a theological nature. Sigman notes that the "withdrawal of extra-terrestrial influence [by the end of the novel] is another metaphorical death of God" (34). Furthermore, the attempt to replace a failed religion with a new one,

Rumfoord's establishment of the humanist/Deist Church of God the Utterly Indifferent, is also fraught with difficulty. While the concluding pages end the novel at a bus stop on a snowy street on Earth where Malachi/Unk dies, the more lasting image is of Chrono, the adopted member of the Titanic bluebirds, "the most beautiful creatures in sight" according to Beatrice (Vonnegut, *Sirens* 312).

As on Titan, humanity also promises to be totally different on Earth in *Galapagos* and *Cat's Cradle*. The "humans" in *Galapagos*, if they can be properly identified as such, are the sea-dwelling descendants of the few survivors of a mysterious apocalypse[9] and the result of one of the survivors', Mary Hepburn's, decidedly unscientific genetic tinkering. The first child born in the new Eden on the remote island of Santa Rosalia is named Kamikaze, ostensibly meaning "sacred wind" in Japanese according to the novel's narrator but undeniably laced with an ironic double meaning. After all, since the narrator also believes that the "survival of humankind to the present day" is "miraculous" and "based on luck rather than intelligence" (Vonnegut, *Galapagos* 297), and since this newest iteration of humankind has wriggled free from the shackles of critical thought, examination of history and intelligence, it seems to be only a matter of time before its luck runs out.[10] On the other hand, these "humans" appear satisfied with their lot and have survived a million years past the supposed End of the World, so perhaps this concern over luck is unwarranted. *Cat's Cradle*, another novel featuring an isolated group of remnant humans on an island, is also guilty of a certain amount of ambiguity. The subtitle of elusive philosopher Bokonon's *Fourteenth Book* is "What Can a Thoughtful Man Hope for Mankind on Earth, Given the Experience of the Past Million Years?" The text of the book is a single word: "Nothing" (Vonnegut 245). This is revealed to the reader just before the world's oceans are infected with *ice-nine*. The few survivors, having hidden themselves in what the title of Chapter 117 identifies as a "sanctuary," emerge after seven days to survey the world that humans have created for themselves. While, as in *Galapagos*, humanity persists, this may again not necessarily be a victory. That *Cat's Cradle*'s Dr. Hoenikker, inventor of *ice-nine* and de facto creator of the new world, is not a very good father and raises children who become physically and psychologically impaired adults making questionable choices is surely not insignificant. Bokonon's truths, the foundation of a kind of religion, are simple but often childishly so, rendered in rhymes or songs that do not adequately reflect reality. It would seem that a regression to a less complex, more tribal kind of life would be required for Bokononism to truly catch on. Hope is not as tangible in the postapocalyptic world of *Cat's Cradle,* whereas Vonnegut's other novels suggest a greater possibility of it. In no other novel is this hope among the ruins more apparent than *Slaughterhouse-Five.*

PART TWO: HOPE AMONGST THE RUINS OF DRESDEN, OR, "POO-TEE-WEET?"

In *Beyond the Waste Land* Raymond M. Olderman writes that

> hovering above the abyss of total destruction, reminding us that there is little to say about massacres, and nothing to say about Purpose and Meaning, Vonnegut continually pictures a small bird asking eternally a small question: "Poo-tee-weet?" If such a question means anything, it probably means "so what"; but it also means "I see the dimensions of human life and I survive!" (198–99)

The central occurrence of Kurt Vonnegut's *Slaughterhouse-Five* is, of course, the firebombing of Dresden during World War II.[11] Of course, Vonnegut himself defies readers to arrive comfortably at definitions for terms like "central occurrence," but it is safe to say that Dresden is Vonnegut's seminal apocalyptic event. His decision to tell his story in such an untraditional, nonlinear way is one that has been replicated by successive writers; postmodern texts, in particular those postmodern texts that deal with war and the aftermath of war, often engage nonlinearity as a narrative technique. Tim O'Brien, for example, consciously uses nonlinearity in his storytelling about his Vietnam experience in *The Things They Carried* (1990) as a way to give textual representation to his fragmented and war-torn mind. And Vonnegut's inclusion of the science fiction element, as previously mentioned, is hardly unexpected, given the cultural zeitgeist of the period: hundreds of films, mostly low-grade ones, were produced in the 1950s and 1960s, borne out of the intensification of the space race and the cold war; Frank Herbert, Robert Heinlein, Philip K. Dick, Ursula LeGuin, and Anthony Burgess were busily writing; and television's *Star Trek* had just concluded its brief but culturally significant three-year run.[12] Insofar as *Slaughterhouse-Five* features an annihilation event—one that is manifested by the symbol of purification, fire, no less—the novel, without question, qualifies as a work of apocalyptic literature.

Billy Pilgrim survives several events that could easily have killed him—a plane crash, alien abduction—but Dresden is his crucible. The novel ends just after the firebombing, with Billy Pilgrim

204 ❖ CHRIS GLOVER

surveying the wasteland for bodies to dispose of. As Edgar Derby's trial and execution make clear, a new world order has begun. As Billy takes this all in, he notes that "Birds are talking. One of them said to Billy Pilgrim, 'Poo-tee-weet?'" (Vonnegut, *Slaughterhouse-Five* 215). This last nonword is exactly what we expected to see, because the narrator tells us at the end of the novel's first chapter that it would be there. But the context in which we first see the word is one created to evoke a sense of nonsense: "There is nothing intelligent to say about a massacre" (19), Vonnegut's surrogate says to his war buddy in the introductory chapter, although this sentence quickly falls victim to deconstruction as the reader of the novel continues to read about Dresden. As a result, Vonnegut's spirit of nihilism is definitely undercut once the reader reaches the final page. Now posed as a question, "Poo-tee-weet" becomes less of a meaningless animal vocalization to Billy Pilgrim and more of an invitation to the reader, alongside Billy, to make a conscious decision about how to interpret this new world.

In many ways *Slaughterhouse-Five* is not a novel that is easy to write about, but this is probably par for the course for Vonnegut, if not the notion of the "postmodern novel" altogether. T.J. Matheson notes that "most critics are agreed that *Slaughterhouse* is a carefully structured work, while at the same time recognizing how difficult it is to determine the reasons behind the novel's structural pattern" (228). Matheson and many others have offered speculation, but none so concrete as to surpass further questioning. Textual interrogation often comes up wanting when it is even present to begin with; but it is probably safe to say that given Vonnegut's generally grim, Twainesque view of the human race, the novel's depiction of World War II is not a singular upheaval of a previous state of relative stability, but rather the result of humanity's inexorable progression toward its destruction. This progression only heightens the dramatic nature of the question on the last page—suddenly, after so much sarcasm and negativity, however playfully disguised it may be, the narrator lets us decide what happens next. We get the chance to press the world's *reset* button.

Oftentimes, given this chance, pop-culture representations of humanity are ready to prove it has learned its lesson. To cite just a few examples, in *The Day After Tomorrow* (2004) we realize that we were wrong to doubt global warming and its ability to change the face of the planet. In 1951's *When Worlds Collide* a few of us survive by leaving the doomed planet Earth and flying our hastily constructed rockets, heavy-handedly dubbed "arks," to another planet, where we vow to live in peace. However, the reset button has been less kind to other fictional worlds. Rudolph Wurlitzer's underground classic novel *Quake* (1974) opens with the title event dramatically shaking its unnamed protagonist out of bed one morning and literally collapsing the world around him. As he stands amidst the rubble in front of his broken mirror, assessing himself in a drawn-out moment of obvious and again heavy-handed symbolism, he must decide who he will be in this frightening new world. The best of intentions soon fade as he finds himself occupying a world full of looters, self-righteous and self-appointed law enforcers, rape gangs, sexual deviants, and other representatives of the worst of humanity's bad qualities. The unnamed man-child in *A Boy and His Dog* (Harlan Ellison's short story was first published in 1969; Hollywood's adaptation was released in 1974) has no choice because choices have been made by his immediate ancestors: the post–World War IV world has no place for those not willing to rape and kill, pillage and plunder. Vonnegut himself pushed the reset button several times, but in *Slaughterhouse-Five*, though, it is up to Billy, so it is up to us.

We are forbidden to find refuge in religion—Vonnegut would have none of that, naturally, and any hint of religion in *Slaughterhouse-Five* is laced with poisonous derision. The novel's epigraph suggests a decided lack of religious efficacy: "The cattle are lowing / The Baby awakes / But the little Lord Jesus / No crying He makes," besides being the words from an age-old Christmas carol, also serve to suggest the power of humanity to bring on the apocalypse without divine assistance or predestination. It also implies God's silence in the matter—perhaps even his inability to help. Vonnegut the humanist would have it no other way, no doubt dismissing such a silly belief as "foma," a term essential to *Cat's Cradle* that refers to the harmless, meaningless lies about the universe humans have a knack for telling each other. *Slaughterhouse-Five*'s narrator notes in the novel's final chapter that "On Trafalmadore, says Billy Pilgrim, there isn't much interest in Jesus Christ. The earthling figure who is most engaging to the Trafalmadorian mind, he says, is Charles Darwin—who taught that those who die are meant to die, that corpses are improvements" (Vonnegut 210). The narrator ends this commentary with the familiar refrain "So it goes." If we need further proof of the inability of God or faith to assist, we can certainly find it in the text. At one point, Billy Pilgrim hears "Golgotha sounds" off in the distance, sounds so described as to conjure up parallels to the construction of the cross to be planted on the hill of Golgotha, where Christ was crucified. But we are quickly told that they are only the distant sounds of latrines being built. At another point, the narrator takes note of a "ghastly crucifix" on the wall, but Billy Pilgrim is certainly not Catholic. He was not one to subscribe to "hope constructed from things found in gift shops" (Vonnegut, *Slaughterhouse-Five* 38–39). Even the Trafalmadorians, who, it can be argued, are a kind of ersatz gods in that they transcend time and possess the ability to see all things at once, are themselves ultimately responsible for accidentally destroying the entire universe.[13]

So it may seem, then, that my argument for hope for humanity hinges on the novel's final word—which is a question, no less— and nothing else. But there is other evidence. For one thing, the Trafalmadorians' insight, to which Billy Pilgrim eventually comes to ascribe, admits room for the "So it goes" philosophy. In fact, they are coiners of the phrase, and Billy learns to see, even to preach, that this approach is a satisfying and fulfilling one. Knowledge of the specifics of the ultimate demise of the entire universe should not prevent one from appreciating life as it is. The Trafalmadorian vision, then, is preferable to the earthly one, and indeed Billy's post-Dresden life as a philosophically minded optometrist is certainly suggestive. Vonnegut the author may well be trying to convince his readers that God, the author of the universe, is a sham, but that a belief in something beyond our mortal conception, even taken with its limitations, has its merits, especially if it helps us achieve a more inclusive worldview. Vonnegut the humanist would have no problem with such "foma" if a gentler "granfalloon" (a network of connected people) were achieved because of it.

Another piece of evidence of the existence of hope is that Billy Pilgrim does, after all, survive the war. In fact, he lives quite a long life afterward. His eventual death, which is never in question throughout the course of the discontinuous novel, because the Trafalmadorians have shared, are sharing, and will share the details of this event with Billy, is not the result of worldwide hostility or epic destruction. Instead, it is the result of one lunatic's desire for payback—an aberrant event, in other words, not a typical or ordinary kind of death. Billy dies under atypical circumstances, yes—shot by a former comrade-in-arms years after the war as he gives a lecture on the existence of UFOs—but not globally malicious or naturally cataclysmic ones. Humanity would have been responsible for Billy's death had he been one of the possibly 135,000 killed at Dresden. But humanity was not responsible for Billy's death; one lone gunman, a stray human, was. Billy's death—as are ours—were never in doubt. So it goes. But the world goes on.

PART THREE: VONNEGUT'S POSTAPOCALYPTIC LEGACY

The world also goes on for the anonymous man and his son in *The Road* (2006). Cormac McCarthy's American landscape is one of formless gray as far as the eye can see during the day, and a blinding, oppressive blackness at night. Only one of the sections in this novel is a flashback to the event that created this world, and the description of this memory is presented to the reader with a chilling minimalism, as we see the man staring out his window and wisely, instinctively, fill the bathtub with water: "What's going on?" his wife asks. "I don't know," he answers. "Why are you taking a bath?" "I'm not" (52–53). (This scene is reminiscent of the opening scene in Ian McEwen's *Saturday* (2005), in which protagonist Henry Perowne stands naked at the window in the middle of the night, watching an airplane, engine on fire, come in for an awkward landing at Heathrow. Of course, the plane's future is as uncertain and tenuous as Henry's, as is ours.) The End of *The Road* is clearly our fault, even if the exact details are unknown. Ultimately, whether it was intentional or accidental destruction to blame is irrelevant. Man's creation, whatever it was that created the "dull rose glow in the windowglass" (52), brought about his end.

As it is in many of Vonnegut's novels (like *Galapagos*), the extent of *The Road*'s apocalypse is unclear, because our point of view never leaves the two travelers, whose sole mission—whose sole reason to exist—is to continue traveling. What they hope to find is equally unclear, because the man never says why they must travel southward on the road toward the ocean or what he expects they will find if and when they get there. But we readers know fully well that the chance of finding a habitable world, some pocket of the earth that Armageddon has somehow left untouched, is impossible. This is not that kind of story, McCarthy not that kind of writer. Perhaps, the man continues on merely for the benefit of his son, who, it rapidly becomes clear, is the father's only cause for living. At any rate, whether the apocalyptic event has left the entire globe in this state of gray or just the North American continent, we do not know. Of course, when the travelers finally reach the road's conclusion, which comes very near the novel's, they find nothing remarkable, and since there is physically nowhere else to go, nowhere preferable to here, this is where the book ends.

But it isn't *how* the book ends. Notwithstanding the terrible bleakness of the American landscape and the seeming utter hopelessness, the novel insists that hope is not unrealistic. The America represented in *The Road* is the firebombed Dresden, but on a larger scale. In attempting to not only merely survive but also to be a good parent, the man seems to try his best at not filling his son's head with negative thoughts; but his world is full of dichotomies: safe versus unsafe, life versus death, day versus night. One of those dichotomies is particularly, if inadvertently, pernicious, as he tells his son several times that they will survive because they are the "good guys" and that they should not stop for fear of the "bad guys," while at the same time forcing his son to take possession of their gun, much to the latter's horror and refusal, whenever he leaves him. At one point the boy asks if his father is always brave, and the man answers that he is as long as he always expects trouble. Also, the man bears no small amount of anger toward God, if he exists, and others of the "grown-up" generation agree with him, committing unspeakable acts of cruelty toward their fellow humans, giving new meaning to the term "extremist," and insisting, as one of their fellow travelers does, that "there is no God and we are his prophets" and "where men can't live gods fare no better" (McCarthy 170, 172). The physical surroundings are gray and bleak, but the existential outlook is equally desolate.

But the boy, the one more willing to help his fellow man and concerned with the welfare of others, is the one who survives *The Road* trip. The end of the novel deposits the boy at a place where the gray of the clouds is indistinguishable from the gray of the ocean, a place where the firmament of the Genesis story has yet to be separated, humanity has yet to be created. This new world is full of possibility, as we watch the boy meet up with a cadre of survivors who offer to help him; the boy suppresses his father's suspicion, surrenders his gun, and decides to trust. After a painful farewell with his father, and after interrogating the newcomer—"Are you carrying the fire? . . . You don't eat people" (283–84)—the boy joins forces with the stranger. Of course, it is possible that this stranger represents a cadre of survivalists who, like others we have seen previously in the novel, are not honest scavengers like the protagonists but are instead prone to rape, murder, and cannibalism; but McCarthy closes out the novel writing about the deep forests and glens that "hum of mystery" (287), and that hum may just represent a form of faith. McCarthy's hum is Vonnegut's bird, daring us to hope in the face of overwhelming evidence to the contrary, no matter the odds.

The odds are literally what Keith Neudecker is playing in his post-9/11 life as a professional poker player. Poker is the analogue to the hum and the bird, as DeLillo leaves his readers with a self-reinvented Keith—formerly a lawyer, now a full-time card shark. Like baby Wilder in DeLillo's most famous novel *White Noise* (1985), Keith undergoes a life-altering experience and regresses to an immature state. "Mystically charged," Wilder manages to ride his tricycle across a busy, multilane highway; when he reaches the other side, far from home and confused about what has just happened yet aware it is something existentially substantive, he bursts into a primeval, "profound" howl (*Falling Man* 322–23). Keith can't howl in such a profound way, as *Falling Man* (2007) is a novel with a much different tone. (As it often is in Vonnegut's work, existential profundity is subdued in *Falling Man*.) Instead, he seeks fulfillment in basic human needs: companionship with his son and his estranged wife, sex with a fellow survivor that doesn't—can't—be meaningful for either of them, because sex can't be representative of the intimacy they share. Because he can't find fulfillment here, he has to reinvent himself completely, taking one aspect of his former life, poker, and planting it as the base of his new one.

All plots end in death, DeLillo is fond of reminding his audience, in both of these novels and in other novels such as *Libra* (1988), which concerns the events leading up to the JFK assassination. But Wilder and Keith defy the odds and do not die. In the opening chapter of *Falling Man,* the twin towers fall, and Keith is among those left to reconstruct order from the chaos, walking aimlessly in shock down the streets of New York. From this moment on, Keith struggles to discover who he is. In poker he finds comfort because he finds a kind of stability. After all, in cardplaying unpredictability and randomness operate within parameters of order. There exist only so many possibilities; win or lose, the game is subject to rules. Having experienced firsthand that terrorist plots do in fact end in death, Keith retreats to a new world where the worst possible outcome is a mathematically inevitable loss. Like Jack Gladney, chair of the Hitler Studies Department at the College on the Hill in *White Noise* who withdraws into the world of the German leader because he finds him "solid" and "dependable" (unlike the rest of the world), Keith leaves reality behind for something more comfortable.

And his hope is there. The book opens and closes with the events of 9/11, as DeLillo revisits the scene at the novel's end in what Sven Birkerts, writing for the *Los Angeles Times* book review in May 2007, called a bend of the narrative line "into a circle in an assertion of authorial fiat. Having opened in the midst of the chaos ... he moves to a close in the same place" (R4). It may be the same physical and temporal place, but the psychological place differs. On the book's final page, DeLillo describes an apocalyptic scene:

> The windblast sent people to the ground. A thunderhead of smoke and ash came moving toward them. The light drained dead away, bright

day gone. They ran and fell and tried to get up, men with toweled heads, a woman blinded by debris, a woman calling someone's name. The only light was vestigial now, the light of what comes after, carried in the residue of smashed matter, in the ash ruins of what was various and human, hovering in the air above. (*Falling Man* 246)

Great attention should be given to the mention of the "light of what comes after"—after all, if there *is* light at all, not all is extinguished. DeLillo literally offers a glimmer of light; it is dimmed by horrible human truths, but it is there. By bending his novel back to the beginning, he manages to frame Keith's post-9/11 life, slightly and subtly, in a positive way.

The term "apocalypse" may be misleading, but its use as a literary device is a time-honored one. From Jonathan Edwards' famous sermon "Sinners in the Hands of an Angry God" to *Slaughterhouse-Five* through to *The Road* and *Falling Man*, some of us always stubbornly survive. We will also survive 9/11, which, fictionally speaking, reimagines the horrifying possibilities of life-altering death on a large scale, but also confirms the notion that Americans will persist. After the bombing of Dresden, Billy Pilgrim notes casually that "somewhere in there was springtime"(215); hope is subtle, even creeping in and manifesting itself without his noticing, but it is there. The apocalypse is not the end.

Notes

1. This speech also appears as "Up Is Better Than Down" but has here been taken from the 1989 printing of *Wampeters, Foma, and Granfalloons*.
2. From "Excelsior! We're Going to the Moon! Excelsior!" which also originally appeared elsewhere but is here taken from *Wampeters, Foma, and Granfalloons*, 1989 ed.
3. In *Mother Night,* Joseph Goebbels remarks, "We are never as modern, as far ahead of the past as we like to think we are" (19).
4. Vonnegut closes by meshing the words of Christ, the satire of Voltaire, the philosophy of Marx, and the politics of Eugene V. Debs, suggesting socialism as a possibility because, after all, "if we start drinking heavily and killing ourselves, and if our children start acting crazy, we can go back to good old Free Enterprise again" (168).
5. Vonnegut's fictional stand-in, Kilgore Trout, owns a parakeet in 1972's *Breakfast of Champions*; talk between these two often turns to the fate of humanity. "Trout supposed that when the atmosphere became poisonous," writes Vonnegut, "Bill would keel over a few minutes before Trout did" (18).

6. Of 1950s' Hollywood science fiction, Geoff King and Tanya Krzywinska write, "During this period—now often described as the 'classic' era—science fiction was largely produced in low-budget 'B' formats, designed for a predominantly teenage audience. Such films built on the success of science fiction as a popular literary form, particularly in magazines such as *Astounding Science Fiction* (1930–1996), *Weird Tales* (1923–1954) or EC comics" (4).

7. *Wampeters, Foma, and Granfalloons*, 1989 ed.

8. Interestingly, Malachi Constant's first name is also the name of the final book in the Old Testament, just as the Bible sits on the verge of a world-altering event (the birth of Christ).

9. Captain Adolf von Kleist believes meteorites to be the culprit; a more intelligent guess would probably be mutual assured destruction prompted by economic unrest and global panic.

10. *Timequake* takes this notion one step further, as humans, having been robbed of their free will for ten years, must learn how to reapply these faculties once they get them back again.

11. Of course, Vonnegut defies readers to arrive comfortably at definitions for terms like "central occurrence"; still, Dresden is Vonnegut's seminal apocalyptic event.

12. Many *Star Trek* episodes are famous for including obvious metaphors to contemporary culture and its issues, and many feature time travel as a plot device.

13. As they do in *The Sirens of Titan*, the Trafalmadorians come up short in *Slaughterhouse* when it comes to omniscience.

Works Cited

Berryman, Charles. "After the Fall." *Critique: Studies in Contemporary Fiction* 26.2 (1985): 96–102.

Birkerts, Sven. "In a Darker Place." Rev. of *Falling Man*, by Don DeLillo. *Los Angeles Times* 13 May 2007: R1+.

DeLillo, Don. *Falling Man*. New York: Scribner's, 2007.

———. *White Noise*. 1985. New York: Viking-Penguin Putnam, 2001.

Edwards, Jonathan. *Sinners in the Hands of an Angry God*. 1741. Pennsylvania: Whitaker, 1997.

Ellison, Harlan. "*A Boy and His Dog*." *The Essential Ellison: A 50 Year Retrospective*. Eds. Terry Dowling, Richard Delap, and Gil Lamont. California: Morpheus, 2001. 951–84.

Freese, Peter. "Surviving the End: Apocalypse, Evolution, and Entropy in Bernard Malamud, Kurt Vonnegut, and Thomas Pynchon." *Critique: Studies in Contemporary Fiction* 36.3 (1995): 163–76.

Kalfus, Ken. *A Disorder Peculiar to the Country*. London: Pocket, 2007.

King, Geoff, and Tanya Krzywinska. *Science Fiction Cinema: From Outerspace to Cyberspace*. London: Wallflower, 2000.

Klinkowitz, Jerome. "*Mother Night, Cat's Cradle,* and the Crimes of Our Time." *Critical Essays on Kurt Vonnegut.* Ed. Robert Merrill. Boston: G.K. Hall, 1990. 82–93.

Krauss, Nicole. *Man Walks into a Room.* London/New York: Penguin, 2002.

Matheson, T. J. " 'This Lousy Little Book': The Genesis and Development of *Slaughterhouse-Five* as Revealed in Chapter One." *Studies in the Novel* 16.2 (1984): 228–40.

May, John R. *Toward a New Earth: Apocalypse in the American Novel.* Notre Dame: U of Notre Dame P, 1972.

McCarthy, Cormac. *The Road.* New York: Random, 2006.

McEwan, Ian. *Saturday.* London: Vintage, 2006.

Mustazza, Leonard. *Forever Pursuing Genesis: The Myth of Eden in the Novels of Kurt Vonnegut.* Lewisburg: Bucknell UP, 1990.

Olderman, Raymond M. *Beyond the Waste Land: A Study of the American Novel in the Nineteen-Sixties.* New Haven: Yale UP, 1972.

Robinson, Douglas. *American Apocalypses: The Image of the End of the World in American Literature.* New York: Johns Hopkins UP, 1985.

Scholes, Robert. "[History as Fabulation:] *Slaughterhouse-Five.*" *Critical Essays on Kurt Vonnegut.* Ed. Robert Merrill. Boston: G.K. Hall, 1990. 37–39.

Sigman, Joseph. "Science and Parody in Kurt Vonnegut's *The Sirens of Titan.*" *The Critical Response to Kurt Vonnegut.* Ed. Leonard Mustazza. Westport: Greenwood, 1994. 25–41.

Updike, John. *Terrorist.* London/New York, 2007.

Vonnegut, Kurt. *Breakfast of Champions.* New York: Delacorte-Seymour Lawrence, 1973.

———. *Cat's Cradle.* 1963. New York: Bantam Doubleday Dell, 1998.

———. *Galapagos.* 1985. New York: Dell-Random, 1999.

———. *A Man without a Country.* 2005. New York: Random, 2007.

———. *Mother Night.* 1961. New York: Dial-Random, 2006.

———. *Palm Sunday.* 1981. New York: Bantam Doubleday Dell, 2001.

———. *The Sirens of Titan.* 1959. New York: Dial-Random, 2006.

———. *Slaughterhouse-Five.* 1969. New York: Laurel-Bantam Doubleday Dell, 1991.

———. *Wampeters, Foma, and Granfalloons.* 1974. New York: Bantam Doubleday Dell, 1989.

———. "Why They Read Hesse." *Wampeters, Foma, and Granfalloons.* 1974. New York: Bantam Doubleday Dell, 1989. 107–15.

Wurlitzer, Rudolph. *Quake.* 1974. New York: Serpent's Tail, 1995.

CHAPTER 12

Wampeters and Foma? Misreading Religion in *Cat's Cradle* and *The Book of Dave*

Claire Allen

In this chapter I suggest that specific similarities can be identified between Kurt Vonnegut's *Cat's Cradle* (1963) and Will Self's *The Book of Dave* (2006). In particular, I focus on the manner in which both Vonnegut and Self examine how Western society engages with religion during a time of fear. For Vonnegut, writing in the 1960s (and 1970s), there was significant widespread fear concerning the scientific developments of the nascent military-industrial complex, exemplified primarily in the form of the Atomic Bomb. For Self, writing in a post-9/11[1] world, the prominent fear is that surrounding the contemporary "War on Terror." Key to both authors' exploration of religion is its use as a means of comfort. Indeed, such is Vonnegut's particular interest in the soothing properties of religion in *Cat's Cradle* that he invents a set of terms to define how it can be used in this capacity: "A wampeter[2] is an object around which the lives of many otherwise unrelated people may revolve. The Holy Grail would be a case in point. Foma are harmless untruths, intended to comfort simple souls" (*Wampeters, Foma and Granfalloons* [1974] xiii).

Both texts also explore the concept of narrative and language and how the misreading of supposedly religious texts can lead individuals into problematic situations. This preoccupation with religion as narrative and the subsequent ability for humans to misinterpret such texts (either intentionally or unintentionally) should, perhaps, not come as a surprise, given the proclivity of both writers for playing around with language. Vonnegut's novels are infused with fictional, made-up words and languages, while Self is contentiously renowned for his urbane erudition and linguistic "abilities" as one critic has noted:

> Self's technique cannot be reduced simply to his vocabulary, however impressive, or annoying its range might appear to his readers. His prose style often leaps between journalistic declarative sentences and rapid verbal riffing, expanding the dimensions of his extended metaphors and descriptive catalogues. (Hayes 4)

Both Vonnegut and Self depict characters who "misread" what is perceived to be religious dictum. For both authors, there are significant consequences attached to such a form of misunderstanding; however, I hope to suggest that Vonnegut, writing before religious fundamentalism attracted such attention (in terms of the modern post-9/11 era), expresses an ambiguous stance regarding "misreadings" of religion. Whereas Self, writing post-9/11, produces a much more damning depiction of religion and extremism.

Both authors work within the apocalyptic or postapocalyptic genre in their respective novels. Critic Jerome Klinkowitz (1982) refers to *Cat's Cradle* as "a mock-apocalyptic novel, satirizing such doomsday books as *On the Beach* and *Seven Days in May*" (52). Klinkowitz suggests that Vonnegut writes *Cat's Cradle* in order to "confront the largest possible issue: mankind's threatened self-destruction" (52), namely the creation of the atomic bomb, and the concomitant fear of global disaster as a result of nuclear weapons. Similarly, Self writes *The Book of Dave* at a time of perceived threat initiated by the 9/11 attacks and the resulting continued fear of terrorist activity. The events in New York and Washington are prevalent in the minds of Dave's customers, especially those who have taken recent trips to or from America. In the opening chapter of the twenty-first–century section of Self's book, it is immediately apparent that terrorism is at the forefront of the public's thoughts. Dave predicts it will be a topic of conversation with his American passenger, who has recently traveled from the United States: "He'll start on fucking Afghanistan in two minutes" (29). Dave correctly predicts this to be the topic of most concern for his "fare":

> He was thinking about his family—and Afghanistan.
> "Kinduv weird being in Europe."
> "I imagine you'd rather be at home, what with all this business—"
> "In Afganistan, you bet I would. Sure, it's crazy to think you're any more at risk here, or your family's any more at risk if you're not there, but still—" (29)

Both texts are concerned with a fictive faith and its followers. In Self's *The Book of Dave*, this takes the form of Dävinanity, which is based on the insane ramblings of the central character of Dave in the contemporary part of the novel's double-helix time system. Dave writes two books; the first is the culmination of his depression and is written during Dave's drug-induced psychotic episode in which he hears voices telling him that he is a prophet: "*There is no god but you, Dave, It whispered, and you can be your own prophet*" (original italics 345). Dave writes the book because the voices tell him that there should be rules on how people should live their life: "*There has to be a Book of Rules....A Set of instructions you can follow to the letter*" (original italics 345). The book contains the anger he feels at his relationship breakdown and the hatred he now feels toward his ex-wife: "these dribs and drabs of humdrum misogyny flowed together into a mighty Jordan, nothing less than A COMPLETE RE-EVALUATION OF THE WAY MEN AND WOMEN should conduct their lives together. Which, as the Driver saw it, was mostly apart" (348). Dave considers himself "A messiah mushing through the two-millennium-old city" (348), thinking what he is producing is a set of "Epistles, the intent of which was to SET THE RECORD STRAIGHT" (348) for his son. Dave has this book transcribed onto metal plates and buries it in Carl's back garden for him to discover when he is a grown man.

In the alternate time-helix of Self's text, England of the distant future, or "Ingerland" as it is referred to, has suffered a great flood, from which only isolated parts of the country survive. These remaining areas have atavistically regressed into a type of dystopian feudalism. The people of "Ham" (one of the areas to have survived the floods) lead simple lives; they do not have all the "mod cons" of the twenty-first century. They are farmers, growing wheat and collecting gulls' eggs for food. They rear "Moto's," a genetically modified herbivore that combines the characteristics of a pig, a cow, and a two-year-old child. "Hamsters" live in small huts, having basic cloaks for clothes. The first book Dave wrote is discovered in this distant future, in the founding years of a new civilization. The book is believed to be prophetic, and, therefore, forms the basis of this future society's development.

Despite the faith that the book inspires in its fictional future readers, for its actual contemporary audience the twenty-first–century section of Self's novel reveals that Dave is suffering from mental illness. This becomes more apparent to those around him, such as one of his passengers who happens to be a psychiatric doctor: "Dr Bernal allowed her professional detachment to come to the fore. *He's ill,* she thought as he turned off at Chiswick Lane and worked his way through Shepherd's Bush to the A40. *He's ill and he doesn't even know it"* (original italics 55). After receiving medication for his depression, which induces psychotic episodes, Dave suffers a complete mental breakdown. Eventually, Dave receives the correct treatment and begins to recover: "Since coming off the anti-depressants he still felt the elbow-jabs of reckless thoughts—but mostly he felt better" (393–94). Dave realizes the insane nature of the content of his book and wishes to recover it, but he is unable to do so; it is lost, concealed underneath Michelle's (Dave's ex-wife's) recently landscaped garden.

As consolation for being unable to recover the book, Dave, with the help of his new partner, writes a second book in which his revised, saner philosophy on life is prescribed. In the distant future, after 500 years or so of civilization following the angry, insane ramblings of Dävinanity, Dave's second book is found. This discovery causes a great upset for the original followers of Dävinanity, because the second book entirely refutes the teaching of the first:

> the second book...might yet have the power to shake the PCO[3] to the very core. It might explain us to ourselves...undermine the pretended claims of the davidic line...circumscribe the very turning circle of the PCO itself...(434)

In *Cat's Cradle* Vonnegut also depicts a fictionalized land (the island of San Lorenzo) whose inhabitants follow a fictional religion (Bokononism). Bokononism, like Self's Dävinanity, consists of the teaching of one man (Bokonon). Bokonon is an outlaw and has attained this position because the worshipping of the religious teachings of Bokonon has been banned on San Lorenzo. The ban was imposed at Bokonon's own request, in the belief that this would increase the popularity and potency of the faith, a fact that his followers have not been made aware of.

In both novels a whole culture has developed around the religion, including its own unique language, traditions, and rituals. Vonnegut tells us of the Bokononist mantra: "We Bokononist believe that humanity is organized into teams....Such a team is called a *karass* by Bokonon, and the instrument the *kan-kan*" (*Cat's Cradle* 11). In *The Book of Dave* a common language has developed from the writings of Dave's first book. To the followers of Dävinanity, reflecting the stereotypical life of a twenty-first–century taxi driver, a hot meal is known as a "curry," water as "evian," and the sun as a "foglamp."

Such wordplay reveals Self's and Vonnegut's interest in the close association between language, narrative, and faith. Both authors appear to share an interest in the capacity individuals seem to have to manipulate religious narrative, for positive and negative ends.

The postapocalyptic society Self devises uses the discovery of the first book of Dave as a momentous marker for the beginning of their civilization, and as such, narrative can be said to occupy a significant position for the people of Ham. Similarly on San Lorenzo, a new religion is formed by Lionel Boyd Johnson and Corporal Earl McCabe, two travelers washed up on the island, who decide to commandeer San Lorenzo, an island with a long history of being conquered due to it consistently being "lightly held" (Vonnegut, *Cat's Cradle* 88–89) since "God, in His Infinite Wisdom, had made the island worthless" (89).

The fact that the narrator uses the well-known phrase "God, in his infinite wisdom" highlights the irony embedded in the idea that the raison d'être for the establishment of a false religion can somehow be attributed to "God" (and by implication, a system of faith). This underlines the ambiguity with which Vonnegut confronts religion. He simultaneously critiques the possible fictiveness of faith and its reliance on ambiguous narrative and contradictorily has the narrator assert a belief in a divine power.

When McCabe and Johnson arrive on the island, they find the inhabitants to be

> persons far worse off than they. The people of San Lorenzo had nothing but diseases, which they were at a loss to treat or even name. By contrast Johnson and McCabe had the glittering treasures of literacy, ambition, curiosity, gall, irreverence, health, humour and considerable information about the outside world. (87)

Initially, their attempt to improve the situation on the island consists of rejecting religion: "When Bokonon and McCabe took over this miserable country years ago," reports Julian Castle, "they threw out the priests" (118). Vonnegut examines interpretations of faith and religious teachings in an objective manner, refusing to offer an absolute damnation of religion. We are told that after Bokonon violently expelled the island's existing religious figures, he then "cynically and playfully, invented a new religion" (118).

In place of debunking humanity's need for religion, Vonnegut's novel considers the potential for comfort in the belief in a divine power. Perhaps reiterating for Vonnegut's own humanist beliefs,

Bokonon suggests that life is the same with or without religion but that the human desire to have religion may in fact have a positive effect. Klinkowitz suggests Bokonism "helps the people create happy meaning for their otherwise pitiful lives" (53).

When John, the narrator of *Cat's Cradle*, reads the history of San Lorenzo, he learns that as Johnson and McCabe's plan came into effect, Bokononism was generally seen in a positive manner, placating the islanders:

> As the living legend of the cruel tyrant in the city and the gentle holy man in the jungle grew, so, too, did the happiness of the people grow. They were all employed full time as actors in a play they understood, that any human being anywhere could understand and applaud. (Vonnegut 119)

This belief system, however, is not seen to result in any quantifiable improvement in terms of the living conditions of the islanders: "McCabe and Bokonon did not succeeded in raising what is generally thought of as the standard of living" (119).

The religious texts both Vonnegut and Self create are subject to mis/interpretation. Self's characters Antony and Carl believe in a different way of life to the one the majority of the future, "Hamsters," are following. Though they believe that Dave is their god, Antony and Carl believe that families should be able to live together in harmony and that women should not be treated as badly as they are, based on the words of Dave, who poignantly reveals his misogynistic attitude:

> I tellya, mate, you're better off never going near fucking women [...] Once they've squeezed one aht they ain't worf dipping yer wick in anyway [...] When they're mummies they ain't got no sense....When they get older iss worse still....Fucking boilers. (348)

Through the discovery of the second book, Antony and Carl try to prove that their way of life is more accurate to the word of Dave. However, Self depicts how religious text, like any narrative, can be interpreted differently, misinterpreted, and used for an individual's own needs. Some sections of society in the distant future are reluctant to accept any other version than the one they have for so long been following. Many of the religious leaders dismiss the ideas of those seeking any alternative, preferring to follow their existing beliefs. An example of this can be seen through the treatment of the rebellious character Luvvie Joolee Blunt. Luvvie Joole is exiled to

Ham by the Lawyer of Chil (another area that survived the floods). A Lawyer is akin to a Lord, defined in Self's Glossary as "dads who have large land holdings" (490). Carl's grandmother recounts the story: "Everyone knew why Luvvie Joolee had been exiled. She and her husband, the Lawyer of Blunt, had fallen foul of the PCO by living together, with their children, under the same roof." Their actions are seen as irreligious, "loathsome conduct," for which Luvvie Joolee and her husband were punished. Though this did not stop Luvvie Joolee from preaching what she believed in, there is no room for contrary beliefs in this future society, and so a fierce punishment is prescribed: "Mr Hurst, had made it clear to her that were she to continue, he would have no alternative but to return her to London for formal judgment. Understanding that this would mean torture, and very likely breaking upon the wheel" (118).

People who do not follow the rules of Dävinanity are branded "fly-ers," a name Dave in the twenty-first century gave to his least favored kind of passenger, referring to those who wanted to be dropped off at the airport, as Dave despised being trapped in the terrible traffic around it. In the distant future, "Flyers" is the name given to what society perceives as the worse kind of people, those who go against the word of Dave. These heretics are punished severely, sometimes exiled, just as Luvvie Joolee is, in an attempt to stop her ideas from spreading to others in the population.

The punishment proscribed for Luvvie Joolee is "breaking upon the wheel." "The Wheel" is an instrument of torture, sometimes exe-cution, on which perpetrators are spun until injury or death occurs. Dave, while he drives around the capital during the twenty-first cen-tury, considers the tourist attraction The Millennium Wheel: "The Millennium Wheel slowly revolved on the South Bank, its people-pods ever threatening to dip into the silty wash" (46). Here, Self provides us with an example of the ambiguous nature of narrative, as although the reader is not provided with the book Dave writes, which the religion is based on, the suggestion is that the text is informed by his daily activ-ities. Therefore, it is likely that the instrument of torture in the distant future is a misrepresentation of the giant fairground ride, which Dave has written about during his psychotic episode and which has been misrepresented or misinterpreted as a form of punishment.

Both Self and Vonnegut critique the integrity of religious leaders, and the manner in which these leaders can misread or manipulate reli-gious texts for individual gain. As is the case when Bokonon requests that his religion is banned, and he is outlawed in order to "give the religious life of the people more zest, more tang" (Vonnegut, *Cat's*

Cradle 118). Bokonon and McCabe work together to create the belief that the president dislikes Bokonism, when in reality McCabe is fully aware of how essential Bokonon is to the smooth running of the island. This is why no serious attempts are ever made to capture Bokonon: "McCabe was always sane enough to realize that without the holy man to war against, he himself would become meaningless" (120). Those at the head of Dävinanity do not want the feudalistic system in which Dävinanity operates to change, as this would challenge their position of power and privilege. It is for this reason that they do not want Dave's first book to be expelled in favor of the second book, which promises to "undermine the pretended claims of the davidic line" (Self 434).

In *Cat's Cradle* it is fear, and particularly one man's fear of death, that initiates the catastrophe at the end of the novel. The president of San Lorenzo, suffering from incurable cancer, opts to imbibe a portion of the chemical *ice-nine*, which has been given to him by Frank Hoenikker. *Ice-nine* is a material that when it comes into contact with water, it turns into ice. On his deathbed, the president consumes *ice-nine*, wishing to end his life quickly. However, because of a plane crash, the president's body falls into the sea, causing the entire earth's supply of H_2O to freeze. As with the atomic bomb—created, Vonnegut suggests, by a whimsical scientist, who has an almost childlike level of naivety—it is not the actual scientific product that is dangerous, but rather people's misuse of this power. As the narrator of *Cat's Cradle* suggests, " 'What hope can there be for mankind,' " I thought, " 'when there are such men as Felix Hoenikker to give such playthings as *ice-nine* to such short-sighted children as almost all men and women are?' " (164). Vonnegut seems to suggest that metanarratives, be they religious or scientific, can be dangerous when they are allowed to go unchecked. It is crucial that humanity is able to critique and revise such narratives lest they run out of control.

In *Cat's Cradle*, at the time of the initial disaster, John and Mona (John's wife to be) retreat to the safety of an oubliette. They leave this refuge after a few days to see what has happened. To their shock, what awaits them is not the devastation they were expecting: "I wondered where the dead could be. Mona and I ventured more than a mile from our oubliette without seeing one dead human being"(Vonnegut 181). John eventually discovers all of the town's former residents gathered at the top of the mountain that dominates the landscape of San Lorenzo: "In that bowl were thousands of dead. On the lips of each decedent was the blue-white frost of *ice-nine*" (181). As the narrator then goes on to explain, what Mona and John witness is not the aftermath of the "frightful winds." Because the bodies were so neatly gathered into one place, their deaths must have come after the initial impact: "and since each corpse had its finger near its mouth, I understood that each person had delivered himself to this melancholy place and then poisoned himself with *ice-nine*" (181). At the center of the gathering, John describes finding a note, which states that the survivors of the winds that followed the freezing of the sea "made a captive of the spurious holy man named Bokonon. They bought him here to tell them exactly what God Almighty was up to and what they should now do" (182).

The people of San Lorenzo took these events to be an act of God, rather than science, and turned to their holy figure for an explanation. Bokonon gave them an answer: "The mountebank told them that God was surely trying to kill them, possible because He was through with them, and that they should have the good manners to die" (182). Evidently, they followed his advice, even though it is clearly stated within Bokononism that any attempt to understand or believe to understand the wishes of a higher being would be futile and foolish. In *The Books of Bokonon* the story of a lady who believed that she could "understand God and His Ways of Working perfectly" (13) is told. *The Books of Bokonon*'s response to such a claim is the following: "She was a fool, and so am I, and so is anyone who thinks he sees what God is doing" (13).

Seemingly, at a time of great disaster, the society of San Lorenzo turned to their spiritual leader, even though if they truly adhered to the tenets of the religion, they would have known not to. As the narrator recounts the words of the religious book, "All of the true things I am about to tell you are shameless lies" (14). Mona comments on Bokonon's absence from the death pile: "He always said he would never take his own advice, because he knew it was worthless" (182). These people in desperation believed that Bokonon did know the word of God, and so they followed his advice. It was not the chemical per se that caused their deaths, but their belief that the wishes of God can be known and accurately followed. Bokonon did not kill himself, as he recommended the people he addressed should do; instead, John finds him alive at the end of the novel.

Cat's Cradle concerns a society that is aware that what they are choosing to partake in is a communal lie, but knowingly still chooses to do so:

> When it became evident that no governmental or economic reform was going to make the people much less miserable, the religion became

the one real instrument of hope. Truth was the enemy of the people, because the truth was so terrible, so Bokonon made it his business to provide the people with better and better lies. (Vonnegut 118)

As David Simmons (2008) comments, whilst *Cat's Cradle* critiques religion, and the manner in which those in authority use it as a tool to deceive the masses, "the novel seems to imply that science has an even greater potential for misuse" (129). By the conclusion of the novel, it is science that seems to represent the greatest threat. Though Johnson and McCabe may have misled many people, it is clear that they are not responsible for causing any actual physical harm to the island's inhabitants. This is in opposition to the antics of the Hoenikeer family who, between them, have succeeded in freezing the earth's supply of water and nearly killing its entire population.

As Bokonon writes in the conclusion of *The Books of Bokonon*, he would "take from the ground some of the blue-white poison that makes statues of men; and I would make a statue of myself, lying on my back, grinning horribly, and thumbing my nose at You Know Who" (Vonnegut, *Cat's Cradle* 191). These closing remarks suggest a certain degree of ambiguity in terms of Vonnegut's critiquing of religion. Bokonon's open acknowledgment of both his own failings (he continually says that he wouldn't follow his own advice) and the fallibility of any religious leader shifts the blame for the mass suicide to the individual. Vonnegut still retains the notion that there is a divine power, one that Bokonon himself acknowledges; but he seems at least partially to suggest that followers of any such narrative, be it religious or scientific, must preserve a critical attitude to it, judging it in terms of their own humanist sense of moral right and wrong.

The Book of Dave seems somewhat less ambiguous with regard to its critique of the misinterpretation and misuse of religious texts. Self's future civilization misread Dave's narrative as a religious text, in a manner that allows them to justify their barbaric actions.

Indeed, both authors suggest that the act of interpreting any written text is fraught with difficulty and susceptible to misunderstanding. In *Cat's Cradle* Vonnegut questions the idea that anything can be accurately represented in the written form: "Write it all down," Bokonon tells us. Vonnegut goes on to ironically suggest that "without accurate records of the past, how can men and women be expected to avoid making serious mistakes in the future?" (159). Similarly, Self makes a cautionary point in terms of the fallibility of interpretation. The reader knows that Dave writes his first book in a state of madness, and so the reader is encouraged to take this circumstance of production into consideration. However, those reading Dave's book in the distant future do not know this to be the case. Misreading and misinterpreting information has two significant consequences. Not only does a whole civilization develop from the insane ramblings of a man on (prescription) drugs but also misreading and misinterpretation allows people, quite literally, to get away with murder.

The Book of Dave ends with the death of the eponymous Dave. All the characters presume that Dave has committed suicide when his body is found with a gun shot in his side, as all the available evidence suggests this to be the case; but as the reader knows, this is not true. Misinterpretation allows for Dave's murder to be concealed, and narrative is at the heart of this misinterpretation. Dave's murderers successfully stage Dave's death to look like suicide, aided by Dave's careless notes on the newspaper he was reading at the time:

> There was an article on the vacant fourth plinth in Trafalgar Square, rubbishing the proposals for the arty sculptures that might be poised there. The paper editorialized that this prime position should only be afforded to the image of a mighty national hero [...] Dave had a biro in his hand and annotated the newspaper, scrawling in the blank linchets between rips of text and photos: EMPTY, I'VE HAD ENOUGH. TAKING THE PLUNGE. (468)

This note is misinterpreted by his family to be a suicide note, when in fact it was just Dave scribbling a response to the newspaper article.

The misinterpretation of this written text eventually allows individuals to get away with murder. During his period of mental instability, Dave borrows money to have his first book printed onto metal plates. This leads him into debt, a debt that Dave is unable to repay. The moneylenders track Dave down: "He knew they were only there to put the frighteners on him, *smack me about a bit*" (original italics 469). But things don't go to plan, because Dave happens to have his farmer friend's gun in the house: "*so why am I reaching for Fred's gun? Why? P'raps I've simply 'ad enuff?*" (original italics 469). The thoughts of Dave here are indistinct; "*'ad enuf*" seems to refer to Dave having had enough of running away from his debtors because he feels it is unjust that he has to pay them: "*why should I pay that cunt back, why? I was off my bleedin' rocker*" (original italics 469), yet, of course, "*'ad enuff*" may be understood as Dave's declaration that he has had enough of life and so doesn't mind if he ends up getting killed during this unfortunate debacle. A third means of interpretation may be that Dave has had enough of being chased for money, and he simply isn't thinking clearly when he reaches for the gun, meaning his own death is far from his mind. Murder seems to be far from the minds of those seeking to retrieve the money Dave owes also. The events that lead to the fatal shot seem to be unintended by all involved:

> For a while there was a mercilessly inefficient struggle, neither one gaining advantage—so that when Rifak did manage to get hold of the shotgun, it was with that element of shocked surprise with which a younger brother wrests a toy from his older sibling. Still in the giddy grip of his accomplishment, Rifak pulled both triggers—really just to see what might happen—and a smoky flame tore a big chunk out of Dave's middle. (469–70)

The evidence of the murder is quickly concealed: "taking the dying man's hands carefully in his own, [Mustafa] arranged everything so Dave held the trigger guard and the stock, while the gory muzzle was rammed in his chest cavity" (470). The plan works: "No one— not even Phyllis Vance [Dave's new partner]—seriously doubted that Dave Rudman had taken his own life" (472). All the pieces seem to fit together to suggest suicide: "the heavy history of depression, the toxic jungle of his brain chemistry, the loss of both son and career, the opportunity, the scrawled notes in the margin of the newspaper: EMPTY, I'VE HAD ENOUGH, TAKING THE PLUNGE" (472). Dave's innocent scribbling is taken as proof of his suicidal state of mind, reflecting the possible consequences of misunderstanding the written word. While in the twenty-first century, the misinterpretation of Dave's words results in the injustice of Dave's murderers escaping punishment, for a whole civilization in the distant future, the consequences for misinterpreting Dave's words are far greater: Torture, capital punishment, misogyny, and the division of family are all meted out to those that disobey.

"Wampeters and Foma" are prevalent in both Vonnegut's and Self's texts, and in both any attempts to interpret them culminate in erroneous or disastrous ramifications. These two novels both reveal the power of narrative to create comfort as well as question the ability for such narratives to be misread in order to cause harm. While Vonnegut's *Cat's Cradle* is ambivalent toward the act of misreading sacred texts, with the novel suggesting both positive and (very) negative consequences, Self, writing post 9/11, produces a harsher critique of the wanton misreading of religious narrative.

NOTES

1. 9/11 refers to a series of coordinated suicide attacks by al Qaeda on America on September 11, 2001.
2. Wampeter and Foma are invented words by Vonnegut used within *Cat's Cradle*; they also form two-thirds of the title Vonnegut gives to a collection of his essays, reviews, and speeches, *Wampeters, Foma and Granfalloons* (1974), in which Vonnegut defines the terms in the preface: "A wampeter is an object around which the lives of many otherwise unrelated people may revolve. The Holy Grail would be a case in point. Foma are harmless untruths, intended to comfort simple souls. An example: 'Prosperity is just around the corner.' A granfalloon is a proud and meaningless association of human beings" (xiii).
3. The PCO are described as a "Priestly Hierarchy" in the glossary that accompanies *The Book of Dave*. Essentially they are an authoritarian, corrupt elite group who control the population of Ham by claiming and exercising religious authority.

WORKS CITED

Hayes, M. Hunter. *Understanding Will Self.* Understanding Contemporary British Literature. Matthew J. Bruccoli, series ed. South Carolina: U of South Carolina P, 2007.

Klinkowitz, Jerome. *Kurt Vonnegut.* Contemporary Writers. Malcolm Bradbury and Christopher Bigsby, gen. eds. London: Methuen, 1982.

Self, Will. Introduction. *Riddley Walker.* By Russell Hoban. London: Bloomsbury, 2002.

———. *The Book of Dave: A Revelation of the Recent Past and the Distant Future.* London: Viking, 2006.

Simmons, David. *The Anti-hero in the American Novel: From Joseph Heller to Kurt Vonnegut.* New York: Palgrave Macmillan, 2008.

Vonnegut, Kurt, Jr., *Cat's Cradle.* New York: Dell, 1963.

———. *Wampeters, Foma and Granfalloons.* 1974. New York, Dell, 1999.

CONTRIBUTORS

Elizabeth Abele (PhD, Temple University) has published essays on American culture and masculinity in the journals *College Literature*, *American Studies*, *Journal of American and Comparative Popular Culture*, and *Images* and in the book collections *Best American Movie Writing 1999* (edited by Peter Bogdavonich) and *Annie Proulx and the Geographical Imagination* (edited by Alex Hunt). She currently teaches English and women's studies at SUNY Nassau Community College and is executive director of the Northeast Modern Language Association.

Claire Allen is currently writing her PhD at The University of Northampton on literary representations of London at the millennium. The central research question for this study is to consider the implications of the transformation of fiction that concerns itself with London during the millennial period. Recent publications include "Young Protagonists in the Contemporary London Novel: Hanif Kureishi and Rupert Thomson," *Literary London*, December 2008 and regular contributions to the Routledge Annotated Bibliography of English Studies.

Professor Lawrence R. Broer is an internationally acclaimed scholar of modern and postmodern American and British literature. He has published widely in critical collections and professional journals and has authored or edited eight books, including *Hemingway's Spanish Tragedy* (The University of Alabama Press, 1973), *Sanity Plea: Schizophrenia in the Novels of Kurt Vonnegut* (UMI Research Press, 1989; revised edition, The University of Alabama Press, 1994), *Rabbit Tales: Poetry and Politics in John Updike's Rabbit Novels*, ed. (The University of Alabama Press, 1998), and *Hemingway and Women: Female Critics and the Female Voice*, coedited with Gloria Holland (The University of Alabama Press, 2002). Professor Broer is presently working on a full-length study of Kurt Vonnegut and Ernest Hemingway, entitled *Writers at War: Vonnegut's Quarrel with Hemingway*.

Todd Davis teaches creative writing, environmental studies, and American literature at Penn State University's Altoona College. He is the winner of the Gwendolyn Brooks Poetry Prize and the author of two books of poems, *Some Heaven* (Michigan State University Press, 2007) and *Ripe* (Bottom Dog Press, 2002). In addition to his creative work, Davis is the author or editor of six scholarly books, including *Kurt Vonnegut's Crusade, or How a Postmodern Harlequin Preached a New Kind of Humanism* (State University of New York Press, 2006) and *Postmodern Humanism in Contemporary Literature and Culture: Reconciling the Void* (Palgrave Macmillan, 2006).

Susan E. Farrell is a Professor of English at the College of Charleston where she teaches courses in American literature, contemporary fiction, and women writers. She has published articles on Toni Morrison, Alice Walker, Jane Smiley, Alice McDermott, and Tim O'Brien, among others. She is also the author of the 2008 book *Critical Companion to Kurt Vonnegut: A Literary Reference to His Life and Work.*

Since earning his master's degree in 2005, **Chris Glover** has taught composition (and literature when he is lucky) at Long Beach Community College in Long Beach, California. He also has worked extensively in LBCC's writing and learning centers, in both faculty and administrative roles. He has written or presented on authors such as Don DeLillo, Mary Wilkins Freeman, Eugene O'Neill, and Thomas Malory as well as on topics related to writing center administration and theory. Glover spends his free time obsessing over baseball.

Lorna Jowett is a senior lecturer of American studies and media at the University of Northampton, United Kingdom, where she teaches some of her favorite things, including science fiction, contemporary literature, and film and television. Recent publications have focused on genre and gender in science fiction and horror texts across fiction, television, and film. Her monograph, *Sex and the Slayer: A Gender Studies Primer for the* Buffy *Fan,* was published by Wesleyan University Press in 2005, and she is on the editorial board of *Slayage: the International Online Journal of* Buffy *Studies.*

Jessica Lingel received an MA in literary theory and gender studies from New York University and an MLIS from Pratt Institute. She is currently working on a collection of autobiographical disease narratives from twentieth-century women authors. She lives and works in Brooklyn, New York.

Rachel McCoppin (PhD, Indiana University of Pennsylvania) is an assistant professor of literature at the University of Minnesota, Crookston. Her publications include "Questioning Ethics: Incorporating the Novel into Ethics Courses" published in *Teaching* *the Novel across the Curriculum* (Greenwood Press, 2007) and edited by Colin Irvine and "Existential Endurance: Resolution from Accepting the 'Other' in J. M. Coetzee's Disgrace" published in *The International Journal of Existential Literature.* She has also coauthored an article entitled "Being Actively Revised by the Other: Opposition and Incorporation" in the book *Teaching Ideas for the Basic Communication Course* (Kendall Hunt Publishing, 2006).

Robert T. Tally, Jr., is an assistant professor of English at Texas State University, where he teaches American literature, world literature, and critical theory. He is the author of *Melville, Mapping and Globalization: Literary Cartography in the American Baroque Writer* (Continuum Books, 2009). Tally holds degrees in law and in literature from Duke University and the University of Pittsburgh.

An associate professor of education at Furman University since 2002, **Paul L. Thomas** taught high school English for eighteen years and holds an EdD in curriculum and instruction from the University of South Carolina. Thomas has focused throughout his career on writing and the teaching of writing. His major publications include volumes on Barbara Kingsolver, Kurt Vonnegut, Margaret Atwood, and Ralph Ellison in the series *Confronting the Text, Confronting the World* (Peter Lang, various). Coauthored with Renita Schmidt, *21st Century Literacy: If We Are Scripted, Are We Literate?* (Springer) is his newest work for 2009.

Philip Tew is professor in English (Post-1900 Literature) at Brunel University. His major publications include *B. S. Johnson: A Critical Reading* (Manchester University Press, 2001); *The Contemporary British Novel* (Continuum Books, 2004; revised edition, 2007); *Jim Crace: A Critical Introduction* (Manchester University Press, 2006); and *Re-reading B. S. Johnson* (Palgrave Macmillan, 2007), coedited with Glyn White. Svetovi Press published a Serbian translation of *The Contemporary British Novel* in 2006. Tew is the founding director of the UK Network for Modern Fiction Studies. Forthcoming are four books: *Zadie Smith* (Palgrave Macmillan, 2009); *Re-Envisioning the Pastoral* (Fairleigh Dickinson University Press, 2009), coedited with David James; *Beckett and Death* (Continuum Books, 2009), coedited with Steven Barfield and Matthew Feldman; and *Modernism Handbook* (Continuum Books, 2009), coedited with Alex Murray. Tew is a fellow of the Royal Society of Arts.

INDEX